52 Weekends in New Jersey

52 Weekends in New Jersey

From Rodeos to Air Shows to Biking Back Roads

MITCH KAPLAN

THE COUNTRYMAN PRESS
WOODSTOCK, VERMONT

We welcome your comments and suggestions. Please write to: Editor, The Countryman Press, P.O. Box 748, Woodstock, Vermont 05091, or e-mail countrymanpress@wwnorton.com.

First Edition

Library of Congress Cataloging-in-Publication Data
Kaplan, Mitch.
    52 weekends in New Jersey : from rodeos to airshows to biking back roads / Mitch Kaplan.—1st ed.
        p. cm.
    Rev. ed. of: 52 New Jersey weekends. c1996.
    Includes index.
    ISBN 0-88150-658-3
1. New Jersey—Tours. I. Title: Fifty-two weekends in New Jersey. II. Kaplan, Mitch. 52 New Jersey Weekends. III. Title.
    F132.3.K36 2005
    917.4904'044—dc22

                                                                            2004059368

Book design and composition by Dawn DeVries Sokol
Maps by Paul Woodward, © 2005 The Countryman Press
Cover photograph © Jeffrey Greenberg
Interior photographs by the author unless otherwise specified

Published by The Countryman Press, P.O. Box 748, Woodstock, Vermont 05091

Distributed by W. W. Norton & Company, Inc., 500 Fifth Avenue, New York, NY 10110

Printed in the United States of America

10 9 8 7 6 5 4 3 2 1

To Penny for infinite patience and support.

CONTENTS

Summer

Fall

❄
Winter

INTRODUCTION

TO MANY PEOPLE, NEW JERSEY is nothing more than an exit off a toll road—an ugly industrial landscape off the turnpike or an overpopulated little place wedged between New York City and Philadelphia.

I grew up here and raised my kids here. Still, it wasn't until I began working on the first edition of this book that I began to appreciate one very clear fact: New Jersey hides a wealth of wonderful places. And I do mean hides. The trick is to get past the tollbooths, the malls, the look-alike suburban developments, and the industrial "parks." Look a bit deeper. You'll be amazed at what's available out there.

I was.

For instance, a canoe trip in the Pinelands revealed a wilderness adventure that started right under a highway viaduct. In the heart of urban Jersey City hide a hive of artists hard at work and one of the most pleasant urban waterfront parks anywhere. And just a few miles from the southern terminus of the New Jersey Turnpike a real Western rodeo has been riding for years.

All of these adventures were news to me when I first encountered them, as were others—like the plethora and range of activities to be found on the Camden riverfront—revealed in recent travels around the state. I hope this book will make these hidden wonders of New Jersey somewhat less hidden.

As I worked on this project, a lot of people I told about the book reacted with the typical, pejorative "Jersey Joke" attitude, saying something along the lines of, "Can you *find* fifty-two things to do in New Jersey?" On the contrary. The problem lay in choosing *only* fifty-two; to paraphrase the old Jimmy Durante line, "I found a million of 'em."

Think about this: according to a newsletter item published by the

State Division of Travel and Tourism, New Jersey contains 1,056 places that are listed on the National Historic Register.

Obviously, visiting historic places alone would require a lot of weekends.

Still, I'll go on uncovering the state's cache of treasures, and I'd welcome information on additional worthwhile places to visit, things to do, or events. They're out there—just beyond the next exit ramp or behind that shopping mall.

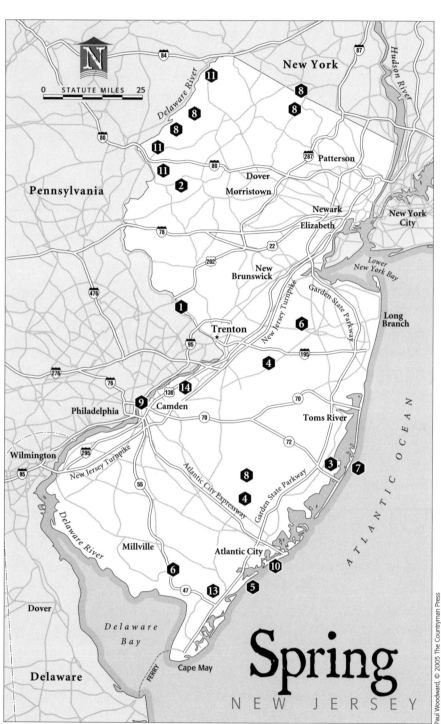

Spring

The Shad Festival
Lambertville

A SHAD IS A FISH. And a bony one at that. About twenty years ago, the shad had all but stopped their spring run up the Delaware River because the river was a mess. But slowly, through persistent conservation efforts, the water began to clear, and gradually the shad returned. In 1981, the village of Lambertville (population 4,000) decided to celebrate the shad's resurgence, and the Shad Festival was born. Now, for one weekend in late April, thousands of people come to Lambertville to shop, eat shad, listen to music, dance, learn about river ecology, and watch Fred Lewis.

Fred Lewis?

Fred Lewis is New Jersey's sole licensed, commercial, inland fisherman. He lives and works on a minuscule island. The island sits, oh, maybe 50 feet off the New Jersey bank. It's connected to the "mainland" by a private footbridge. This island—along with the fishery—has been in the Lewis family for more than 100 years.

Now, six days a week, from mid-March to mid-May, Fred and his crew seine the river for shad with their big net. It takes about six guys to complete the operation—more if the haul is particularly good. The townsfolk purchase the day's catch. If Fred's had any luck. On Saturday and Sunday afternoons during Shad Festival, Fred performs several seining demonstrations. Shad hauling, he calls it. It's a technique taught to

On the banks of the Delaware River at the Lambertville Shad Festival

New Jersey's early European settlers by the local Native Americans. I joined about 250 other people who crossed over to his island via his rickety, handmade bridge to watch him work.

There was no formal announcement, no starting ceremony or gun. Most of us couldn't even tell which one of the seiners was Fred. But the crowd lined the riverbank with great anticipation, and when a grizzled-looking man in a bright orange slicker began hauling a tangle of rope up the riverbank, we figured out two things: one, that was Fred; and two, the fishing had begun. Fred dragged that net about a quarter-mile upriver, while his helpers, midstream, sat by in a rowboat. Upon reaching an appointed spot, Fred tossed the net into the water. His aides grabbed one side and, with Fred providing on-land resistance, they dragged the net slowly downstream toward the concrete-and-iron bridge that crosses over to Pennsylvania. As Fred passed the rock upon which I sat, deliberately placing one muddy boot in front of the other, his body angled radically back, someone in the crowd called out to him.

"How's it lookin'?" barked the friendly voice.

"Won't know till I pull 'er in," Fred said without missing a step.

Having marched the net to the little island's southern tip, they hauled her in. The entire process took about 20 minutes. Fred caught four fish. Just goes to show you—even the pros get skunked.

The news of Fred's poor catch was passed on to the crowd waiting to cross the bridge for the next demonstration, but nobody was deterred. There was a party mood in town.

Indeed, the Shad Festival really amounts to an enormous block party. North Union Street is closed and filled with booths offering everything from shad chowder to fine crafts to silly trinkets to a putt-putt golf fund-raiser for the sixth-grade educational fund. Bands play continuously. A historical tour of the town runs sporadically. Or, you can tour town in an horse-drawn carriage. Children romp in the KidZone. The Budweiser Girls serve beers and sandwiches. On Sunday, three seatings are offered for the traditional Shad Dinner—ten bucks buys you grilled shad, fish chowder, baked potato, coleslaw, buttered roll, and a beverage.

But shad hasn't always been Lambertville's claim to fame. The town was a late-19th century industrial center: the bobby pin was invented here; wooden wagon wheels, rubber boots, railway cars, locomotives, and bottled beer were made here. Today, the town holds a reputation for having one of the state's finer collections of antiques stores. Filled with fascinating Federal- and Queen Anne–style houses, narrow tree-lined streets, quaint shops of many descriptions, galleries, cozy bed & breakfasts and a selection of excellent restaurants, Lambertville remains small-town America.

The town's shops reflect grass-roots commerciality. Collectibles, crafts, art, and antiques are displayed in a loving but rough-edged manner that says this is where the craftspeople not only sell, but live—so c'mon in and have a look-see. Places like the Antique Center at the People's Store (a co-op) and the 5 & Dime, which houses an outstanding collection of antique toys, are more fun and fanciful than the typical overpriced high-brow antiques shops. And Joseph Finkle & Son bills itself as "the world's most unusual hardware store."

Unlike many of New Jersey's historic districts, Lambertville's buildings span many styles, giving the town a timeless feeling, and a small historical museum offers tours and a glimpse into the village's rich past. Take the building at 44 Coryell Street, now an enchanting bed & breakfast; it was built in three sections, starting before 1800, and with a knowledgeable eye, you can track its evolution.

Tired of shopping and playing tourist? Need something active to do? Ride or walk the bike path that parallels the river and the Delaware & Raritan Canal.

Like Lambertville, the Shad Festival has evolved, from a small get-together to one of the state's most popular springtime events. It has been said that if you want to be at the big block party, you should visit the town during festival weekend, but if you want to see the real Lambertville, come around some other time. Luckily, Lambertville's open year-round, so you can do both.

❋ ❋ ❋ ❋ ❋ ❋ ❋ ❋

DETAILS

For Shad Festival dates and schedule, or general Lambertville information: *609-397-0055; www.lambertville.org.*

Directions to Lambertville: *From the north take US 202 south to the last exit in New Jersey and get on NJ 29 south. From the south, take the New Jersey Turnpike or I-195 to I-295 north, circumventing Trenton, and exit onto NJ 29 north.*

❋ ❋ ❋ ❋ ❋ ❋ ❋ ❋

2

THE PEQUEST TROUT HATCHERY

Oxford

T'S A SATURDAY IN APRIL, about 7:45 AM. I'm performing my daily morning run through the local county park. The running path parallels the creeklike Saddle River. I run this route four times a week. I seldom see anyone except other runners or walkers.

This morning the riverbanks are lined with dozens of people—mostly men. All are dressed like they've stepped from the pages of *Field & Stream*. All hold fishing poles. But not one of them is fishing. They merely stand and wait.

I ponder them as my run takes me along a park access road, past a playground, and then back onto the path and over a footbridge. I see more of them. Some chat idly, one or two smoke, but nobody makes a move toward the water. Why are these folks lined up by the dozens, in a place where I'd only occasionally seen schoolkids working five-and-dime rods and reels? Why are they holding fishing gear but doing nothing? What is going on?

That morning's newspaper, which awaits me in my driveway, holds the answer: "Trout Season Starts Today" reads a small headline in the sports section. At 8 AM. They'd been anxiously but lawfully waiting for the Official Start.

The fish those sportsmen sought to snare were all hatched and raised at the Pequest Trout Hatchery in Oxford. The state hatchery annually stocks more than 200 bodies of water (like the Saddle River) with some 600,000 brook, brown, and rainbow trout. The money anglers paid to obtain their fishing licenses fund that process. Because so many of the fish New Jersey anglers catch are given life at the Pequest Trout Hatchery, it's an appropriate place to begin exploring New Jersey freshwater fishing.

In front of the hatchery's visitors center—a modern, angular building with a facade of glass and variegated, mock-sandstone block—a small fish raceway has been cut into the sidewalk. The group of adult trout of various species who live in it greet visitors indifferently. But they illustrate what this place is all about. When my wife, Penny, and I arrived, a handful of boys wearing Cub Scout uniforms was lined up along the raceway, shouting and pointing with fascination. "There's one!" "Look at that one!" "Here's a big one!" Mind you, these trout were doing nothing more than slowly lolling from one end of the trough to the other. Of course, just being a trout may be extraordinary enough. Especially to small boys.

Inside, this place is all about trout. A video explains the entire spawning process. They're particular creatures, these fish. They need very, very clean water that's just the right temperature, and they demand only the best food. Here they get it. "These fish live in water that's got to be the purest in all of New Jersey," wildlife education specialist Paul Tarlowe told me.

Out back, we saw it all in action. The water purification and pumping plant. The long, large raceways, which literally bubble with jumping fish. The nursery, where the fry (baby fish) grow up in special cradling tanks.

But this hatchery is devoted to more than just fish. All areas of conservation are given attention. Back inside, displays show the wildlife that inhabits the surrounding area, explain the various branches of the state government that deal with conservation, and afford an opportunity to bird-watch. One particularly effective presentation chronicles how New Jersey has become a leader in preserving endangered species. Developed to commemorate the 30th anniversary of New Jersey's Endangered Species Conservation Act of 1973, the interactive exhibit illustrates the successes and challenges involved in managing endangered wildlife. The highlights include a so-called interactive I-Wall containing a collage of video, audio, and graphic displays. Another cool aspect: seeing a bald eagle, peregrine falcon, and osprey close-up.

I confess that I'm just as fascinated by watching fish swim seemingly aimlessly as were those boys we encountered in front of the building, and I was mesmerized by the main display area's enormous aquarium containing representatives of each fish species raised here. And, while stuffed animals might not be everyone's cup of tea, for those who enjoy taxidermy, the displayed mounts include examples of all the wildlife found on this wildlife management area.

The hatchery also offers classes. We attended a session entitled "So, You Want to Take Up Fly-Fishing," which reviewed the basics of equipment and fish behavior. Those Cub Scouts were on their way to a session called "Tracks," in which they would trek into the adjacent woods to find and identify various kinds of animal sign. During the year, the hatchery offers hands-on programs ranging from bird-watching to bow-hunting and fly-fishing to spin-casting. Almost all of them free.

One week before trout season opens (late March or early April) the hatchery mounts its annual Open House. The event features a full weekend of family games and activities, as well as an encampment by the New Jersey Muzzle Loading Association, displays by and information from sportsmen's groups, archery, and BB shooting ranges—and a chance to meet Smokey the Bear.

Set on the Pequest Wildlife Management Area's 1,600 acres, the hatchery offers hiking trails, a picnic area, access to the Pequest River, and a stocked pond where beginners can practice their techniques. ("Remember, we call it fishing," said Tarlowe when asked about his students' success. "We don't call it catching!") With its proximity to the Pequest and Delaware Rivers, the hatchery is a natural jumping-off place for both new and experienced anglers.

✽ ✽ ✽ ✽ ✽ ✽ ✽ ✽

DETAILS

Pequest Trout Hatchery & Natural Resource Education Center hours *are 9–4 daily, closed holidays. Some evening programs are offered. The hatchery is a good source for fishing information and regulations. For an event schedule or other information:* 908-637-4125; *www.state.nj.us/dep/fgw/pequest.htm; Pequest Trout Hatchery, 605 Pequest Road, Oxford, NJ 07863.*

Directions: *The hatchery is located on US 46 in Oxford, about 10 miles west of Hackettstown. From I-80, take exit 19 onto CR 517 south to Hackettstown, approximately 5 miles. At the first traffic light you come to (downtown Hackettstown) turn right onto US 46 west. Go approximately 8 miles to the hatchery entrance on eastbound side. From I-78, take exit 17 onto NJ 31 north approximately 17 miles to its end at US 46. Turn right onto US 46 east. The hatchery entrance is approximately 2.5 miles up on the right.*

✽ ✽ ✽ ✽ ✽ ✽ ✽ ✽

EDWIN B. FORSYTHE NATIONAL WILDLIFE RESERVE

Brigantine

LOOKING FOR THE FORSYTHE REFUGE just north of Atlantic City, I spotted a sign along US 9 that said SCOTT'S LANDING. It pointed east along an unremarkable road that appeared to go out to sea. In a few miles, another sign pointed to the right. The pavement soon gave way to dirt, and a large sign warned of dire consequences to any who entered the refuge before or after the appointed hours—those being essentially summer daylight hours.

Immediately, the road was enshrouded by a primeval forest—old, scraggly, bent trees ensnared by strangling vines and tangled in under-growth. At the end of the track, in a small clearing, a quartet of pickup trucks, each attached to a boat trailer and each looking a little worse for wear, stood like trusty steeds, idly waiting for the return of their masters. The bed of each held various seafaring and fishing items—old netting, bobs, gas cans, and the like.

A small dock stood to the right, abutting a low concrete wall beyond which in three directions a sea of swamp grass held itself tall and still in the heavy air. The ocean was not visible here, only various tidal creeks running to it. Two men stood on the dock, now staring out across the grasses, now fidgeting with lines they had dropped into the water. As I approached, a dark, oblong object scurried across the dirt. It came to rest at the base of the low wall. A crab. Pincers opening and closing nervously,

Edwin B. Forsythe National Wildlife Reserve

it stood ready for trouble. Five feet away, a large plastic bucket overflowed with his (her?) brothers and sisters.

"These crabs belong to you guys?" I asked the two.

"Yep."

"One's making a getaway," I noted.

"That's okay," the one in the red shirt assured me. "Those are all too small anyway. They're going back."

That's when I noticed the half barrel standing a few yards closer to the water. "Those are the keepers," said the other, a middle-aged fellow in a white baseball cap.

We chatted, these two gentleman and I. They'd been crabbing since the tide had started climbing up at about 10 this morning. It was, they declared, a nice way to kill a day. They dropped a trap dockside, and pulled up another that held one keeper out of four. The younger guy held the squirming crustacean carefully between his fingers, and showed me how to tell male from female.

"Got a favorite recipe?" I asked.

25

"Sure," he replied. The recipe involved a carefully mixed marinade of beer, water, vinegar, red pepper, and several other spices. The already steamed crabs should, it was strongly recommended, soak in that concoction overnight in the fridge. "They get tastier that way," he reasoned aloud. "They pick up extra flavor from the shell."

I left them at that point, their bucket overflowing, the older gentleman hustling after a keeper who was trying to scurry back to freedom. Overhead, hundreds of birds flew in great circles, looking for a dinner of their own.

Back on US 9 South I found another sign. This one said FORSYTHE REFUGE. Again the road bent sharply, but this time I found several small buildings and one larger administrative-looking edifice. FEE COLLECTED EVERY DAY a sign warned.

I parked near the small cluster of outbuildings and approached one that promised visitor information. Looking through the front door glass, it appeared to be nothing more than a wall with a door—like a Hollywood set comprised only of building fronts. I opened the door and understood why. The far wall, overlooking the vast expanse of swamp, was made of glass. A shelf ran across it at tabletop height. On the shelf rested a registry book, a bird-watching log, and bird-spotting survey forms. Also available were brochures explaining the refuge, a self-guided driving tour, and a list/scorecard of birds to be seen. I took one of each.

About to get back into the car, I noticed the James F. Akers Trail. A marker promised a quarter-mile, self-guided hiking loop. Walking time required would be one-half to one full hour, depending on my level of interest.

I followed the path. Not 10 yards into the woods, I was enveloped by hungry bugs. The bug repellent? In my suitcase at the hotel. I'd have to make this quick. Even walking swiftly, pausing little, and continuously swishing my arms around like a horse's fly-swatting tail, I was able to learn from reading the trailside annotations the difference between black and white oak, that red cedar was really a juniper, that the ubiquitous vines were either Virginia creeper or greenbrier, and that poison ivy ran rampant in this area. Poison ivy? DON'T TOUCH, the sign admonished. I didn't.

Safely back in my insect-free, air-conditioned car, I embarked on the self-guided driving tour. The dry, dirt road took me through dark and mucky surroundings. This thoroughfare, my printed guide revealed, was constructed on an abandoned railroad bed that once sustained tracks to Brigantine Island. Now the dirt track topped a dike that had been strategically constructed to reclaim this ocean wetland and allow the creatures of the air and water to live naturally.

Birds swooped and dove, ascended and flew off into the distance. An abundance of sandpipers pecked at the sands. A small portion of beach was littered with dead horseshoe crabs. They resembled miniature army tanks that had been stopped in their tracks by an unseen force and were now being picked over by ravenous scavengers.

The drive covered 8 miles. The printed guide nicely explained how wetlands reclamation worked, if not much about the actual animals I was seeing. But my strongest impression was the prevailing contrast: a foreground of quiet wildness and undisturbed shore; a background of boisterous, manmade Atlantic City wildness that loomed so closely down the coast.

❋ ❋ ❋ ❋ ❋ ❋ ❋ ❋

DETAILS

The Edwin B. Forsythe National Wildlife Refuge *is open year-round and encompasses 39,000 acres. Park headquarters are open 8–4, weekdays; Wildlife Drive and walking trails are open daily from sunrise to sunset. The entrance fee is $4 per vehicle, $2 per bicycle. A seasonal guide to wildlife activity is available from the park's head-quarters.* **Information:** *609-652-1665; http://forsythe.fws.gov/; Great Creek Road, P.O. Box 72, Oceanville, NJ 08231.*

*   * **Directions:** *The Brigantine Division, home to the refuge's headquarters and self-guided driving tour, is just north of Atlantic City; turn east off US 9 onto Great Creek Road. The Barnegat Division is located along the western shore of Barnegat Bay—follow US 9 south and turn left on to Lower Shore Road, then turn right at the second fork, Collinstown Road. The Holgate Division covers the southern tip of Long Beach Island.*

❋ ❋ ❋ ❋ ❋ ❋ ❋ ❋

THE NEW JERSEY WINE TRAILS

WHEREVER A GRAPE CAN BE GROWN, man will turn his hand to winemaking. New Jersey is no exception. Indeed, it ranks fifth among all wine-producing states. More than two dozen wineries and vineyards operate here, producing upward of a quarter-million gallons of wine per year in more than 40 varieties, generating some $36 million.

You'll find wineries to visit in 10 of the state's 21 counties. Among them:

RENAULT WINERY—EGG HARBOR CITY

The Renault Winery can be wonderous, but you have to get past the confused, kitschy architecture first. The overall goal is to effect a Mediterranean villa. Cutesy elements like exterior staircases and ramps ensconced in mock wine barrels, as well as tunnel-like interior walkways that are meant to recall, no doubt, great wine cellars, create a gaudy, Disneyesque effect. It's all a bit much.

But, having been in operation for more than 140 years, Renault contains historical interest. An impressive collection of antique wine-making equipment is displayed, and the Champagne Glass Museum—a roomful of flutes collected from every part of the world and every era—displays its treasures in built-in cabinets of beautiful workmanship underneath a striking Renaissance-style ceiling.

The winery's history is fascinating (it was founded in 1864), and its telling makes the tour worthwhile. But is the wine any good? In the tasting room (decorated like the inside of a wine barrel), I sampled a few. The dry whites were nice, but a bit too sweet. The Royal Rouge came across well. Renault is perhaps best known for its sparkling wines. The Blueberry Champagne is the sole American champagne of its kind, and it does offer a distinctive taste.

Perhaps the best reason to visit Renault, however, is its food. On weekend evenings, the winery offers a six-course dinner that has gained a wide reputation for excellence. The Sunday brunch is no less satisfactory. Lunch is served daily at their Garden Café.

FOUR SISTERS WINERY—BELVIDERE

Matarazzo Farms and its associated Four Sisters Winery specializes in festivals. With everything from Hike the Hills Day to celebrations of the

Renault Winery

strawberry, wines in spring, Father's Day (with a pig roast), the peach, bluegrass music, the fall harvest, wines in fall, as well as a cross-country skiing get-together in midwinter and Native American powwows, this enterprise has become a major northwestern New Jersey tourist attraction. What's more, they have a great bakery.

I have to confess that I didn't taste any wine at Four Sisters. I'd just come from another winery, and I'd had my fill. But the Matarazzo family's wines have won a number of awards, and reliable word-of-mouth promises that they are palate-worthy. Wine tasting is done in a small, pleasant building attached to the farm store. Professional art and photography grace the walls, and there are terrific views of the surrounding fields, vineyards, and hills through the large windows and from the adjacent deck.

In addition to the standard winery tour, the vineyards are explored and explained, and special classes are given regularly.

Four Sisters/Matarazzo's strength lies in its appeal as a family-centered event specialist. If you've got kids, and you want to keep them happy while you do your wine tasting, visit during any of the farm's festivals. There's always something going on—music, storytelling, hayrides, hay bale mazes, pick-your-own veggies or pumpkins, grape stomping, dancing—you name it.

CREAM RIDGE WINERY—CREAM RIDGE

You've got to like Tom Amabile. He likes what he does, and his enthusiasm is infectious. A former systems specialist for Public Service Electric & Gas, Tom has allowed a kitchen hobby to sweep him into an entirely new second career—master vintner.

You've got to like Cream Ridge Winery, too. Set up in a large, barnlike structure, it's designed as if Tom and his wife, Joan, simply let the business grow like a runaway vine out of the family kitchen. In the front parlorlike room, you find a pleasant gift and wine shop. Behind, in an oversized garage, you find the winery. One side of the garage is overlooked by a balcony. Wine tour participants gather on the balcony while Tom stands among his machinery and explains what he does.

What Tom does is create some unique fruit wines. The man is clearly a born tinkerer, and he loves to tinker with different fruits to see how he can develop them into wine. His cherry and cranberry wines have won gold medals at the New Jersey Wine Competition. But it's the Cream Ridge Black Raspberry that leaves people talking. Why? It's dry. Tom uses a cold fermentation process; the unique dryness is derived from oak-barrel aging. "Aging fruit wines in oak is unique," he quips. "Not too many folks do that." The results are hard to describe. Best to head on over to Cream Ridge and sample a bottle.

❋ ❋ ❋ ❋ ❋ ❋ ❋ ❋

DETAILS

The Garden State Wine Growers Association, through its web site, offers a range of information on everything related to New Jersey wine. They offer 11 Wine Trails, which are excellent guides to discovering and visiting member wineries, and they provide a directory of fairs and festivals. **Information:** *609-588-0085; www.newjerseywines.com; Box 2631, Hamilton Square, NJ 08690.*

Renault Winery: *609-965-2111; www.renaultwinery.com; 72 N. Breman Avenue, Egg Harbor/Galloway, NJ 08215.* **Directions:** *Take the Garden State Parkway to exit 44, make a sharp right onto Moss Mill Road (CR Alt. 561), go 5 miles to Bremen Avenue, turn right, and drive a quarter-mile.*

Four Sisters Winery & Matarazzo Farms: *908-475-3671; www.foursisterswinery.com; 10 Doe Hollow Lane, County Route 519, Belvidere, NJ 07823.* **Directions:** *From I-80, take exit 12, turn left onto CR 519 at the bottom of the ramp, and go 6.5 miles; from I-78, take NJ 31 north until it ends, turn left onto US 46. At the first light, turn right onto CR 519 and drive for 2 miles.*

Cream Ridge Winery: *609-259-9797; www.creamridgewinery.com; 145 Route 539, P.O. Box 98, Cream Ridge, NJ 08514-0098.* **Directions:** *From the New Jersey Turnpike take exit 7A to I-195 east. Get off at exit 8, then follow CR 539 south 3 miles.*

❋ ❋ ❋ ❋ ❋ ❋ ❋ ❋

LAUGHING ALL THE WAY

Ocean City

WHO CAN RESIST A RESORT TOWN that has a sense of humor? Take, for example, the annual Miss Crustacean Beauty Pageant, complete with a miniature, mollusk-sized runway surrounded by all the traditional pomp and circumstance normally reserved for human beauties. Or the annual Twins Contest—those who look most and least alike win. Or the Hermit Crab Day celebrations, in which a character named Martin T. Mollusk, described in his news releases as "a testy hermit crab addicted to stale pizza crust and rancid swamp water," appears on the beach in search of his shadow. Should he see it, so it is told, summer comes one week early that year. It is no coincidence that in nearly twenty years of this riotous ritual, Martin has never failed to see his shadow.

What can you say about a seaside resort that can see beyond the sun, sand, salt, and water to provide some silliness? You've gotta love Ocean City.

Ocean City stages funny and fun special events nonstop. Weekly happenings begin with the town's Easter parade, run right through the early October Indian Summer Weekend, and keep going till New Year's Eve, with the shore's biggest First Night celebration (see chapter 51). In June, the action moves into high gear, and throughout the summer a special contest, celebration, or parade of some kind takes place almost daily. The events are good old-fashioned, wholesome, clean fun, aimed at families.

The Ocean City boardwalk

Few seaside resorts cater better to Mom, Dad, and the kids. Why? Because this town's family roots run deep.

Ocean City was founded in the 1870s by the three Lake brothers— Methodist ministers all—who were dedicated to the notion that such

The Music Pier at Ocean City

profligacies as gambling and drinking had no place where families gathered. In 1879 they signed a covenant banning such vices. Today, the town remains liquor-free and devoid of games of chance.

Walk Ocean City's boardwalk and you'll find enough shops selling T-shirts, saltwater taffy, used books, and swimwear to supply yourself with these items for a lifetime. But, unlike the more carnival-like boardwalks of Wildwood, Atlantic City, Asbury Park, and Seaside Heights, you won't be harangued by hawkers trying to entice you to "take a chance" at this game or that. Yes, there are video games, and there's a small, child-friendly amusement arcade at the boardwalk's north end. But, you'll find a low-key atmosphere, a live-and-let-live feeling. And you'll discover the Music Pier.

The Music Pier takes you back to the 1930s, the time of marathon dance contests. A marvel of period architecture, the pier underwent a $4 million renovation in the mid-1990s, but for lectures and musical events, you still sit on folding chairs. Many gatherings there—like the Artisans Band Concert or the Youth On Stage performances—sustain a smile-inducing but thoroughly enjoyable homemade quality. Professional concerts are staged as well. Indeed, the Ocean City Pops is the Jersey shore's only resident professional orchestra. They play everything from Sousa to Victor Herbert to Beethoven, and at times they accompany special performances, like a fully mounted production of South Pacific or presentations by the New Jersey Ballet.

Other unique Ocean City items of note: the town has its own 9-hole golf course, fosters a small airport, and offers shopping in a true downtown environment. Remember, nearly 20,000 people call Ocean City home year-round; it's a real place, not just a tourist trap. You can wander along Asbury Avenue and find a plethora of fine shops supplying not-so-touristy items, such as Oriental rugs, antiques, and furniture, and you'll find a series of small, storefront restaurants that offer good fare at reasonable prices where you'll feel comfortable with your toddler, your teenager, or your date.

Downtown is home to the Discovery Sea Shell Museum, a collection of more than 10,000 shells, including the famous, one-of-a-kind, Siamese twin–helmet shell.

Ocean City's spirit, however, is best captured by its dedication to crabby special events—the Miss Crustacean Beauty Pageant, Hermit Crab Day, and the World Championship Hermit Crab Races. To capture that spirit, let me finish with a descriptive quote from an obscure tome entitled *The Martin Z. Mollusk Story (Rhyme & Punishment)*:

Miss Crustacean, USA
The pageant where a vast array

Of lovely shellfish meet to vie
For Queen of Crabdom, how they try
To bump and grind in gaudy dress

To smile and otherwise impress

The judges on the pristine sand
Of Ocean City, that's a grand
Resort upon the Jersey shore . . .
This pageant siphons crabs galore

From every state where crabs exist,
From every cove where crabs persist
In doting over daughters whom
"Look beautiful," I presume

Are beautiful, at least to fish . . .
They come in droves, it is their wish,
Nay, more than that, it is their duty
To be proclaimed "Crustacea's Beauty."

The epic, poetic history goes on like this for many chapters. But you get the point: folks in Ocean City know how to laugh.

❋ ❋ ❋ ❋ ❋ ❋ ❋ ❋

DETAILS

Ocean City *is located south of Atlantic City. Information and event schedules: 800-232-2465; www.njoceancity.com; www.oceancitychamber.com.*

*   **Directions:** *From the Garden State Parkway southbound, take exit 30; northbound travelers use exit 25. Ocean City lodging runs the full range, from bed & breakfasts to full-service resort hotels.*

❋ ❋ ❋ ❋ ❋ ❋ ❋ ❋

6

BIKING THE BACK ROADS

*In a car, you're always in a compartment, and because you're used
to it you don't realize that through that car window everything you see
is just more TV. You're a passive observer and it is all moving by you
boringly in a frame.*

*On a cycle the frame is gone. You're completely in contact with it
all. You're in the scene, not just watching it anymore, and the sense of
presence is overwhelming.*

—Robert M. Pirsig,
Zen and the Art of Motorcycle Maintenance

Pirsig was talking about the joys of driving a motorcycle. But he just
as easily could have been talking about pedaling a bicycle. Indeed, if anything, his observations are even more true for bicycling, because you're
not only in the scene, you're in it under your own power. Biking affords
contemplative possibilities simply not available at greater speeds.

Any cycling enthusiast should take the time to visit the U.S. Bicycling
Hall of Fame in Somerville. The collection of antique bikes and biking
paraphernalia is fascinating, and if you can be in the area during
Memorial Day weekend, you can take in the oldest continuously operating
major bike race in the country, the Tour of Somerville.

If you're a doer rather than a watcher, New Jersey affords a surprising
variety of biking terrain. Hilly rides, flat rides, waterside rides, and urban

rides are all possible here. The Department of Transportation prints pamphlets describing nine individual rides that together cover most of the state. The following offers a glimpse at two of those rides, plus another of my own fancy.

ROUND VALLEY ROUNDABOUT

Tucked just to the south of busy I-78 and US 22, Round Valley Reservoir is the centerpiece of Round Valley State Recreation Area, a popular weekend getaway spot. You can begin this 28.5-mile ride at the recreation area, or start at the East Whitehouse Fire Station in the small town of Whitehouse, just south of US 22. The overall circuit covers moderately hilly terrain and, since it sticks largely to back roads, only a few spots are busy with auto traffic. You pass through some surprisingly rural countryside.

Along the way you'll pedal through Oldwick, a tiny town established circa 1740 that boasts a number of fine antiques shops and a old-fashioned general store. When you arrive in Mountainville, you can stop in at the Kitchen Kaboodle for a gourmet box lunch, and a visit to the General Store, in business since the mid-1800s, is a must.

For those who start in Whitehouse, several miles after leaving Mountainville you'll pass under I-78 and US 22 and then skirt the Round Valley Recreation Area's western edge. It's a good spot for a picnic or a swim, but be cautious of traffic on weekends. Continuing south, the route heads toward the microscopic town of Stanton. Before you get to the village, however, a turn onto CR 618 can lead you into the Hunterdon County Arboretum, a converted commercial nursery in which a variety of trees are grouped into single-species groves. In Stanton, another classic country general store provides an opportunity to stop for food or drink.

BATTLE OF MONMOUTH RIDE

Monmouth Battlefield State Park marks the site of the longest battle of the American Revolution. It's also the start for this 28-mile loop through rolling countryside that passes a full range of New Jersey scenery—horse farms, suburban tracts, orchards, and woodlands. The route allows for battlefield exploration and goes to Holmdel County Park, home to yet another garden, the Holmdel Arboretum. The 20-acre arboretum contains nearly 500 species of plants. Pick up a plant index as you enter and see how many you can identify.

In Freehold, a stop at the Monmouth County Historical Society on Court Street will give you an overview of the area's significant historical role in U.S. history.

A DEEP SOUTHERN EXCURSION

I discovered this route while exploring the so-called Delsea region. The roads are good and traffic is light. The going is fairly flat and the environment has a subtropical flavor. If you're riding in the heart of summertime, be sure to carry water, bug repellent, and sunblock.

Start in Mauricetown (pronounced Morris-town), a small village sited at a crook in the Maurice (pronounced Morris) River. Riding out of town on Haleyville Road, turn left onto NJ 47 for a few hundred yards. Then go

❋ ❋ ❋ ❋ ❋ ❋ ❋ ❋

DETAILS

The New Jersey Department of Transportation prints maps and descriptions of nine bicycle tours on water-resistant paper that folds to fit in your pocket. The maps contain directions and information about parking, food, and other local amenities. These can be ordered online or downloaded as PDF files. Clicking on the "Getting Off on the Right Foot" and then "Publications/Books" links delivers an impressive list of books on New Jersey bicycling, and general biking times, as well.
30 Bicycle Tours in New Jersey *(Countryman Press).* **Information:** *www.state.nj.us/transportation/commuter, then link to "Biking and Walking." Department of Transportation phone for general inquiries: 609-530-8059.*

❋ ❋ ❋ ❋ ❋ ❋ ❋ ❋

right on CR 670 (also marked as Alternate 47), which will take you to the edge of Belleplain State Forest. Follow CR 550-Spur, the Delmont-Belleplain Road, south. When CR 550-Spur turns right, continue straight ahead into Delmont. Hook up with NJ 47 there, take a right, staying on NJ 47, go a mile or two, then go left on CR 616, Grade Road, which will take you into Heiserville. Follow CR 616, now called the Heiserville Road, as it winds north and parallels the Maurice River. It will pass through Leesburg and then into Dorchester. Both towns sit right on the river and make good spots for a scenic riverside break. North of Dorchester, CR 616 will take you back to NJ 47. Turn left, then right back onto CR 670, Haleyville Road, and you'll return to Mauricetown.

Throughout the region, farmlands mix with densely overgrown woodland areas with junglelike undergrowth, combined with marshes that characterize the Delaware Bay and the silica-rich sandy soils that fostered the region's great glassmaking industries. You'll not find anything like it anywhere else in New Jersey.

A DEEP-SEA FISH STORY

Barnegat Light

THE *DORIS MAE IV*, owned an operated by the brothers Eble, sets sail three times daily out of Barnegat Light. Trips that start mornings at eight and afternoons at one are for half-day fluke fishing. The hard-core fishermen (and women) come aboard at 7 PM for the nighttime bluefish run. This is a boat that, clearly, never rests.

We've all heard the vicious rumors about "those party-fishing boats." That they're nothing more than an excuse for foolish landlubbers to consume enormous amounts of beer. That the "party" in the name is much more important than the "fishing." That nincompoops regularly climb aboard and spend the entire trip too seasick to do anything but wish they'd stayed home.

Now let's make a couple of things perfectly clear. *Doris Mae's* patrons—like most other party-fishing boat patrons—come aboard because they love to fish. And most people who venture to sea and spend the entire time seasick are not fools. They just have, perhaps, more sensitive inner ears than most.

At least that's my story. I can't vouch for the two other people who spent the evening lying near me on padded benches in the main cabin fighting tooth and nail against the overwhelming nausea. But I've always been too easily victimized by dizziness and vertigo. This trip was no exception.

The anglers began to gather at the dock some two hours before sailing time. They loitered by their automobiles, sipping beer and soda from cans and picnicking in the parking lot.

"Why," I asked my friend Bob, "are they here so early?"

"They want to be sure they get the 'good spot' on the boat."

Some, it seems, believe that good luck comes only from fishing the boat's stern. Others insist on a place along the bow. You claim a spot by setting your pole into one of the holders along the main deck's rail. Then you wait.

The ride out to sea took about an hour; sometimes it runs an hour and a half, depending on where the fish are purported to be. Captain Ron Eble, equipped with the best sonar fish-spotting equipment (which can help him differentiate among fish species) and the best rumor-sorting ear (which can help him determine which fish reports from other boats are meaningful) sailed to a predetermined spot.

Below, some customers stood on deck and stared at the dark water or peered into the night. Others rode inside, eating hot dogs and burgers grilled by a deckhand or food from their own coolers. Folks chatted idly

❋ ❋ ❋ ❋ ❋ ❋ ❋ ❋

DETAILS

The *Doris Mae IV* sails daily, March through January.

Information: *609-494-1692, 609-494-7468; www.dorismae.com.*

Directions: *Take the Garden State Parkway to exit 63 and NJ 73 east onto Long Beach Island. When the road ends, turn left onto Long Beach Island Boulevard and drive 8.3 miles. Turn left onto 18th Street. Go to the end; the boat dock is right in front of you.*

The New Jersey Division of Travel & Tourism's *web site contains a directory of charter and party-fishing boats (www.state.nj.us/travel/fishing.shtml).* **General information:** *1-800-VISITNJ, 609-777-0885.*

❋ ❋ ❋ ❋ ❋ ❋ ❋ ❋

or watched a large TV screen that went fuzzy each time the captain's radio was activated.

Suddenly, the ceaseless rumble of the dual diesel engines changed cadence, a bell rang, and like alerted firemen, everyone ran on deck and manned his or her post. The fishing began.

I didn't fish. I didn't even attempt to stand up. I drifted in and out of a Dramamine daze. But, between my own nauseated groans, I did listen. The people were quiet. Quiet like that, I quickly learned, means bad fishing. After a while, the bell rang, the engines started, and we steamed farther into the night.

At stop number two, infrequent and sporadic shouts were heard. "I got one!" "Whoa!" "Hey! That guy got a shark!"

The frustrated drifted indoors to crack open a beer, eat another prepackaged hoagie, and bemoan their fishing fate. "I'm just out here on a thirty-five dollar boat ride," complained one.

"Did you see that guy next to me?" another asked rhetorically. "He's pulling them in left and right. Left and right. And me, I got exactly nothing!"

"It's the green light," another luckless one stated unequivocally. "All the guys who are landing fish got those green lights." The mysterious green light, my friend Bob later explained to me, affixes to the end of the line, and is reputed to attract fish, although no one can exactly say how or why.

"See that guy?" said the luckless, green light-less one, pointing out the window. "He's getting 'em like crazy. I'm going to check it out. I give you ten-to-one he got the green light."

A moment passed. The boat rolled with a wave. My stomach waved with the roll. The disgruntled angler returned.

"No light!" he proclaimed joyously. "No light! There's hope! We better get back out there!"

Near my sick-man's roost a young woman slept. "I'm the designated driver," she told Bob between twenty-wink stints. "We have a two-hour drive when we get back, so I sleep on the boat."

The bell rang. The boat moved. Thank goodness, I thought, we're going in.

But, no. The engines fired back, the bell rang still again. And everyone's luck changed.

A constant refrain of "I got one!" now emanated from the deck. Although Captain Ron was fully out of earshot of thirty-five-dollar-boat-ride complaints, he was obviously aware that most of his customers were being skunked. With a professional's smarts he brought them to this place, home to a large school of bluefish. We stayed there for an hour. By the time we docked, the clock said 4:30 AM. We'd been scheduled to return at about two. But, contrary to hearsay, these folks had come not to party but to fish. And the captain worked the extra hours to make them happy.

All the ship's passengers ate fresh bluefish that night. Except me. I had Pepto Bismol with a Maalox chaser, and was just thankful when the floor stopped rocking under my feet.

HIKING
North...

THE APPALACHIAN TRAIL, possibly the best-known hiking trail on the continent, rambles more than 2,000 miles from Georgia to Maine. Traveling south-to-north, the trail enters New Jersey at the Delaware Water Gap and follows the Kittatinny Ridge for more than 40 miles to High Point. There, the trail moves sharply east and crosses through the heart of Waywayanda State Park and Hewitt State Forest. When it approaches Greenwood Lake, it veers to the north and disappears into New York.

You can hop on the trail at many places for short hikes of varying degrees of difficulty. Anywhere you join it, the trail is marked by its signature white blazes.

Casual walkers should remember that, while the mountains of New Jersey may not be regarded with the same awe as the Rockies, or even those in New England, this is still hill country, and in many places the traveling involves fairly strenuous uphill and downhill scrambles.

THE KITTATINNY RIDGE

The walk along the Kittatinny Ridge, from the northern side of the Delaware Water Gap National Recreation Area to the southern boundary of Stokes State Forest, offers wonderful views of horse and farm country to the east and fine glimpses of the Delaware Valley to the west. Winter hikers with sharp eyes—or a good pair of binoculars—might spot bald eagles sitting high in the trees overlooking the river.

Parking is available at a trailhead just south of Millbrook Village along CR 602, and a bit more than 4 miles north, where CR 627 intersects the trail. If you're looking for a longer trek, arrange a pick up at Culver's Gap in Stokes State Forest, about 12 miles north. Walking north, the eastern highland vista is pockmarked by small lakes—Farview, Swartswood, Plymouth, and Owassa, to name a few—that attractively enhance the views. A side trip into Millbrook Village, a re-created 19th-century community, adds another kind of texture to the trek.

WAYWAYANDA

Waywayanda State Park offers a wealth of hiking and history. Approximately 2.5 miles south of the Appalachian Trail lies Lake Waywayanda, where you'll find the remains of a charcoal blast furnace that produced iron to make shovels and swords during the Civil War; an abandoned iron mine can be found near the junction of the Appalachian Trail and the side trail that leads south to the lake. In the eastern section of the park, the trail touches upon and intersects with other trails that penetrate a dense hemlock forest, a veritable untamed jungle that is unique to the region. Still farther east, the park holds a swamp thick with tall white cedars and showy rhododendron more normally associated with coastal marshlands.

...and South

THE BATONA TRAIL

The name Batona is an acronym for Back to Nature. The name was adopted by the Batona Hiking Club, the organization that created in the early 1960s this pathway through the heart of the Pine Barrens. It's the longest of southern Jersey's blazed trails. In contrast to the Appalachian Trail's more alpine nature, Batona wends its ways through lowland wilderness dense with wild berries (huckle, blue, winter, and choke), orchids,

The reward at High Point State Park

and some 100 other species of herbaceous plants. Watch out for the thick colonies of poison sumac and poison ivy.

Abundant cedar trees are what first attracted European settlers to the region, and the trail travels through and past several cedar swamps. The trail also winds through an area known as The Plains, a fascinating tract of stunted forest filled with scrub oak and pine that grows, at best, to heights of about 4 feet.

The Pine Barrens, of course, are anything but barren. The name derives from the fact that the wet, sandy soils were not conducive to raising the traditional crops that European settlers grew. That by no means meant that the land had no commercial value. Along the Batona Trail you'll discover the remnants of various human settlements. The most prominent of these is Batsto Village in Wharton State Forest. Batsto functioned first as a bog-iron and glassmaking center, and later, under the ownership of Joseph Wharton, as a gentleman's farm. This 100,000-acre tract sits atop one of the continent's largest subterranean water supplies, the Cohansey Aquifer, estimated to hold some 17 trillion gallons. Wharton thought of the aquifer as a gargantuan underground reservoir. His plan was to dam the main streams and rivers and sell water to the nearby cities, especially Philadelphia. Luckily for us, he was thwarted by politics.

The Batona Trail continues north from Batsto—just follow the pink

---

❋ ❋ ❋ ❋ ❋ ❋ ❋ ❋

DETAILS

The Appalachian Trail: *For information on the trail in New Jersey State Parks: www.state.nj.us/dep/parksandforests; 973-948-3820 (Stokes State Forest); 973-875-4800 (High Point State Park); or 973-853-4462 (Waywayanda State Park).*

Delaware Water Gap National Recreation Area information: *908-496-4458, 570-828-2253; www.nps.gov/dewa.*

The Batona Trail: *For information on the trail in New Jersey State Parks, visit www.state.nj.us/dep/parksandforests. This site offers a comprehensive list of the parks and their hiking opportunities. For state parks in the Pine Barrens, call Bass River State Forest (609-296-1114), Brendan T. Byrne State Forest (formerly the Lebanon State Forest, 609-726-1191), or Wharton State Forest (609-561-0024). The New Jersey Pinelands Commission prints a guide called "5 Hikes and 5 Bikes" with detailed hiking routes along the Batona Trail and other Pinelands treks; information: 609-894-7300; www.state.nj.us/pinelands.*

Special needs: *A number of parks around the state offer hiking and walking trails for the disabled. Among them are: the Braille Trail at the Frelinghuysen Arboretum in Morristown (973-326-7600, www.arboretumfriends.org), Cattus Island Park in Toms River (732-270-6960, www.ocean.nj.us/parks/cattus.html), and the Trailside Discovery Trail at Watchung Reservation in Mountainside (908-789-3670).*

❋ ❋ ❋ ❋ ❋ ❋ ❋ ❋

---

blazes. Its path crosses a number of local and county roads, which makes it easy to access the trail for shorter out-and-back hikes. Its northern terminus is at Ong's Hat in Brendan T. Byrne State Forest. Camping, swimming, and other recreations can be pursued in these state parks and forests, and the old sand roads make for excellent mountain biking.

The combination of the sandy soil and the abundant water create the area's essential swampy character—an environment bugs love. Be sure to carry plenty of bug spray.

Waterfront Revival

Camden

J UST HOW SORRY HAD CAMDEN'S reputation become? Let me put it this way: I'd not bothered to travel there since 1974. Now, whether or not this former manufacturing dynamo is as bad as its reputation doesn't really matter. Perception is reality, is it not?

Well, the perception is changing. And the change has begun at Camden's dynamic waterfront, where the views of the Ben Franklin Bridge and downtown Philadelphia—equivalent in their own way to northern New Jersey's views of New York City from Jersey City and Hoboken—create delightful vistas. Amusements and sites worth traveling to are being developed. And the traveling itself is being made easier.

I came to Camden aboard River Line train, boarding in Bordentown with my friend Jill, her nine-year-old daughter, Leah, and Leah's friend Shannon. The cars were spanking new and clean, the ride smooth and relatively quiet, and the scenery, on the train's west side, where the Delaware River parallels the tracks, often eye-catching. The route travels to the heart of Camden, terminating at the waterfront.

THE AQUARIUM

We disembarked at the New Jersey State Aquarium stop; the platform stands just two short blocks from the aquarium's entrance. We passed through the main gate, and en route to the aquarium front door, we

New Jersey State Aquarium

encountered a flock of penguins. "Can I have one?" Leah immediately asked. "They're so cute." Well, who can resist those waddlers, seemingly dressed in tuxedos for the prom? How these denizens of Antarctica can survive outdoors in the New Jersey summertime heat may seem a puzzlement, but if you show up for the regularly scheduled penguin feedings, you find out that they do just fine.

Inside, the facility's main tank—all 760,000 gallons—immediately caught the girls' attention. My eye went to the mini-submersible that hung from the ceiling surrounded by a slowly rotating, sparkling fish mobile. But, hey, how can a piece of art compare with a tankful of barracuda, Atlantic bonito, huge loggerhead turtles, and of course, sharks? Excited as they were, the girls encountered the problem that most kids face when confronted with a building full of wonderment: What to look at first?

We adults tried to instill some order. The displays on the first floor encircled the big tank. Why not follow them around the loop? Good idea—except that it was time for the seal show. Back outside we traipsed to a small amphitheater that faces windows in the seal tank set below water level. The seal show's volunteer host nicely involved everyone, kids and adults alike, while conveying facts and ideas about seals' lives in the wild. Then, using a special whistle and some large cut-out letters, he called on volunteers to lead individual seals in various behaviors by the tank window. It was all very cute and a big hit with the audience.

Back inside, we circled the lower floor, then explored the upper. Two displays stood out. One was a pair of small tanks with odd-looking creatures called sea dragons. They resembled some kind of a cross between free-floating, severed tree branches and stick-figure dragons. Bizarre. The other was the shark/ray touch tank. It took all parental powers of persuasion to get the girls to leave those little sharks.

Children's Garden

When finally we were able to convince them to dry their hands and move on, we returned outdoors to visit the Camden Children's Garden. A not-for-profit display by the Camden City Garden Club, this tiny gem ranks among Camden's best attractions. Indeed, its 4 acres crammed with more than a dozen themed, fantasy gardens rate it among the state's outstanding surprises. Although it's attached to the aquarium and admission is included in the aquarium entry fee, the garden functions independently and can be visited separately.

No sooner had we wandered into this fantasy plantland than the kids disappeared. Gone. Whizzed right past the Dinosaur Garden and vanished into a maze called Red Oak Run. We found them, of course, but not until we'd marched in circles for a while. Regrouped and everyone accounted for, the girls then tore off to investigate the Storybook Gardens, where we soon found them sitting in gigantic tea cups and later in a chair that revealed, no doubt, how Alice felt when she was very, very small. Then—zoom!—it was off again, this time to investigate the carousel and a miniature train ride that encircled the Railroad Garden through which traveled five G-scale model trains.

It's truly a wonderment, this garden for kids, a place for them to romp merrily, climb onto and into things, and to investigate nature. I personally favored the Butterfly Garden, an indoor insect aviary in which some 15 species of the beautiful, multi-colored creatures fluttered all around us.

The Railroad Garden at the Camden Children's Garden

Other special spots at the Children's Garden include the Picnic Garden, in which edible plants are highlighted and gigantic, sculpted ants march; the Trout Stream, complete with real fish; and the Frog Grotto, where frogs have been known to turn into princes. Special events, too, are a forte here. The calendar is full of them from April through December. We're talking gatherings like Dino Day, the Cinco de Mayo celebration, BlueBEARy Blast, Mum Madness & Pumpkin Parade, and even Goblins in the Garden at Halloween. It all culminates in December with the Holiday Festival of Lights, in which more than 100,000 lights, including animated light sculptures, brighten the place in true holiday spirit.

BATTLESHIP *NEW JERSEY*

I left my ladies at the gardens. They had to catch the train to return home. My Camden exploration was just beginning. I hopped on the free jitney that runs along the waterfront. When I got off before me stood an enormous, intimidating, and downright righteous Gray Lady. Her guns seemingly still at the ready, the battleship *New Jersey* guards the Camden–Philadelphia harbor in a most majestic manner.

The more than 60,000-ton vessel came to the Camden waterfront in October 2001 and has quickly become one of the mainstays of the city's revitalization. Built in 1942, she is the country's most decorated warship, seeing action in World War II, Korea, Vietnam, and the Middle East. Its onboard technology evolved through all the advances of those periods, from classic 16-inch guns to Tomahawk missiles.

Now, before I prattle on, seeming like a warmongering fool, let me say this: You need not be a militarist or even a civilian "hawk" (a peacenik from the old school, I certainly don't qualify as either) to appreciate an enormous machine like this. But, like it or not, the military is most often the proving ground for the technologies that make our daily lives what they are today—be it computerized video games or supersized jets—and there's an undeniable fascination in examining this veritable floating city.

"Women tend to be most interested in how the sailors lived on the ship," Jack Willard, the ship's information "officer," told me when I asked him to whom the floating museum had appeal. "Men want to see the technology." Okay, it sounds clichéd, but those kinds of commonalities create clichés. For me, the whole phenomenon of a battleship holds fascination.

Jack led me on a merry tour, reciting the ship's numbers as we went: 887 feet, 7 inches long; 108 feet, 1 inch wide; 11 stories high; originally built with nine 16-inch, .50-caliber guns, twenty 5-inch, .38 caliber, dual-purpose guns, sixty-four 40-mm antiaircraft guns (the number later increased to eighty), and forty-nine 20-mm antiaircraft guns (increased during World War II to fifty-seven); a ship's company that at one time included 120 officers and 3,000 enlisted men; and most impressive of all, just one casualty during the ship's entire active use.

A variety of themed, guided tours are offered on the *New Jersey;* a self-guided tour is available as well. Colored lines painted on the decks mark the way. In addition to touring the outer decks and pretending to be gunners, my guide and I visited the captain's quarters, the admiral's quarters (there had to be one, just in case an admiral happened to come

The battleship New Jersey

aboard), the officers' mess, the bridge, the enlisted men's mess, and the bunk rooms. As a guy who gets seasick from just looking at the ocean (see chapter 7), living on board and sleeping in a bunk barely big enough to contain a large child, no less a six-foot man, was hard to envisage.

Deep in the vessel's innards we ventured into a pair of intriguing operations units. The Communications Center illustrates how contact among the ship's myriad stations and functions was maintained, and includes a unique voice-activated phone system that was devised to handle situations in which electrical power might be lost. (This, in 1942—and you thought your voice-activated cell phone was modern!) The Combat Engagement Center is dark. Very dark. All decked out in black, innumerable screens flicker along the walls. This was the nerve center for Tomahawk missile launches, and simulated launches are a highlight of any ship's tour.

But for me, the real highlight was hearing about the overnight Family Encampments. Open on specific occasions to adults and children age seven and up, campers tour the ship and eat and sleep on board. Meals, slopped onto plates by the kids themselves, are served in the enlisted men's mess, and shipboard announcements, too, are delivered by kids. It's a chance for a mildly adventurous, hands-on learning experience that's unique in the state.

Our tour concluded, Jack tried to lure me into the museum's latest exhibit—the 4-D Flight Simulator Ride. Located on the promenade next to the ship's visitors center, this gadget re-creates the sights, sounds, and movements of a plane. "There are even points in the ride," Jack said, "where you feel the wind through the cockpit." The simulator's featured program is "Seahawk: Battle for Iwo Jima," in which guests ride over Iwo Jima in a World War II Seahawk prop plane launched from the New Jersey's deck, avoiding antiaircraft fire while engaging the enemy in a dog fight. Other programs include "Desert Storm, Desert Attack," which puts riders in a Navy jet, and "Wild Africa," in which you fly from space into Africa to encounter elephants, rhinos, spiders, bats, and all manner of critters.

Citing my lightly triggered motion-sickness tendencies, I politely declined Jack's offer. But I promised to be back for one of the Family Encampments, duffle bag and all.

FERRY TO PHILLY

The afternoon was waning. I was tiring. I also had some time to kill before my next date, a Camden Riversharks minor-league baseball game. Why not a mini-cruise to relax?

The *RiverLink* Ferry runs between a dock near the aquarium to Philadelphia's Penn's Landing. It offers a great way to extend your Camden waterfront explorations into Philly, adding en route terrific views of both city skylines, the Ben Franklin Bridge, the battleship, and the aquarium building.

I boarded the Philly-bound boat with just a few other passengers. We soon passed the *New Jersey*, which afforded me a chance to appreciate the ship's size. Just as we rolled past, two guys sped past on a pair of wave runners, riding fast between us and the battleship. Interesting juxtaposition: the World War II–built heavyweight dwarfing a pair of zipping, 21st-century water gnats.

On the other side of the river, Penn's Landing presents its own variety of intriguing activities. Here you can tour the Independence Seaport Museum, which includes the cruiser *Olympia* and submarine *Becuna*, as well as a variety of museum exhibits; indulge in many dining options; take a sailing cruise; play at the 25,000-square-foot skate park; or walk to Philadelphia's downtown and historic sites.

Me, I just sat there and watched the ferry load for the return to Camden. The line was long and an inordinate number of boarding passengers were dressed with country-and-western flair. Young ladies in tight jeans and cowboy hats, gents in cowboy boots. What was this all about? Seems that country-western star Tim McGraw was performing that evening at the Tweeter Center.

The Tweeter Center at the Waterfront stands adjacent to the battleship *New Jersey*. It represents, according to its creators, "a revolution in amphitheater technology." As an outdoor venue, it can hold as many as 25,000, utilizing a huge lawn with giant video screens and state-of-the-art computerized sound system. In winter, it converts to a fully enclosed theater with seating ranging for 1,600 to 7,000, depending on the event. A

* * * * * * * *

DETAILS

For general information on the Camden waterfront: *856-757-9400; www.camdenwaterfront.com; Camden Waterfront Marketing Bureau, One Port Center, 2 Riverside Drive, Suite 102, Camden, New Jersey 08103.*

New Jersey State Aquarium *is open mid-September through mid-April, Monday through Friday from 9:30 to 4:30 and Saturday and Sunday 10–5; mid-April through mid-September daily from 9:30 to 5:30. Information: 856-365-3300; www.njaquarium.org; 1 Riverside Drive, Camden, New Jersey 08103-1060.*

Admission to the Camden Children's Garden *is included with entry to the aquarium, but one may buy garden admission alone. The garden is open mid-April through mid-September weekdays from 9:30 to 5:30; mid-September until mid-April weekdays from 9:30 to 4:30; year-round weekend hours are 10–5. Information: 856-365-8733; www.camdenchildrensgarden.org; 3 Riverside Drive, Camden, NJ 08103.*

The battleship *New Jersey* *is open in January and February, Friday through Monday from 9 to 3; daily in March from 9 to 3; daily April through September from 9 to 5; and daily October through December from 9 to 3. Information: 1-866-877-6262; www.battleshipnewjersey.org; 62 Battleship Place, Camden, NJ 08103.*

Camden Riversharks game schedule and ticket information: *1-866-742-7579, 856-963-2600; www.riversharks.com.*

The RiverLink Ferry *normally operates from 9:40 AM to 5:20 PM with departures every 40 minutes from Philadelphia and Camden; later runs are made when events are being held at the Tweeter Center. Information: 215-925-5465; www.riverlinkferry.org.*

RiverPass is a combination ticket that allows admission to Independence Seaport Museum, the cruiser Olympia and the submarine Becuna, and the New Jersey State Aquarium in Camden with round-trip passage on the RiverLink Ferry. Contact any of the venues involved for information and pricing.

Tweeter Center information: 856-365-1300; www.tweeter center.com/philadelphia; 1 Harbour Blvd., Camden, NJ 08103.

River Line trains are operated by New Jersey Transit. They run every 15 minutes during rush hours and every half-hour otherwise. **Information and schedules:** *1-800-331-9791 or, in New Jersey, 1-800-582-5946; www.riverline.com.*

❊ ❊ ❊ ❊ ❊ ❊ ❊ ❊

variety of concerts, Broadway productions, and family entertainments are presented.

Now I was conflicted. Long a country-music fan, I was tempted to forgo the ball game to see McGraw. But no, I had a friend coming to meet me at the ballpark. It would be baseball tonight.

PLAY BALL

As I strolled from the Camden ferry dock to the ballpark, I found myself walking among a group of people wearing name tags. I struck up a conversation with two of them. They had sailed over from a sports editors' conference being held in Philadelphia to watch the Camden Riversharks. I was impressed, but not overly surprised. The renaissance of minor-league baseball is a nationwide phenomenon, and the Riversharks just might be New Jersey's poster children for the movement. Their stadium, Campbell's Field—so named because it stands on the site of a former Campbell's Soup factory—has twice been voted Ballpark of the Year.

And what a beauty it is. Tucked just beneath the Ben Franklin Bridge, the architecture recalls baseball's halcyon days, revealing great views from all its seats and outfitted with all the modern amenities. There are any number of reasons for attending a minor-league ball game (see chapter 27), but the accessibility, low-key friendliness, and commitment to pure fun stand out. Indeed, while I waited for my friend Jim to meet me at the front gate, the Riversharks one-millionth fan passed through the turn-stiles. Music played, trumpets blared, confetti and ribbons flew through the air. Later, on the field, prizes were awarded to the lucky fan.

Jim and I wandered the ballpark, indulged in some ballpark-style food, observed the sunset over Philadelphia, and watched the colored lights illuminate the Ben Franklin Bridge as we sat through a most enter-taining Riversharks victory.

On a normal day, the 5 PM ferry that I rode would be the day's last. On Tweeter Center event nights, however, the boats run until the concert crowds have gone home. So, the sports editors I met walking to the ball-park were able to take the ferry back to the city. Not so for weekday River Line train riders like me, however. Because the trains share the tracks with Conrail's nighttime freight trains, they stop running by 9 PM on weekdays. I would have had to leave the game by the fourth or fifth inning to catch the last train. Luckily, Jim, who had driven to Camden, was willing to chauffeur me to my car in Bordentown. That was the day's sole glitch, one that could be conceivably corrected if the River Line gains enough rider-ship. And it might well increase. Because Camden is indeed on the rise.

CHANGE CONTINUES

As this book goes to press, major changes are in the offing for the Camden waterfront. The aquarium will emerge in spring 2005 from a long winter's nap, having morphed into something twice its previous size. In addition to increased exhibit space will be a 4-D Imax Theater. Several huge parking lots are slated to be replaced with a riverfront promenade, retail shops, restaurants, and even some residential development. The aquarium's main gate will move into the new wing. While this will change the specific dynamics of a visit to the aquarium and Children's Garden, chances are the entire experience will improve, offering more sights and entertainment options. Visit the web sites on page 58 to keep abreast of all these changes.

NOT JUST GAMBLING (YOU CAN BET ON IT)

Atlantic City

TLANTIC CITY HAS LONG REIGNED as an American vacation icon. Many elements that symbolize a shore visit were first conceived here. The boardwalk, for example. It was first constructed in 1870 to provide a place to walk easily by the sea, shop, eat, and be merry. So merry, in fact, that the boardwalk was soon extended out over the water, and the amusement pier was invented. The year was 1882, and Atlantic City's heyday had begun.

The good times lasted well into the 1950s. But by the mid-1960s, "AC" had badly deteriorated from the Queen Resort to an aging matriarch. Until the casinos came.

Today tourists make more than 30 million visits to Atlantic City. The vast majority come to play the slots, shuffle the cards, roll the dice, or spin the roulette wheel. The boardwalk bustles. The night sky blazes with neon fire. There are those who condemn Atlantic City's casino-fed rebirth. But it has brought new life to the city, and an excitement that runs along the 4-mile-long boardwalk spills over onto Atlantic and Pacific Avenues.

I'm not a gamer—a "player" as they say—so I'll not attempt to differentiate among the grand casinos. I'm sure that regular visitors can discern the nuances that separate the Trump Marina from the Trump Taj Mahal from the Trump Plaza, or Bally's from the Tropicana; I'm sure that folks have their personal favorites, just as I, an avid skier, have my favorites among ski resorts. But I will say that the action moves nonstop, and there's never a time where the slot-machine bells aren't tingling or the croupiers dealing, and that if you're attracted to this kind of action, you'll find a happy home here.

What if you're not a gamer? What can you do in Atlantic City? Well, for one thing, you can eat very, very well. Most of the casinos offer sumptuous, lavish buffet spreads for extremely reasonable prices. Each casino contains about a half-dozen restaurants, and the culinary styles span the world—from Chinese to Japanese and French. Outside the casinos, places like Abe's Oyster House and Dock's Oyster House, both on Atlantic Avenue, carry on the city's longstanding tradition of purveying superb local seafood.

World-class entertainment can keep the non-gambler happy. In the casino's big rooms and lounges, you find names like Kid Rock, Mary J. Blige, Lou Rawls, KISS, and—well, you name it. If you like lavish musical productions, Atlantic City's stage shows can match the Las Vegas reviews any day.

The entertainment goes beyond gaming houses to a number of annual festivals and events. The Miss America Pageant, of course, remains the city's best-known happening. Again, enjoyment is a matter of taste; ardent feminists and their sympathizers will find no joy in the pageant, but the collection of pretty young women, the pressure of chasing some ambiguous championship, and the ongoing high jinks add nicely to the city's mindless frolic. Little known to those familiar only with the televised finals: almost all the preliminary events are offered for free or for a minimal fee. A traditional favorite is the Show Me Your Shoes Parade, in which the contestants glide down the boardwalk on floats and in cars lifting a leg high when spectators shout "Show us your shoes!"

Come spring, the town mounts a seafood festival that attracts thousands. In summer, jazz performances pervade the boardwalk. The nearby Stockton Performing Arts Center, on the Stockton State College campus, presents a full range of music and theater performances. And the annual Antiques and Collectibles Show, staged in both the spring and fall, is billed as the world's largest antiques fair. Presented in the Atlantic City

Boardwalk Convention Hall, it features nearly 7,000 exhibitors. Anyone with even the mildest affection for antiques will find something to marvel. In February, antique cars fill the bill on an equally grand scale.

Indeed, the Boardwalk Hall itself is worthy of a visit. Built in 1929, it was the world's largest auditorium constructed without interior posts. Renovated in 2001 to the tune of $90 million, the hall seats 13,800 for concerts, sporting events, and family shows, and its main exhibition space spans 300,000 square feet under a 137-foot arched roof. Now home to the Boardwalk Bullies hockey team, indoor collegiate football was once played in here.

Located right on the boardwalk, the Atlantic City Historical Museum is approachable in size and affords a fascinating look at the city's past. Just a bit north of town stands one of the state's outstanding art museums, the Noyes Museum of Art in Oceanville. Included in the permanent collection and rotating exhibits are contemporary American art, crafts, and folk art. In town, the Atlantic City Art Center has ongoing exhibits in a full range of visual disciplines. And then, for something a bit more arcane, there's an installation of the Ripley's Believe It or Not! Museum chain.

Despite the neon and high-rise buildings, nature is not forgotten. In Brigantine, the Brigantine Sea Life Museum and Marine Mammal Stranding Center provides a close look at rescued whales, dolphins, seals,

DETAILS

For general information, *contact the Convention & Visitors Bureau: 1-888-228-4748; www.atlanticcitynj.com.*

Directions: *To reach Atlantic City by car, take the Garden State Parkway to the Atlantic City Expressway. The city is served by Amtrak, and a variety of bus companies from all over the region run day trips. The airport is served by USAir, United Express, Northwest Airlink, and other regional carriers.*

and sea turtles. The Ocean Life Center in the town's Gardner's Basin section contains a ton of tanks—fish tanks, that is. Eight tanks to be exact, holding 29,800 gallons of water and 100 varieties of fish and marine animals. The Touch Tank is always a hit, and the Ocean Life Education Center affords a chance to gain personalized insight into the living ocean.

Kids are not forgotten in Atlantic City. Classic roller coasters and other rides and amusements are found at TropWorld's Tivoli Pier and the Central Pier on the boardwalk. And, a visit to the gigantic Lucy the Elephant in Margate, located just south of the city, is one of the Jersey shore's longstanding traditions. No kid ever looked at the six-story-high Lucy without dropping his or her jaw. The Children's Museum in nearby Egg Harbor Township is perfect for inclement or just too-hot days.

Need more? You can play golf nearby (see chapter 17), fish from the beach or from a boat, and if the honky-tonk bustle becomes overbearing, you can find peace and quiet at the Forsythe National Wildlife Refuge (see chapter 3).

Atlantic City is not everybody's cup of tea. In 1942, Thorton Wilder chose, in the first act of his Pulitzer Prize–winning play *The Skin of Our Teeth*, to use this "playground by the sea" to represent man's self-indulgent, decadent state just prior to the biblical Flood. The city's popularity, however, goes well beyond the fast-paced, glitzy casino ambience. From simple sunbathing on the white-sand beach to a slow ride in a boardwalk roller chair to an excellent meal or a humongous antiques show, the area offers much more than gaming.

PLAYING ON THE DELAWARE RIVER

The Delaware Water Gap National Recreation Area

THE DELAWARE RIVER runs 390 miles from north central New York State to the Delaware Bay. It's most visually striking section is a treasure shared by New Jersey and Pennsylvania—the Delaware Water Gap. At the gap, the river cuts through the side of Kittatinny Mountain, whose rocks make up the highest ridge in the Appalachians from New York to Tennessee.

We walked along the river for 1½ miles on an old railroad bed now called the Karamac Road Trail. Several well-worn, occassionally steep detours ran down to the water. That's where the kids stumbled upon the abandoned bridge abutments. Finding the stone and concrete slabs, overgrown with grasses and vines, was like discovering an ancient Roman ruin, complete with hieroglyphic graffiti dating to 1979. A perfect place to throw stones or cast sticks into the river and watch them float away.

We drove north on Old Mine Road, a bumpity affair. Anglers lined the water's edge. We stopped at the Copper Mine Trail trailhead. I parked next to the port-a-potty. "There's a tarantula in there!" we were warned by a small boy dressed in a Ninja Turtle raincoat. "Don't go in!" Dan and his pal Aaron immediately opened the door. There it was! Well, if it wasn't a tarantula, at least it was a gnarly-looking, extremely large, black spider.

Suddenly nobody had to go.

We left Mr. Spider alone and went to search for the abandoned copper

Delaware Water Gap Recreation Area

mines that give the trail its name.

The Copper Mine Trail runs up to the Appalachian Trail along Kittatinny Ridge, but the old mines are no more than a quarter-mile up a sidetrack. What a beautiful sidetrack. The earth practically gleamed red, and a stream bounced energetically down the steep hillside, cascading over several small waterfalls, and pooling where the sharply angled slope flattened into shelves. We reached a mine and found the entrance boarded up neatly with heavy lumber. A small doorway was set in the middle.

"Don't open it!" the kids cried, in fear, no doubt, of more tarantulas.

I immediately opened it. Nothing to see but—dark.

Aaron clambered up the trail beyond the mine. The path ascended steeply next to tumbling water, over moss-slick rocks and tree roots. I followed. A crumbling concrete dam pooled water about a hundred feet above the mine. Above that, a larger cascade glinted like flowing diamonds in the sun. We reached a ledge and looked back. A narrow corridor of dense forest was cut by the beautifully singing stream. Aaron wanted to continue up the steep ledge, but I glumly informed him we were out of time.

On the way back, the boys set a block of wood afloat in the stream.

"Where do you think our wood block is now?" Dan wondered when we were about halfway home.

"Imagine if it floated to the ocean and washed up at the beach when we were there in the summer?" Aaron replied.

"It probably floated to Philadelphia and got pulled onto a ship bound for the Orient," I declared.

"Cool," they said in an awed whisper.

TUBING

If a wood block could float the Delaware, so could we. After all, we've rafted the icy waters and Class III and IV rapids of Maine's Kennebec and Colorado's Turner. So, really now, was this *floating* going to challenge us? Was this going to frighten us with excitement? I didn't think so.

My companions, twelve-year-old girls, tried their best to make it otherwise, however. Laina's friend Nancy adeptly worked herself into a nervous frenzy. "I'm so scared. I'm so scared. I'm so scared," she repeated like a mantra. Laina, who had paddled dauntlessly as whirling Maine waters whipped our raft about like a toy tug in a torrent, caught the fever and began professing terror of the Delaware's lazy flow.

"Just hold the tube behind you and fall back on your tush," our guide told us after strapping us into life jackets. "Stay to your right. When you see the campground, that's the take-out point. If you're too far out into the river, you won't get over in time, and who knows where you'll be able to get out. The river's moving pretty fast. About four miles per hour."

Four m.p.h. Huh. A snail's pace compared to the Turner.

The girls stopped their nervous Nellie chattering long enough to flop back onto their fannies. We were off.

Slowly.

But speed was not the name of this game. Relaxing was. Within 5 minutes we began to ease back and allow ourselves to go with the flow. When the I-84 overpass disappeared from sight, the tubes began to passively revolve with the current, and we were lost in a primeval setting in which the riverbanks were thick with trees and undergrowth, the crickets made the dominant noise, and worldly cares slipped away.

Until a gurgling rumble assaulted our ears.

"What's that?" cried Nancy. She'd drifted ahead of us and suddenly remembered that she was supposed to be terrified.

"Rapids," I said.

"Laina!" Nancy screeched. "Laina, let me hold your hand."

I shouldn't have called them rapids. Ripples? Rapettes, perhaps? Whatever you'd call baby rapids. Bobbling through them, we were lightly jostled, then placed back on the river's table-smooth surface. Cute. Once Nancy had stopped screeching.

We drifted on. I lolled into a reverie. An island appeared. Stay to the right. I had visions of pioneers canoeing the river long before campgrounds and highways and summer resorts were invented. I saw the entangled underbrush and trees. I saw myself drifting to the river's center.

❋ ❋ ❋ ❋ ❋ ❋ ❋ ❋

DETAILS

The Delaware Water Gap National Recreation Area *runs for 37 miles along the New Jersey–Pennsylvania border. The southern visitors center is located on the New Jersey side at Kittatinny Point just off I-80. The northern Dingmans Falls Visitor's Center is on the Pennsylvania side at Dingmans Ferry. Both offer extensive programming; contact them for information and a schedule of events. Information: Kittatinny Point Visitors Center (908-496-4458), Dingmans Falls Visitors Center (570-828-2253); www.nps.gov/dewa.*

Throughout the gap there are facilities for launching boats, fishing, camping, swimming, picnicking, hunting, and, in winter, snowshoeing and cross-country skiing. Bicyclists will enjoy the riding along Old Mine Road. Some 20 outfits rent canoes.

Tubing companies: *Indian Head Canoes & Rafts, Newton, NJ, (1-800-874-2628; www.indianheadcanoes.com); Delaware River Family Camping Resort, Delaware, NJ (1-888-543-0271, 908-475-4517; www.drfcnj.com); Kittatinny Canoes, Dingmans Ferry, PA (1-800-356-2852; www.floatkc.com).*

❋ ❋ ❋ ❋ ❋ ❋ ❋ ❋

I saw the water's eddies whorl and move on. I saw a hawk circling. I saw the girls floating in toward the take-out point.

Whoa! Take-out point? What am I doing here in midstream? Whoa! I flapped my arms and kicked my feet like a mad duck. No progress. Suddenly 4 miles per hour wasn't so lazy. The girls were out of the water. But, yikes!, I was going to miss it!

Splush. I tipped myself over and, clutching the tube like a swimming pool kickboard, I kicked and flapped a free arm. I gauged the distance (20 yards?) against the current's strength, then kicked harder. And kicked bottom. Huh? I kicked again. And hit bottom again. I stood up. The water was barely waist high. I stood still and caught my breath. Panic? Who me? Coolly I strolled to shore.

"I thought you weren't going to make it!" Laina yelped.

"Piece of cake," I lied. Did I say tubing wasn't going to be exciting?

Horsing Around

Riding, Breeding, & Racing

Mounting Up

THIS IS ABOUT THE SIZE OF IT—I've never trusted any animal that's significantly larger than I am. Take horses, for example. You never know when one might decide to remind you who's boss. No matter how much you can bench-press in your basement, you'll lose.

Little girls, on the other hand, never seem to have this fear. I don't get it. Within an hour of arriving at a stables or guest ranch, my daughter is addressing every one of the dozens of horses in the corral by name, petting and cooing at them. I'm still calling them Sir and Ma'am when we leave, whether that's three hours or three days later. And, how come my daughter, who has only been on a horse a half-dozen times in her life, is off and cantering before I can figure out how to get my 28-short leg high enough in the air to put my foot in the stirrup? And how come Mom is laughing?

I've ridden—if we can call it that—in exotic locales, such as Colorado, Mexico, and the state of Washington. But, you don't have to go way out West to play cowboy. One early spring day several years ago, we stumbled into a most unlikely looking place just outside Hackettstown, right next to US 46. HORIZON STABLES, the handmade-looking sign read, HORSEBACK RIDING. The place didn't look like much—a barn that seemed to have seen better days was all we could see from the highway. Still, it was such a surprise to see a stable sitting so near to the highway, it had to be investigated.

Following the sign's suggestion, we turned right, drove a few hundred feet, and pulled over. A variety of vehicles and horse trailers were parked in a disorderly fashion. I stepped out of the car and stepped right into . . . it. I'd forgotten. Near horses, you've got to watch your step. And there were plenty of horses around. Most of them stood nonchalantly swiping their tails at nonexistent flies. Plenty of riders were hanging around, too, mostly young and female. Some sat on a fence that surrounded a riding ring. Others fussed over the animals. Beyond the barn, a large open field drifted up a lazy hill. Thick woods loomed in the distance.

Horizon, it turned out, ran full-fledged, trail rides. "Hack riding," Megan LaBrie called it. A 21-year-old equestrienne, Megan was working then as a stable hand at Horizon while she trained in hopes of joining the pro rodeo circuit. Horizon, she pointed out, emphasized Western riding. Western trail rides aren't that hard to find in New Jersey. Legends Riding Stable in Vernon, for one, offers them through the state's northern hills. All-day and even overnight rides can be had at Double D Guest Ranch in Blairstown. (Unlike me, apparently, many people like going out on long rides that meander into remote places.) Another option is offered by Branded RW Ranch in Blairstown—a ride along the Paulinskill Trail, a converted railroad bed.

Now Horizon Stables, like so much that's rural in New Jersey, is no longer with us. But the experience we had there can still be duplicated in a surprising number of places across the state, from suburban settings, such as Bergen County's Overpeck County Park or Franklin Lakes' Saddle Ridge Riding Center, to places at the beach, like Hidden Valley Ranch in Cape May, or in the mountains, of which there are many. For those who are too young or too timid, pony rides are offered by many facilities.

That day at Horzion, we refrained from riding—we had other commitments. But we watched a group go out over the pasture. Like our own kid, they looked like they'd been born atop those enormous steeds. Actually, even if you're a horse sissy like me, there's nothing to worry about. Most of these rent-a-horses run on automatic. They have to. After all, they've got to handle a lot of petrified novices—like me. And, you know what they say about horses. They can feel your fear through the seat of your pants. Which is why I always call them "Sir."

Tailgating at the Far Hills Race Meeting

MOUNTING: BREEDING THE FINEST—CREAM RIDGE

Verdant and replete with gently rolling meadows, hills, and woodlands, Cream Ridge is home to a handful of very special horse farms. Residing in the barns and playing in these farm fields are some of the greatest standardbred horses to ever run a race. Or trot one.

If you're like me and don't know a standardbred from a nag, here's the scoop: Standardbreds are the horses that compete in harness racing, as opposed to thoroughbreds, which run at a full gallop. Harness racers are divided into trotters and pacers, the difference is in their racing gait. Standardbreds and thoroughbreds also differ in their breeding. (And, with racehorses, breeding is of the utmost importance.) Standardbreds can be bred through artificial insemination. Thoroughbreds can't.

I learned all this at Walnridge Farm, where Dr. David Meirs II, veterinarian and founder of the Walnridge equine-breeding program, was proud to show off his prize horses and to talk about the farm that he converted in 1972 from an unsuccessful dairy operation to standardbred breeding predominance.

"The farm has been in the family since 1830," Dr. Meirs told me as we admired the stallions. "We began breeding when the New Jersey Sire Stakes

72

program was instituted. That's a program in which New Jersey harness tracks sponsor a series of races only for horses conceived in New Jersey."

Conceived—that's the important word. A competing horse can live anywhere, but to compete in these races impregnation has to have taken place in the Garden State. Keeping in mind that for racehorses lineage is vital, and that artificial insemination is acceptable for standardbreds, and the importance of the Sire Stakes program becomes obvious—bring your mare to one of these Monmouth County farms, home to the best of the best, have her impregnated here, and the offspring qualify to return to New Jersey to win big money.

We entered a large, rather barren, square room with concrete floors. A large object stood to one side. It looked like an oversized gymnastic pommel horse that had a hollow section and was laden with several contraptionlike attachments. "This is an artificial vagina," Dr. Meirs elucidated. "We train the stallions to use it, and then the semen is put into cold storage until its inseminated into the mares. With artificial insemination, we can fertilize 20 mares a day." The doctor smiled. "There's very little romance involved. We refer to it as drive-by breeding."

At Walnridge, as many as a thousand horses—mares, foals, stallions, and yearlings—are in residence at any time during the year.

Walnridge's barns bring you face-to-face with some of the most successful harness racing horses of all time. In residence here, among others, have been Presidential Ball, a $3 million winner; Beach Towel, the 1990 World Champion; and Niatross, winner of 37 of his 39 races, world-speed record setter, and winner of harness racing's triple crown. They'd all come here to stand as studs, where they had lived a pretty good life, running and playing on 315 acres when they weren't working out on that artificial vagina. It makes the concept of being retired to stud rather appealing.

Show Mounts: Horse Park of New Jersey—Allentown

A short distance from the Cream Ridge breeding grounds, along I-195, the Horse Park of New Jersey operates as a nonprofit, volunteer-run, educational facility. Conceived by state agencies and a consortium of horse industry groups, the site has become a premier equine showplace.

The park contains two large show rings, one of which is equipped with lights for nighttime events. In addition, a grass schooling ring and a fenced outside course are used for training and other riding endeavors.

The Horse Park hosts weekend activities from March through November, including a number of riding events for the disabled; the facility houses twin mounting ramps designed to help the physically challenged. A wide variety of organizations use the place for shows, exhibitions, and competitions. You can also go to an auction at the Horse Park. Standardbred sales are carried on here periodically.

You can't hire a horse here or come to the Horse Park for recreational riding. But for anyone who enjoys watching horses in action, as showplaces go, this facility stands with the best of them.

MOUNTING EXCITEMENT: THE HAMBLETONIAN—EAST RUTHERFORD

There may seem to be something incongruous about horse racing as a family outing, but can 30,000 people be wrong? As many as that—and sometimes more—turn out on the first weekend of August to watch the Hambletonian, a 1-mile trotters' race staged at the Meadowlands Race Track. Among them are a huge number of families, many with young children.

"It looks like a day at the beach," commented Lucky, my next-door neighbor and traveling companion, who'd brought along his kids, 5-year-old Lucky (known locally as Little Lucky) and August, who was 2-plus. Indeed, people streamed in carrying all the accouterments necessary for a beach afternoon or a picnic in the park. Coolers, folding chairs, even folding picnic tables were carted through the gate.

We scurried up the ramp, through the grandstand's main floor, past the betting area, and outside onto a grassy expanse that lay to the grandstand's left. There we discovered a carnival, replete with rides, give-away booths, food vendors, and a performance tent. Only a few folks stood by the rail and watched the horses and drivers strut their stuff in warm-up laps. Those who weren't happily lined up to ride ponies, buy food or play carnival games of skill were spreading out on the grass enjoying their homemade picnics. A clown wandered through the crowd attempting valiantly to induce smiles.

There's historical precedent for this playful, countrified, carnival ambience. The Hambletonian's roots lie deep in the country fairs of western New York and the Midwest.

The inaugural Hambletonian took place in August 1926, at the New York State Fair in Syracuse. By 1930, it moved to Goshen, New York, a small village an hour north of Manhattan. The "Goshen Era" lasted until 1956, when the event became part of the DuQuoin State Fair in DuQuoin, Illinois. In 1981, when the race moved here to the Meadowlands Sports Complex, a commitment was made to continue the longstanding country-fair approach.

Even though the hometown festival atmosphere has continued, the Hambletonian's scope has grown enormously. Coverage of the race in broadcast, print, and electronic media now literally spans the globe. And the race is now prefaced by Hambletonian Festival Week, highlighted by the Hambletonian Parade. Staged several days prior to race day, the parade marches down Rutherford's Park Avenue and includes horses, classic cars, pipes and drums, more music, pony rides, clowns, face painters, a Hambletonian driver autograph session, and booths at which to buy food and crafts.

We missed the parade, but at the track the boys didn't pass up the chance to ride ponies, swoop down a large, multilane slide on potato sacks, eat hot dogs, and be enchanted by the roaming clown. And, just as we were beginning to wilt in the hot summer sun, some live vintage rock 'n' roll and a cold soda provided renewed energy. And if, in the midst of it all, we never actually watched a race being run, it mattered little. Plenty of other people were placing bets, cheering as the steeds raced down the home stretch. When all was said and done, we'd been to the fair and had had a great time.

Could New Jersey harbor any other such event—a horse race in which the actual race takes a back seat to the festivities? Well, in fact there is . . . .

FAR HILLS RACE MEETING—FAR HILLS

"This is the best upscale 'Woodstock' in the country," noted one young gent—who was far too young to have been at the original Woodstock. Could be. But Woodstock didn't have racing horses jumping over water hazards, wooden fences, and shrubberies. The Far Hills Race Meeting has all that and more.

Part of the 36-meet National Steeplechase Association race circuit, the Far Hills Race Meeting, staged in mid-October, includes six steeplechase races, highlighted by the Breeders Cup, the richest race of its kind. More than 50,000 people attend.

Knowing that huge crowds would be clogging Far Hills' country lane–like roads, I decided an early arrival was in order. I drove onto the Moorland Farms grounds several hours before the 1 PM start, but the place was already filling up. It was immediately clear that, more than a major horse race, this might well qualify as the Super Bowl of tailgating. I've regularly wandered the pregame parking lots at Giants Stadium, but I can say authoritatively that the supplies and setups being pulled from the backs of minivans, SUVs, and pickup trucks at this steeplechase reached superlative heights, far exceeding anything I'd ever seen. I'm talking about people who reserve spots up to a year in advance, who bring out the fine crystal, who cover the folding tables with fine linen, and who hire formally dressed wait staff to serve the goods. These tailgaters were dressed to the nines in everything from cowboy hats to fashions worthy of Ascot. They were dancing to live bands (one party built its own stage). Professional ice sculptors worked their magic at a few spots.

And those were merely the tailgaters. What was happening in the corporate sponsored tents could match any grand wedding.

Not everyone puts on the Ritz for this event. By race time the grounds teemed with families and twenty-somethings who streamed in from New Jersey Transit trains and buses, weighed down with blankets, coolers, and sunblock. These blanket people had no less fun. They drank six-packs with gusto, sipped wine with genteelness, tossed footballs, and generally lived large while kids ran amuck playing tag, catch, or well, just running amuck.

To get the full view, I stood atop a high spot overlooking the grounds. The place looked like a veritable anthill decorated with striped awnings, bordered by long lines of blue port-a-potties. I'd never seen so many port-a-potties.

Far Hills Race Meeting

Amid all this activity, the six races were run. Not that too many people noticed. I stopped between races to chat with a gathering of families in the blanket-on-the-ground zone and asked them why they came. "The races, of course," one guy said with a laugh.

Came his buddy's quick retort, "You guys have been here for four years and you've never even seen a horse!"

I thought being able to stand at the rail and watch at close range the gallant steeds vault the jumps and gallop on grass was exhilarating.

There's no official betting at the Race Meeting. But you can bet the house that private betting pools and wagers are common. Common enough that many tailgate parties put up their own wager-tracking scoreboards.

Although admission prices are high (2004 general admission was $50 purchased prior to race day or $100 at the door, and on-site parking runs $30), all the proceeds benefit Somerset Medical Center; more than $15 million has been raised over the years. But a charitable contribution wasn't really necessary to justify attendance. As I left the grounds just before the fifth race, people were still arriving, happy just to be at the party, which would last into the evening, well after the last race had been run.

※ ※ ※ ※ ※ ※ ※ ※

DETAILS

General horseback riding information *is available from the New Jersey Department of Agriculture (609-292-2888; www.state.nj.us/ smug/internet/css/outdoor/horseback.htm; Horse Program, CN 330, Trenton, NJ 08625).*

Horse Park of New Jersey: *609-259-0170, 908-996-2544; www.horseparkofnewjersey.com; Stone Tavern, P.O. Box 548, Allentown, NJ 08501.*

The Hambeltonian Society: *732-249-8500; www.hambletonian.org.*

Far Hills Race Meeting, *908-685-2929; www.farhillsrace.org; 50 Route 202, P.O. Box 617, Far Hills, NJ 07931.*

Stables with Horse Rentals: *Circle A Riding Stables (908-938-2004; 116 Herbertsville Rd., Howell, 07731); Double D Guest Ranch (908-459-9044; 81 Mt. Hermon Road, Blairstown, 07825); Echo Lake Stables (201-697-1257; 55 Blakely Lane, Newfoundland, 07435); Hidden Valley Ranch (609-884-8205; 4070 Bayshore Rd., Cape May, 08204); Lakewood Boarding Stables (908-367-6222; 436 Cross St., Lakewood, 08701); Legends Riding Stable (973-827-8332; Rt. 94, Vernon, 07428); New Horses Around, Inc. (908-938-4480; RD2, Box 302A, Belmar Blvd., Farmingdale, 07727); Rider's Edge Inc. (908-938-7360; 5155 Belmar Blvd., Farmingdale, 07727); Saddle Ridge Riding Center (201-848-0844; Shadow Ridge Rd., Franklin Lakes, 07417); Seaton Hackney Stables (201-267-1372; 440 South St., Morristown, 07960); Slim's Ranch (609-227-9893; 1731 Somerdale Rd., Chews Landing, 08012); Spring Valley Equestrian Ctr. (201-383-3766; 56 Paulinskill Lk. Rd., Newton, 07860); Triangle Acres Equestrian Ctr. (201-831-6767; West Brook Rd., Ringwood, 07456); Triple R Ranch (609-465-4673; 210 Stagecoach Rd., Cape May Court House, 08210); Washington Horseback (riding and pony rides; 908-463-0070/545-6220; 1707 S. Washington Ave., Piscataway, 08854); Watchung Stables (908-789-3665; 1160 Summit Lane, Mountainside, 07092); West*

Milford Equestrian Center, Kebra Ranch (201-697-2020; 367 Union Valley Rd., Newfoundland, 07435); Yellow Rock Farm (908-475-4732; 157 Mountain Lake Rd., Belvidere, 07823).

Horseback Riding for the Disabled: Atlantic Riding Center for the Handicapped (ARCH; 609-926-2233; 214 Asbury Rd., English Creek, 08330); Bancroft, Mullica Hill Campus (609-769-1300; Rt. 581, Box 367, Mullica Hill, 08062); Chariot Riders (908-657-2710; 4004 Quarry Rd., Lakehurst, 08733); Handicapped High Riders (HHR; 609-259-3884; Box 145, Rt. 526, Allentown, 08501); Heads Up Special Riders (609-921-8389; 121 Laurel Ave., Kingston, 08528); R&R Special Riders (609-768-9029; 116 Bramau Ave., Berlin, 08009); Somerset Hills Handicapped Riders, Inc. (SHHRC; 908-234-2024; P.O. Box 455, Bedminster, 07921); S.P.U.R. (908-842-4000/872-2928; Huber Woods Park, Brown's Dock Rd., Locust/Middletown, 07760); Somerset County Therapeutic Recreation Services (908-526-5650; Box 3455, Milltown Rd., North Branch, 08876); Steed (201-327-2284; P.O. Box 84, Allendale, 07401); Thunderbird Riders (609-769-4028; 31 Oechsle Rd., Woodstown, 08098); Unicorn Handicapped Riding (609-953-0255; 40 Cooper-Tomlingson Rd., Medford, 08055); Water Wheel Handicapped Olympian Athletes (W.H.O.A.; 201-347-6514; 11-197 Dell Pl., Stanhope, 07874).

State and County Parks and Forests and Wildlife Management Areas: Many state and county parks allow riding. At some you must bring your own horse. Some require fees or permits. Horseback riding is also allowed on selected wildlife management areas throughout the state; permits are required. **Information:** 609-259-2132; Division of Fish, Game and Wildlife, 386 Clarksburg Robbinsville Rd., Robbinsville, NJ 08691.

✽ ✽ ✽ ✽ ✽ ✽ ✽ ✽

BIRD-WATCHING & DELAWARE BAY

Dennisville

MARTY THURLOW LOVED TO TELL BIRDWATCHER stories. A former Cape May County bed & breakfast owner with his wife, Ann, he gladly regaled me with tales of the ardor, fervor, and obsession displayed by people dedicated to sighting our winged friends. To a person unschooled in the ways of bird-watching, these narratives are fascinating listening.

In the spring, people flock to the Dennisville area. They do it because the birds flock here, and the birds do it because the horseshoe crabs flock here. Some mind-boggling facts: Horseshoe crabs, large-shelled animals that look like miniature Panzer tanks, predate the dinosaurs by about 150 million years and are considered by some to be living fossils. These crabs live only in the Atlantic Ocean and they nest primarily on the lower Delaware Bay. The springtime survival of more than a million shorebirds depends upon the eggs laid by the crabs. The birds consume approximately 300 tons of nutritious horseshoe crab eggs each spring. The Red Knot, for example, flies nonstop for four days from the southern reaches of Argentina to the Delaware Bay feast, makes a two-week rest stop here during which it doubles its weight, and then flies on another 3,000 miles to nest in the Canadian Arctic.

A significant portion of this crab and bird activity takes place at an inauspicious spot called Reeds Beach. The road to Reeds Beach, accessible

Reeds Beach on Delaware Bay

from NJ 47, runs for 2.5 miles through marshes thick with the area's signature wild grasses and reeds, then takes you past an eerie place where the
road is lined on one side with the skeletons of dead trees and on the other
with high, almost desertlike sand dunes. You know you've reached the
famous birding spot when the road ends. (Bring bug spray. Reeds Beach
has also gained fame for its thick mosquito and biting insect
population.)

In truth, there's great birding all along Delaware Bay in this region
that I've come to call the "underbelly of New Jersey." To me, it's the most
remarkable area of a remarkably diverse state. But, like so much of New
Jersey, the region often serves only as a byway to other places. With the
exception of a small handful of fishermen, duck hunters, boatmen, and
birders, most people are just passing through. The birders will tell you,
however, there's a lot of reason to stop and, well, smell the wetlands.

Dennisville's long and active history begins with cedar mining. Long ago, enormous cedar trees grew in the nearby swamps, gaining heights as tall as the famous Western redwoods. But, at some point, a violent storm (or storms) felled nearly all the grand old trees, and they eventually sank into the swamp. Submerged and overgrown with peat, the cedar wood remained remarkably preserved. When Europeans migrated into the area, they discovered the trunks and dug them up. Thus, the term cedar mining, instead of cedar lumbering. From these trees were made many a seagoing ship, and the shingles that top the roof of Independence Hall in Philadelphia. And then, inevitably, one day the cedar was played out.

Sand mines were another enterprise that supported the area's economy. A number of them can still be found nearby along CR 660. The sand was taken up the road to Millville—site of Wheaton Village and the Glass Museum (see chapter 48)—where it was fired into glass.

When you travel to the area today, you enter a world that feels far closer to the rural south than it does to the familiar industrialized environment we most readily associate with New Jersey. Follow CR 553 through the lush overgrowth of semitropical plants to tiny Port Norris, and you'll feel as though you've traveled to the areas outside North Carolina's Hilton Head. Head south from there to the minuscule hamlet

❋ ❋ ❋ ❋ ❋ ❋ ❋ ❋

DETAILS

To reach this area from the north, *take the Garden State Parkway to exit 13, turn north onto US 9, then west on NJ 83 and west again on NJ 47. From the west and the Camden–Philadelphia area, take NJ 55 south to Millville and get onto NJ 47 east.*

For overnight stays in this part of New Jersey, *try any of the wonderful bed & breakfasts in Cape May or try a motel in Millville and add Wheaton Village to your agenda. General information on the region is available through the Southern Shore Regional Tourism Council: 1-800-227-2297 (Cape May County), 856-453-2177 or 1-866-866-6673 (Cumberland County); www.njsouthernshore.com.*

❋ ❋ ❋ ❋ ❋ ❋ ❋ ❋

of Bivalve, and you'll find the remnants of the oystering business that once thrived in the bay; it's making a comeback of sorts, but the locals will tell you it's nothing like it used to be.

Continue east on CR 553 to the tiny town of Dividing Creek, stop in at the marina that sits next to the highway along the banks of the creek, and ask for a boat tour; perhaps you can rent a boat and travel up the Maurice (pronounced Morris) River, through the dense vegetation and unique ecology that has led to the river's being designated as a National Wild and Scenic River, or perhaps you'd rather just keep driving along Methodist Road and down CR 643 to the microscopic bayside community of Gandy's Beach. These small, rural hamlets, proverbial one-horse towns that seem to be from a different time and light years away from New Jersey's helter-skelter, traffic-laden world of suburban shopping malls, are a study in themselves. And they all provide access to excellent birding.

Meanwhile, back at Reed's Beach, you'll find a handwritten sign (assuming it has survived the last winter) that offers bird-watching boat tours. Me, I'd get into one of those boats and watch the birdwatchers. As Marty Thurlow told me, they put on quite a show in their own right.

THE AMERICAN INDIAN ARTS FESTIVAL
Powhaten Renape Nation Rankokus Reservation—
Rancocas

FIVE MEN, DRESSED IN COLORFUL, ceremonial costumes, solemnly encircle the pole and momentarily honor it with ritualistic gravity. Then, methodically, they begin to climb into the sky. At the pole's zenith—one hundred feet off the ground—they adeptly take their places. Four of them seat themselves on a square frame rigged to the pole. The fifth stands on the narrow surface of the very top. Now the top man begins to play a handmade wooden flute and an attached miniature drum. The flute's trilled resonance and the drum's persistent beat float down over the gathered crowd who stare fascinated from below. The flute player dances, rotating in that precarious spot on sure, rapidly moving feet. Suddenly, as one, the four others fall backward, like deep-sea scuba divers dropping into midair. Their fall is abrupt, but short. Just as suddenly, they are dangling from ropes. Slowly, hanging upside down, they rotate gently clockwise around the pole. The flute and drum music continues. Like spiders letting out silk, the ropes grow gradually longer, lowering the four men toward the ground while the flute and drum play on. When they are within reach of the grass, the men flip over as one and touch ground.

The pole dance of Mexico's Totaneko Indians is the most daring event at the Powhaten Renape Nation's American Indian Arts Festival, but it may not be the most spectacular—depending upon your point of view.

You might think, rather, that the fire dance creates more spectacle.

The pole dance of Mexico's Totaneko Indians

Performers dressed in flashy, bright combinations of black and white, wearing colorful ostrich feather headdresses that wave gracefully with their movements, dance dangerously close to fiery flame pots accompanied by hard-driving drums.

Or, perhaps, you find the hoop dancer's intricate movements as she weaves several colorful wooden rings into a variety of geometric patterns more of a spectacle.

No matter. The arts festival's nonstop entertainment conjures up such awe and such a continuing array of visual delights that you're left with little time to ponder what is most daring or spectacular.

The Powhaten Renape Nation's Rankokus Reservation occupies 350 wooded acres along the Rancocas River just a few minutes from a strip of commercial highway that seems worlds away. The Powhaten are one of the oldest documented tribes in North America. They lived, when the Europeans arrived, in the mid-Atlantic region, in what is now Maryland

and Delaware. They hold two of
the oldest treaties signed by Native
Americans and Europeans, including one signed with England in
1646. Although the Powhaten
Renape's forty nations signed a
1677 treaty that gave them rights to
vast amounts of Virginia, they, like
most Native American nations,
were slowly driven off their lands.
In time, many Powhaten settled in
the Delaware Valley. Finally, with
the designation in the mid-1980s of
this tract in South Jersey as the official Rankokus Reservation, these
Delaware Valley Powhaten had a
place to call their own.

Each year during Memorial Day
weekend and again on Columbus
Day weekend, the reservation hosts
the largest juried Native American

*A performer at the American Indian
Arts Festival*

arts festival east of Santa Fe, New Mexico. With sixty booths, a large
performance stage, and many exhibition areas and animal displays, the
reservation's great central field comes alive with everything from art and
buffalo burgers to alligator wrestling and traditional storytelling.

The Powhaten's festival celebrates the Native American way of life.
The art, crafts, blankets, and other works that are judged and sold here are
created in the old ways by working master artists who sell what they make
for a living. The dances, rites, and ceremonies date back to ancient times
and reflect the vitality, excitement, and depth of the Indian traditions.
Tepees and traditional thatch huts illustrate how the tribes lived in harmony with nature. Wisdom Keepers share tribal histories and folklore,
and answer questions about the Native American perception and way of

being. Potters, bow-makers, and mask-makers demonstrate their skills and techniques. Cooks prepare delicious food, including fry bread, alligator burgers, buffalo burgers, and much more.

At each festival, an eagle or an owl that has been nursed back to health after injury is released into the wild. As the majestic bird flies back to freedom, a rush of elation touches all who see him go. The bird symbolizes man's connection to nature. It also serves as a metaphor: The injured people's nation, like the injured soaring raptor, can be returned to health and live life to the fullest once again.

The two arts festivals are the highlight the year's activities on the Rankokus Reservation, but the reservation is open year-round. It houses a small museum that contains seventeen beautiful dioramas. Hand-rendered and -modeled by the museum's founder, Charles Danse, the scenes illustrate the Powhaten Renape Nation's history, lifestyle, and survival techniques. The museum also contains an art gallery that displays some exceptional pieces. Outside, a short nature trail explores the shores of the Rancocas River. A printed guide not only identifies plant species, but helps you understand how the wilderness's plants and animals function within the Indian philosophy of life: that all Earth Creatures live in harmony. A harmony that's easy to imagine in a setting like this.

❋ ❋ ❋ ❋ ❋ ❋ ❋ ❋

DETAILS

The Powhaten Renape Nation's Rankokus Reservation *is located on Rancocas Road in Rancocas. Information on museum hours and the festival schedule: 609-261-4747; www.powhatan.org.*

Directions: *From the NJ Turnpike, take exit 5. Turn right onto CR 541, drive about 2 miles, and turn right onto CR Spur 541. Drive to the next traffic light and turn right onto Rancocas Road; the reservation is just less than 2 miles on the left. From I-295, take exit 45A and follow Rancocas Road toward Mount Holly. The reservation is on the right in about three-quarters of a mile.*

❋ ❋ ❋ ❋ ❋ ❋ ❋ ❋

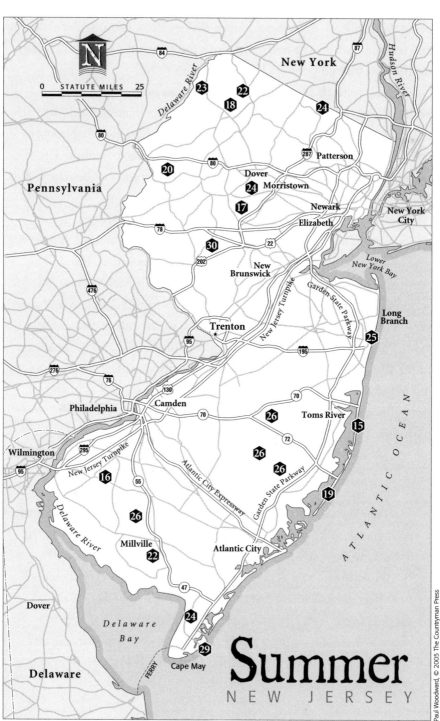

N

0   STATUTE MILES   25

Delaware River

New York

Hudson River

84

87

23

22

18

24

80

287   Patterson

Pennsylvania

20

80

Dover

24   Morristown

17

Newark

New York City

Elizabeth

78

30

22

202

New Brunswick

New Jersey Turnpike

Garden State Parkway

Lower New York Bay

Trenton

★

Long Branch

25

95

195

276

76

130

Philadelphia

Camden

70

70

ATLANTIC OCEAN

Wilmington

295

New Jersey Turnpike

16

55

70

26

Toms River

15

72

26

26

19

Delaware River

26

Millville

22

Atlantic City Expressway

Garden State Parkway

Atlantic City

ATLANTIC OCEAN

47

Dover

Delaware Bay

24

29

FERRY   Cape May

Delaware

Summer
NEW JERSEY

UNFETTERED SANDS

Island Beach State Park

O
F ALL THE 100-PLUS MILES OF NEW JERSEY SHORE, the 10 miles of Island Beach State Park are my favorite. It's quiet, pristine, pleasant, and unpretentious. No place on the New Jersey coast offers you the chance to experience the ocean, the dunes, the wildlife, the native flora—indeed the whole natural package—more completely than this.

Island Beach's tradition as a preserve dates back to the 1930s, when a man named Francis Freeman gained control over the old Henry Phipps estate. Phipps had conceived of developing this oceanside tract into a seaside paradise for the prosperous, but Freeman gave nature's abundance precedence over human affluence. Phipps had constructed three large guesthouses. Freeman, on the other hand, welcomed fishermen, hunters, and strollers, but restricted visitors to those who would act with constraint. No picking the berries, destroying the dunes, or otherwise despoiling the area's natural resources.

During the 1940s the War Department took control of the area and kicked everyone out so they could experiment with antiaircraft rocketry. In 1953 the land became a state park and preserve. Today, the park's condition is not very much different from what the first European explorers might have found.

In my younger years, I was a moody young man and there were more than a few occasions on which I came to Island Beach to seek solace from my worldly woes, indulging in long beach walks and hours of pondering life's imponderables beside the surf's ebb and flow. When I return these days, as a husband, father, and hardworking adult, more given to wrestling with life's day-to-day hassles than its ambiguities, I still find refreshing solace.

The park offers only 2,400 parking spaces, so while the life-guarded beach areas can become crowded, you need not walk far to get away. (Not to swim, however. Swimming from the unguarded beaches is always a bad idea.) The patrolled beaches offer full bathhouses with changing facilities and snack bars. These are clean and simple, in keeping with the overall atmosphere of the park. Even in the swimming areas, tubes and other inflatables are forbidden, and surfing is restricted to the more southerly patrolled areas, which helps to maintain a low-key atmosphere.

Just a short walk from the swimming beaches, the beachcombing and strolling become incomparable. Depending upon the time of year, you'll likely come up with some fascinating shells, sea horses, starfish, and other treasures.

As you wander south, you'll find a lot of surf fishermen. It's legal to drive onto the beach here via four-wheel-drive vehicles, and that makes this prime surf-fishing territory. Casting for blue fish is especially good in the fall, which you might prefer if your ability to handle the sway of the deep water party boats is, like mine, limited (see chapter 7). Fishermen are given to chatting, and they'll probably regale you with fish stories for as long as you can listen to them.

The entire park is just under 10 miles long, with a single two-lane road running right down its middle almost to the southern end.

The welcome center lies a mile from the entrance at the park's north end. Also known as the Aeolium, it offers a wealth of maps and other park information. Just beyond its doors, you can explore the dunes with a short self-guided hike on the nature trail; park naturalists lead guided hikes during the summer. The eel grasses are especially interesting; they were once harvested to make insulation for houses and upholstery stuffing for Model-T Fords. The park's terrain is nearly completely flat, providing casual and relaxing bike riding. Indeed, bike riders enter the park for free.

When you get to the southern end of the park, you're across the inlet from Barnegat Lighthouse, an exceptionally pretty spot. If you're certified to scuba dive and can verify it, the southern oceanfront beach areas offer prime diving.

But, more than anything, Island Beach presents a chance to walk in wonderment, an opportunity to find the Jersey shore in its native condition. It's a throwback to a time when white sand beaches, coastal scrub forest, and barrier sand dunes encouraged wildlife-preserving sanctuary and habitat, not commercial development; it's a place to contemplate the larger powers that work the planet.

What if, after all this naturalness, the urge to get funky and revel in the honky-tonk just cannot be subjugated? Well, the bustling Seaside Park boardwalk is just a few minutes away by car.

DETAILS

Island Beach State Park *is open year-round from 8* AM *to 8* PM. *The beach bathhouses are open from Memorial Day through Labor Day.* **Information:** *732-793-0506; www.state.nj.us/dep/parksandforests/ parks/island.html. Call ahead for information on fishing licenses and diving permits.*

Directions: *Take the Garden State Parkway to exit 82, and follow NJ 37 east across Barnegat Bay. Turn south onto NJ 35 through Seaside Heights and Seaside Park; the road leads directly into the park.*

The Cowtown Rodeo

Woodstown

PROFESSIONAL RODEO? IN NEW JERSEY? You betcha! Every Saturday night, the Cowtown Rodeo rides in Woodstown—no more than 8 miles from the Delaware Memorial Bridge. And, here's a startling fact: Cowtown Rodeo is the longest-running, regularly scheduled rodeo in the country. It started in 1929 and has been a regular Saturday night feature since 1955.

Professional rodeo in New Jersey may surprise most folks, but the locals come out in droves to watch the cowboys and cowgirls rope, wrestle, and ride. Traffic on US 40 backs up for a mile in either direction of the entrance. The glow of the rodeo ring's arc lights can be seen from miles away. Little kids sit with their noses pressed to the wire fence that surrounds the ring. Teenagers, dressed to the country-and-western nines in their jeans, checkered shirts, high-heeled cowboy boots, and yes, their Stetsons, exchange all the appealing and furtive glances and feigned nonchalance that pervade high-school dances. Folks of all ages arrive in their RVs to whoop and holler and make like this was Wyoming.

Arriving just at showtime, my wife, Penny, and I winced when we saw the line at little white-and-red wooden ticket booth. It stretched a good twenty yards. We followed a procession of other late-arriving cars and were directed to a parking spot in a grassy field by a plump young woman in an policelike uniform.

"Do they stop selling tickets at a certain number?" we asked her, unsure if we'd get in after making the long drive south.

"Nah," she replied with a smile. "They'll just keep sellin' 'em till there's nobody left to buy 'em."

"Can we bring our cooler in?"

"Well, little coolers are okay. Just ask at the gate. They'll let you know if it's too big."

While you can buy hot dogs, popcorn, candy apples, soda, hot funnel cake, ice cream, and other vital vittles at the concession stands, the rodeo doesn't sell beer. You're welcome to bring your own, however. Which everyone seems to. If your cooler's too big, well you just leave it by the fence and come back to it when you need to.

We parked our cooler, paid our admission, and wandered up the grassy knoll to join the crowd. The onlookers loomed above us, standing three deep behind those who were seated. Broad-brimmed cowboy hats were silhouetted against the floodlights. We slithered into a spot where we could see the ring. It seemed small. A bright white wooden "grandstand" with blazing crimson trim offered prime "box seat" views high along one side. Just four or five tiers of seats were held within its enclosure.

❋ ❋ ❋ ❋ ❋ ❋ ❋ ❋

DETAILS

The Cowtown Rodeo *rides every Saturday evening at 7:30, Memorial Day through September. Tickets are sold on a first-come, first-served basis. On Sunday, the rodeo grounds hosts one of South Jersey's biggest flea markets.* **Information:** *856-769-3200; www.cowtownrodeo.com; 780 US Route 40, Pilesgrove, NJ 08098.*

Directions: *The rodeo can be reached from New Jersey Turnpike exits 1 or 2. From exit 1, follow US 40 east for 8 miles. From exit 2, take US 322 east to Mullica Hill, then follow NJ 45 south into Woodstown. Turn right when you get into the center of town, and right again onto US 40 west.*

❋ ❋ ❋ ❋ ❋ ❋ ❋ ❋

Ringside, people sat on rows of wooden benches that had been set into the side of a shallow hill. At one end, an announcer's booth overlooked all; at the other, cattle of various sorts stood in pens below ring level patiently waiting to be ushered into the spotlight.

Despite being outdoors, smoke hung heavy in the air. And, of course, the pungent redolence that can only mean horses and cattle pervaded all. Some folks go for that acidic combination of hide, hair, and manure. Not me.

The rodeo started with a grand entry parade. After that, eight events made up the night's card—just about everything you'd expect in a rodeo, from bareback riding to steer wrestling. For the riding events, the program, typed up on a legal-sized sheet of paper, graciously listed the animals names as well as the riders'. Who would dare ride a bull named Jalapeño?!

Our favorite event was the girls' barrel race. Four barrels were set up, and the contestants had to ride from one end of the arena to the other and back again going around each barrel along the way. The young women were excellent riders, but we particularly liked the fact that the event was a straightforward display of skill that didn't exploit animals— no busting, roping, or wrestling some poor beast who'd probably rather be out munching on grass.

Despite continued cajoling by the PA announcer and the antics of the old, reliable rodeo clowns, the crowd didn't appear to be paying a lot of attention. Eating, chatting, and shopping seemed to get a lot of play. Western wear, Western hats, cowboy toys and trinkets, and T-shirts were being sold, and the souvenir stands seemed to be doing a brisk business.

Still, this is true professional rodeo—complete with prize money and talented athletes—and the crowd did get into it and cheered loudly when one performed well. Many of these cowboys have had some success on the major-league rodeo circuit, and their skills were impressive. The only one who gave me pause was a bucking bronco rider who was announced as hailing from the Bronx. An urban cowboy, I suppose.

FORE!

USGA Golf House—Far Hills
(And the State's Best Courses)

I SET MY FEET, TIGHTENED MY GRIP, and lined up the golf club head with the ball. I waggled the club, my feet, and my tush—just like the pros on TV. I checked the fairway one more time, then oh-so-slowly brought the club up and back. Now! I swiped a grand arc forward and down, shooting my good intentions along the club shaft through the head and down to the ball, creating a grand sweeping flow that oozed with power and perfection of form. I anticipated Whack! I got a dull thud. The dirt-scuffed ball dribbled over the blanched ground like a wounded woodchuck, leaving behind a torrent of flying turf and a divot bigger than my swelled hopes.

Why does anyone play this game?

You might not find the answer to that question at Golf House in Far Hills. But you will find some answers to questions like these: How is a golf ball made? How was a golf ball made in 1620? How far will a modern golf ball travel on the moon if hit at a specified force? What is acceptable and unacceptable in the design of golf clubs?

Golf House is the headquarters for the United States Golf Association (USGA), and anyone who generally enjoys golf, or who can appreciate the game as a measure of social history, should visit this extremely pleasant, pastoral site.

Set in a mansion of Georgian Colonial design, amid fittingly fairwaylike

USGA Golf House, Far Hills

lawns, Golf House takes you on a magic carpet ride through the sport's history. The game's roots reach as far back as Rome, but it began to flower at the turn of the 16th century. Golf's first public written mention, we learn, was in the Acts of the Scots Parliament, circa 1497. Did the Scotsmen issue an official state edict outlining proper play? No. They prohibited the game. The decree (obviously) didn't take. All of the Stuart kings and queens (1502–1688), including Mary, Queen of Scots, were hackers.

Golf House presents much more of this fascinating, quasi-social history, reviewing the development of clubs (how a "brassie" became a 2-iron), balls, and golf wear, as well as how the sand tee was replaced by the wooden one.

The USGA is the game's American governing body. Among other things, it sets the rules and standards for equipment and guidelines for course development, and their Research and Test Center is located adjacent to the museum. Visit, and you'll learn how exactingly balls are

✽ ✽ ✽ ✽ ✽ ✽ ✽ ✽

DETAILS

Golf House *is open daily from 10 to 5, closed Thanksgiving, Christmas, New Year's Day, and Easter.* **Information:** *908-234-2300; www.usga.org/aboutus/museum/museum.asp; Liberty Corner Road, Far Hills, NJ 07931.*

Directions: *From I-287, take exit 26 (Mt. Airy Road). Northbound travelers bear right off the ramp, southbound bear left. Drive to the first traffic light and turn right onto Lyons Road Drive about a quarter mile and turn right onto Liberty Corner Road. From I-78, take exit 33. Eastbound travelers turn left off the ramp and drive five traffic lights, westbound turn right off the ramp and go four lights. Turn left onto Valley Road and then left again onto Liberty Corner Road; Golf House is in 1.8 miles.*

The New Jersey Division of Travel & Tourism's Outdoor Guide *lists the state's public golf courses (1-800-847-4865, www.state.nj.us/ travel/orderform.shtml).*

The New Jersey State Golf Association *offers course listings, tournaments, and a plethora of information (973-338-8334; www.njsga.org).*

✽ ✽ ✽ ✽ ✽ ✽ ✽ ✽

made and equally as meticulously tested; what's legal and illegal in club design; and, if the weather's good, you might see Iron Byron working out on the practice tee. Byron's a robot, you see, whose only job is to smack golf balls with such an invariable swing (speed, force, and loft) that the spheres' performance characteristics can be evaluated against a measurable standard.

You really needn't be a golfer to appreciate Golf House. But if you are a golfer, watch out. By the time you leave the grounds, you'll be itching to play. And, there are some very playable public courses in New Jersey. Among them:

NORTH

Crystal Springs Golf Club, Hamburg (973-827-5996, www.crystal golfresort.com) A hilly, challenging course set in an old quarry that lends a very unique character. Crystal Springs has been described as extremely challenging, or as one person put it, "It's a 'must play' but bring lots of balls."

Great Gorge Country Club, McAfee (973-827-5757, www.greatgorge countryclub.com) Great Gorge Country Club contains 27 picturesque holes that combine wooded, lakeside, and quarryside settings and a variety of challenge that will capture any golfer's fancy. *Golf Digest* has rated the course highly. Play-and-stay packages are available at the nearby Mineral Hotel.

The Architects Club, Lopatcong (908-213-3080, www.the architectsclub.com) One of the state's newer courses, each hole at the Architects Club has been fashioned in the style of a famous course designer, from Old Tom Morris to Robert Trent Jones. The result is a fascinating mix of challenges in a most attractive setting.

CENTRAL SHORE

Marriott's Seaview Resort, Galloway Township (609-652-1800; www.seaviewgolf.com) If you like to pitch and putt in a classic club setting, Seaview provides. It was once an exclusive private club where the likes of Dwight Eisenhower liked to play. With two championship courses, a recently renovated, gleaming white, neoclassic building (described in the brochures as "Gatsby-esque"), all the services a first class hotel or country club should offer, and a location 15 minutes' drive from Atlantic City, Seaview has it all. *Golf Digest* ranks Seaview's Pines Course among New Jersey's best. On the Bay Course, the tight, oceanside links with their bunker-fortified greens might have you thinking you're playing the classic Scottish game.

Blue Heron Pines Golf Club, Cologne (609-965-1800, www.blue heronpines.com) Blue Heron Pines aspires to private-club ambience. By all reports, they've succeeded. With an excellent restaurant, clean and comfortable locker rooms, and an understated modern architectural design, the club makes you feel welcome. The courses aren't too shabby either. The West Course was designed by accomplished architect Stephen Kay; the newer East Course by Steve Smyers. This club was the only southern New Jersey site to earn 4½ stars and a quality service rating from *Golf Digest*, and the West Course was also voted among the "Top 100 You Can Play" by that publication, one of only two courses in New Jersey to make the list. The Atlantic City area abounds with excellent courses, and Blue Heron is among the best of them.

CENTRAL

Howell Park Golf Course, Howell Township (732-842-4000, (www.monmouthcountyparks.com/Golf/howell_gc.asp) Despite a tendency to be crowded on weekends, Howell Park engenders rave reviews from golfers of all types. So impressive are the links that *Golf Digest* has ranked it among the top 50 public courses in America. This is a very challenging public course operated by Monmouth County Parks that is well-kept and a pleasure to play.

Hominy Hill Golf Club, Colts Neck (732-462-9222, www.mon mouthcountyparks.com/Golf/hominy_hill.asp) Another Monmouth County Parks operation, Hominy Hill, does Howell one better—it has been ranked in *Golf Digest*'s top 25 public courses in America. A Robert Trent Jones design, the course is considered long and difficult, but it's very playable even when it gets crowded. Many New Jersey golfers will tell you this is the best public course in the state.

SOUTH

Cape May National Golf Club, Erma (609-884-1563, www.cmngc .com) What would you expect from a course that lies near the queen city of the South Jersey shore? Wind, water, and plenty of sand. That's Cape May National. Cape May is a delightful links that includes a memorable par-three set beside a nature preserve.

The Sussex County Horse & Farm Show and the New Jersey State Fair

Augusta

YOU SEE A LOT OF ANIMALS at the Sussex Farm & Horse Show. But me, I could've watched the racing miniature pigs forever. First of all, they're so cute! Second, they're ridiculous. Tiny porkers all done up in little racing bibs, they run around the small oval while their master reports a running commentary. Last, I'm a sucker for miniaturized anything, even pigs.

The Sussex County Horse & Farm Show takes place for 10 days in early August. It may represent the last major gasp in the state's withering attempt to maintain contact with its agrarian roots. The good news is this: A few years back, this event was named the official state fair. Good move. It replaced an anemic gathering that had dwindled to an ephemeral affair attended by few. Now we New Jerseyites have a vibrant, entertaining, authorized event in which to celebrate our New Jersey–ness.

Only once, when I was perhaps seven or eight, did I have the opportunity to attend one of the classic Midwestern state fairs. You know, those large and exuberant gatherings where country music stars sing, where farmers put their equipment and animals to a public test by using them to pull enormous amounts of weight, where blueberry pies (and anything else that can be baked, cooked, or grown) are judged, and where the smarmy farm smells pervade even the food and game midways—and

Prize winners at the New Jersey State Fair

nobody seems to mind. Well, the Sussex Farm & Horse Show is as close as we New Jerseyans come to something like that.

When my older kid, Dan, was just six or so, he went absolutely bonkers over the mud races. That perfectly ordinary folks were trying to drive cars and trucks with gargantuan wheels through a man-made bog seemed totally exciting—but frightfully logical—to him. To me, it was clear that this was just a grown-ups' extension of playing with trucks in the sandbox. But the boy loved it. And so did dozens of other little (and not so little) boys—and even girls, too.

You say you'd rather watch oxen pull stuff than tractors? You can do that, too. And whether you like your pulling done by animals or machines, you'll love destruction carried out by men in machines. For pure, aggressively mindless fun, don't miss the Demolition Derby.

Our girlchild, Laina, preferred the horse ring. The fair puts on a horse show of some kind each day—a Quarter Horse Show, a Welsh and Crossbred Pony Show, a Team Pulling Contest, an Arabian and Half-Arabian Show, and so on.

As for Mom, well, I don't think she had a particular favorite. I think the whole affair reminded her of being a kid back at the county fair in rural California. And I guess that's the whole point of the Sussex Show, the reason it stands out. There's nothing pretentious here. It's refreshing to know that there are still kids out there who raise blue-ribbon rabbits and roosters; that in New Jersey farmers still exist who will transport a heifer for miles in an effort to win Best in Show; that women will cook carefully guarded family recipes just to chase a first-place designation. Sure, the show has a lot of tacky stuff—the usual array of booths filled with buy-it-anywhere trinkets and pseudo-crafts, the requisite junk-food vendors who first soak their wares in grease then soak you if you want to buy them. But, a carnie element is not only to be expected, it's welcomed.

Everyone who has any kind of talent is likely to show up to show off. The Performing Arts Tent echoes with the sounds of music and, well, dogs. A Canine Obedience Demo, Seeing Eye Dog exhibition, Canine Frisbee Contest and, in the past, such headliners as the Tails-A-Waggin' Dog Act and the Corky & Riker Dog Act have been just a few of the typical dog-gone events. Human entertainers range from Beatles and Eagles tribute bands to a Kids' Fiddlin' Contest and the Annual Sussex County Talent Day.

Antique farm machinery, a petting zoo, a milking parlor, and an exhibition building (where photography, home economics, floral, horticultural, and honey shows are featured) are also ongoing features at Sussex.

Now, some debate has been riffling up at our house. Seems the young 'uns want to challenge my notion that miniature pig racing is the top event of the show. They're purporting that the combination event of the Pot Belly Pig Confirmation Show and the Pen Decorating Contest takes the blue ribbon for best attraction. And suddenly Mom, knowing my affection for miniatures, reminds me that the miniature horse show deserves recognition. But I say, you haven't seen anything until you've seen those porklets going around the far turn, dashing for glory and victory. Just take in few of these races, then wander over to the Livestock Area for the Open Swine Show, and you'll know just what it means to be as happy as a pig in [expletive deleted]!

DETAILS

The Sussex County Farm & Horse Show *takes place during early August at the fairgrounds on Plains Road in Augusta.* **Information:** *973-948-5500; www.sussex-county-fair.org; www.njstatefair.org.*

Directions: *Take I-80 to exit 34B, then follow NJ 15 north to US 206 south. Drive 1 mile to Plains Road. Or take NJ 23 north into Sussex and take CR 639 south to CR 565 south. Follow the signs onto Linn Road and thence to Plains Road.*

THE HEARTLAND OF THE SHORE

Long Beach Island

S OME 18 MILES LONG but barely three blocks wide at its narrow points, Long Beach Island, equally accessible from the greater New York and Philadelphia suburbs, ranks among the most popular summer beach vacation spots for New Jerseyans of all stripes. Still, you've got to wonder why such a diminutive island is divided into 21 communities. Some, like Beach Haven Crest and North Beach Haven, stretch for less than 10 blocks. But nobody seems to regard these lines as much more than designations on a map. LBI, as it is commonly known, offers a surprising blend of isolation and access, quietude and activity, and a mix of full-time residents, summer home owners and overnight lodges.

The kids and I left our rooms at the Engleside Inn, a large and comfortable motel in Beach Haven at the island's southern reaches, and began a bicycle exploration. The riding is straight and flat. Bike lanes along Atlantic and Beach Avenues (both are one-way streets) make this section's north–south riding easy and safe, even in the busiest times. In case you've come unprepared but get a sudden urge to ride, a number of island shops rent bikes.

Another kind of riding vehicle can be rented, as well—wave runners, those snowmobiles for water. This isn't a calm or contemplative sport; it's high action. While some regard the fast-flying little vehicles to be as pesky as bees at a picnic, even their staunchest critics must admit that driving them is a lot of fun. Looking for less mechanized action? Windsurfing lessons can be had, and gear rented, at Beach Nutz on 13th Street in Beach Haven. If Jet Skiing is on-water snowmobiling, then windsurfing is on-water downhill skiing.

But our bike ride was meant to be leisurely. We rolled to where the Black Whales are docked and checked the schedules. One boat departs twice a day for a nine-hour excursion and play-day (or night) in Atlantic City. The Black Whales also offer two 1-hour sightseeing rides on the island's bay side.

We turned back toward midisland. At the corner of Beach Avenue and Engleside Street the sidewalk turns to neatly laid red brick. The brick walk leads to the Surflight Theater. Through the summer and into October, the theater offers high-caliber live shows, usually tuneful musicals. Right next door stands Show Place, an ice cream parlor of local renown where singing waitpeople serve your order with an operatic flair.

We drifted across the street to the Long Beach Island Historical Museum, a weathered wooden building that holds a wealth of the area's cultural history. The photos of the 1962 nor'easter, in particular, tell a fascinating tale of nature's devastating power.

Speaking of history, over at 9th and Bay Avenue, the Schooner's Wharf shopping center takes its theme from the two-masted schooner *Lucy Evelyn*. Permanently moored at this spot in 1948 and transformed into a gift shop, the ship is now the focal point of the shopping plaza which, with its planking and weathered woods, has adapted the nautical design. Along with Bay Village across the street, the complex is the island's shopping hub. It also hosts spectacular fireworks for the Fourth of July, and a handful of October events, including the Chowderfest and the Festa di Columbo 18-Mile Run, a combination of Italian cuisine, carbo-loading pig-out followed by a high-energy, calorie-burning atonement.

Next door are Fantasy Island and the Thundering Surf Water Park. Fantasy Island is a family-friendly amusement park. Clean and small, the rides delight young children, and keep their parents from dying of fear for their safety. You pay by the ride here, so it can be as expensive or affordable as the limits you set. A "family casino arcade" offers an electronic mini–Atlantic City. As to Thundering Surf, according to an undisclosed youthful source I know (who has the experience to speak authoritatively), the water park can be classified as "totally cool."

Still, it is the beach that makes LBI special. It's pure, no frills and, importantly, very handicapped-accessible (or barrier-free, as the current terminology would have it). The island contains thirty access ramps, and the various communities combine to provide twenty "beach wheels"— wheelchairs suitable for use on the beach and in the surf, making this one of the most accessible beaches on the shore.

The island's northern end is essentially residential and sedate. From Bayview Avenue on the bay side of Barnegat Light you can board one of several deep-sea fishing vessels (see chapter 7), or just buy yourself some fish. A drive along 12th Street reveals a series of houses built in the 1880s, and a stop at the corner of 5th Street and Central Avenue is always worthwhile. That's the address of the Barnegat Light Museum, formerly a one-room schoolhouse.

Continue up to the northern end of the island and you come to the real Barnegat highlight—the lighthouse. Barnegat Lighthouse State Park

DETAILS

For general, regional information on Long Beach Island, *contact the Southern Ocean County Chamber of Commerce, 265 W. 9th St., Ship Bottom, NJ 08008; www.discoversouthernocean.com; 1-800-292-6372 or 609-494-7211. Useful web sites include: www.longbeachisland .com; www.lbifun.com; and the official Ocean County government web site, www.oceancountygov.com, which has a terrific links page.*

Directions: *From the Garden State Parkway, take exit 63 and follow NJ 72 east over Barnegat Bay. You'll arrive on the island in Ship Bottom at the midpoint—Brant Beach, Beach Haven, and Brighton Beach are to the south, Barnegat Light, Loveladies, Surf City, and Harvey Cedars are to the north.*

covers 31 acres on the island's tip. It has been renovated, and the barrier-free facilities offer picnicking, fishing, and pleasant seaside strolling. Of course, you can climb the lighthouse steps. The lighthouse, known to the locals as "Old Barney," stands 172 feet high; it overlooks Barnegat Shoals, the site of some 200 shipwrecks over the years. Indeed, the name "Barnegat" derives from the Dutch name for the inlet, "Barendegat," which meant "inlet of breakers," an homage to the treacherous nature of the narrow water passageway that connects Barnegat Bay to the ocean.

A quiet island with spectacular scenery, historical sites, and a user-friendly beach that's walking distance from almost anyplace, unfettered by commercial glut and yet offering plenty of mercantile necessities? No wonder New Jerseyans flock here.

HOLY FLYING CHICKENS, BATMAN!

Triplebrook Campgrounds, Hope

IN THE END, IT WAS A CHICKEN by the name of Tiger who won it. Won it big time, she did—flying away from the competition. A big chicken, she was. A Pennsylvania Flyer, according to the kid who'd brought her to the campground. And fly she did. Two hundred and twenty-five feet by someone's measure. Roosted high up in a tree, too. We're never going to know how far she'd really have gone if she hadn't lit in that tree. Next best in the contest was the featherweight-class winner—name of Winner of all things—who managed only 22 feet, 3 inches.

The International Chicken Flying Meet at Triplebrook Campground is just one of the events that attract campers, and sometimes the public, all summer long. People flock (pun intended) to private campgrounds like Triplebrook from all over, seeking the combination of bucolic setting with friendly social environment.

Private campgrounds are an anomaly, really. They're a mix of summer camp, resort, camping, and the ongoing American love affair with being on the road. People visit for a weekend, a week, or the entire summer. Some purists argue that campground camping is not camping at all, but something more akin to traveling as a self-contained motel. Well, yes, many of the live-in RVs do come equipped with all the amenities of home, and some are literally as big as a small house. While purists may insist that campgrounds are far too cushy, that doesn't preclude purists

Chickens fly at Triplebrook Campgrounds

from camping at commercial campgrounds. Tents are welcome and, if desired, most campgrounds can place you up at a campsite in a beauti- fully wooded area just far enough from the washrooms and showers to resemble roughing it.

At Triplebrook, for example, a working 250-acre farm with about 100 acres set aside for camping, the campground contains 200 hook-up and tenting sites, many set deep in the woods. If you don't own your own RV but are disinclined to endure the uncertainties of tenting, you can rent what they call a "cozy cabin."

In addition to the living arrangements, Triplebrook's amenities include two side-by-side swimming pools (one for adults only), a tennis court, a well-stocked country store, a coin laundry, a basketball court, a barnyard full of farm animals, an elaborate model train display, a private lake fully stocked with fish, paddleboats and two plastic kayaks, an RV repair shop, and a lifeguard staff that doubles as kiddie camp counseling crew on rainy— ("Don't say the 'R' word!" Triplebrook proprietor Brenda James admonishes visitors). Okay then, "precipitational days." If that's not enough to keep you occupied, the Jameses print a calendar of the area's special events and nearby recreational options.

Triplebrook, like many of campground operations, is a family affair. Operations run by families tend to understand family vacationing needs, especially the need to find a facility that attracts other families so your kids will have other kids to play with. On that chicken-flying Saturday, the campground overflowed with children. Adults, too, for that matter. And most importantly, everyone was having a good time. During the egg-tossing contest, the two lines of entrants covered enough ground for several

❀ ❀ ❀ ❀ ❀ ❀ ❀ ❀

DETAILS

Triplebrook *is located in Hope; reservations are recommended on weekends. Information: 908-459-4079, www.triplebrook.com.*

Directions: *Take I-80 to exit 12 and turn south onto CR 521. Drive 1 mile and turn right at stoplight onto CR 609 west. Drive 3.5 miles and turn right onto Nightingale Road. After 1 mile turn right onto Honey Run Road. Or take I-78/US 22 to Clinton, then NJ 31 north approximately 15 miles to US 46 west. Drive about 8 miles to Marshall's Farm Market (on the left) and turn right onto CR 616 north. Drive 2.5 miles and turn right onto Nightingale Road; Honey Run Road will be on the left in 0.5 mile.*

The New Jersey Campground Owners Association (NJCOA) *represents privately owned, commercial campgrounds. It produces and distributes an annual, free, consumer camping guidebook (800-2-CAMP-NJ; www.gocampingamerica.com/newjersey/njcoa.html; www.beachcomber.com/Nj/campnj.html).*

❀ ❀ ❀ ❀ ❀ ❀ ❀ ❀

first downs in a football game and enough of an age range to qualify for everything from day care to Social Security.

The major problem in picking a campground is deciding on the location that best suits you. According to the New Jersey Campground Owners Association, the state harbors nearly 150 private campgrounds in every kind of setting—from an urban location just 15 minutes from Times Square, to oceanside, to mountainside, to riverside. If you'd like to add a bit of an international flavor, you'll find an enclave of *"Nous parlons francais"* campgrounds in the Cape May area, which for some reason has long been a popular destination for the French-speaking Quebecois.

Campground camping, by the way, is not limited to summertime. A number of sites offer winter camping, with activities like cross-country skiing, snowmobiling, and ice fishing.

But back to those chickens. If your bird didn't win, you still had a chance to make up for it by making like a chicken yourself. The little kids went ape over the Chicken Scratching Contest, in which they searched with only their toes for Hershey's Kisses scattered on a plastic tarp covered with sawdust. And everyone seemed willing to make fools of themselves for the Rooster Crowing Contest and the Chicken Legs Chicken Walk Contest. It was as simple as cock-a-doodle-doo.

21

LIVING HISTORY

THE STATE IS ALIVE WITH THE SOUND OF HISTORY. The sights, smells, tastes, and feels of it, too. New Jersey provides an abundant opportunity to see everyday life from many time periods re-created and reenacted. Different from restorations or museums, living-history installations feature artisans at work using the tools of yesteryear; you can learn about a historic period by talking to people who are "living" it.

Some re-creations are more elaborate than others. All of them make fascinating time travel.

The Historic Village at Allaire, Allaire State Park (732-919-3500 or 732-938-2371; www.allairevillage.org; www.njparksandforests.org/parks/allaire.html; P.O. Box 220, Route 524, Farmingdale 07027) An 1830s ironworks and mining village, Allaire is also home to the Pine Creek Railroad, where narrow-gauge trains are pulled by historic steam and diesel engines, and the New Jersey Museum of Transportation, an organization that restores and preserves antique railroading equipment. Village life is depicted with superb reality, and visitors find hard at work such trades- and craftspeople as carpenters, blacksmiths, tanners, gardeners, quilters, and wheelwrights. Open daily 11–5, Memorial Day through Labor Day; 10–4, Labor Day through December and in May; closed January through April.

Batsto Historic Village (609-561-0024; www.njparksandforests
.org/parks/wharton.html; Route 542, Hammonton) Another mining
community, Batsto was a principal source of iron for ammunition production during the Revolution. It was also a glass-making center that
thrived from 1766 to 1867. Today, the village is a part of Wharton State
Forest, and it contains remnants of a combined industrial and agricultural enterprise dating from the late 19th century. The grounds are dominated by Joseph Wharton's mansion, an eerie building that looks like
something from the movie *Psycho*. House tours are given during summer. The original workers' cabins are located across a footbridge from
the visitors center and the mansion. There, a small nature center provides
information on the local flora and fauna, and a few doors down, a potter
and a weaver demonstrate their craft. Open daily, 8–4:30, year-round.
Call ahead to ascertain if the mansion renovation has been completed
and that it is open for tours.

Batsto Village

Cold Springs Village (609-898-2300; www.hcsv.org; 720 Route 9, Cape May 08204) Cold Springs is a 20-building collection that depicts life in a 19th-century South Jersey farming village. The reception building is decked out in a nautical theme, and in re-created, below-deck sailing schooner decor, visitors watch an orientation video that reviews the history of the Cape May region, tying the sea and agricultural lifestyles together. The "citizens" of Cold Springs Village (from the tinsmith to the school marm) display excellent knowledge of their livelihoods and their roles in village life. I particularly enjoyed the rope-making demonstration, in which a nifty, antique mechanical device wove three lines of hemp into a simple rope. And we found the Village Bakery's edible goods irresistible. Open 10–4:30 on weekends Memorial Day Weekend through mid-June; Tuesday through Sunday mid-June through Labor Day weekend; weekends from Labor Day until mid-September.

Fosterfields (973-326-7645; www.parks.morris.nj.us/parks/ffmain.htm; Kahdena Road and Route 24, Morristown) Fosterfields takes you to a more recent time—the turn of the 20th century—to explore life on the farm. Visitors are treated to a glimpse of farming the way it was when the Garden State was truly that, including frequent special events and demonstration days (everything from pressing flowers to threshing and harvesting) that illustrate the use of period tools. In addition, the grounds hold a 125-acre arboretum with self-guided trails, including one documented in Braille, and tours are offered of Willows Mansion, a home built by Paul Revere's grandson. Open 10–5, Wednesday through Saturday, and 1–5 Sunday, from April through October.

Howell Living History Farm (609-737-3299; www.howellfarm.com; Valley Road, Hopewell) Howell is another turn-of-the-20th-century working farm, offering a pleasant country hayride in summer. Open Saturday 10–4 with programs from 11–3; Sunday 12–4, April through November for self-guided tours only; Tuesday through Friday 10–4 February through November; closed Monday.

Longstreet Farm (732-946-3758; www.monmouthcounty parks.com/parks/longstreet_revised.asp; Holmdel Park, Longstreet

Road, Holmdel) Rural life as lived by the Longstreet family during the Gay Nineties (the 1890s, that is). Open daily 9–5, Memorial Day through Labor Day; otherwise, 10–4 PM.

Millbrook Village (908-841-9531; www.nps.gov/dewa/InDepth/ Sites/MV.html, www.njskylands.com/hsmillbrookvillage.htm; Old Mine Road, Millbrook) A highly recommended side trip for anyone exploring the natural beauty of the Delaware Water Gap, Millbrook presents 19th-century village life. At its height, Millbrook was home to just 75 people, but among the town's "populace" today you'll find a blacksmith, weaver, and several other craftspeople at work. The Garris House tour describes a typical mid-19th-century woman's day. On summer weekends—until the restoration is completed—the town's original grist mill is being rebuilt using period tools. During the first weekend in October, Millbrook Days is staged; more than 150 volunteers demonstrate 19th-century crafts and rural living skills. Open daily 9–5 from mid-April through mid-October.

Miller-Cory House (908-232-1776; 614 Mountain Avenue, Westfield) A 250-year-old farmhouse where 18th-century crafts come to life on Sunday afternoons 2–5 mid-September to December and March to mid-June; 2–4 in January and February.

New Sweden Farmstead Museum (856-455-9785; www.co.cumber land.nj.us/tourism/new_sweden_farmstead_museum/; 50 East Broad Street, Bridgeton) The city of Bridgeton contains the largest historical district in the state and, based on the number of buildings, the third largest in the country; it includes some 2,200 buildings, a 1,100-acre park, four museums, and a zoo. The small, rustic New Sweden Farmstead is located within the park. It depicts a 17th-century farmstead typical of those built by Swedish immigrants. Costumed tour guides escort visitors hourly through the bath/smokehouse, threshing barn, blacksmith residence, animal barn, and farmstead home. Open from mid-May through Labor Day, 11–5 Saturday and noon–5 Sunday; the last tour is at 4.

Waterloo Village and Lenape Indian Village (973-347-0900; www.waterloovillage.org; Waterloo Road, Stanhope; see also chapter 28) Waterloo was a main lock station on the Morris Canal. Today it is home

Cold Springs Village store

to the New Jersey Canal Society and is one of the few places where you can see every element of the technology that made that canal an engineering colossus. The village also offers a close look at small-town life in the early industrial age. The adjacent Lenape Indian Village depicts the region's Native American lifestyle from the time before the Europeans arrived. Open July and August 11–5 Saturday and Sunday and 11–4 Wednesday through Friday, closed Monday and Tuesday; open weekends in June, September and October, 11–5 .

Wheaton Village (1-800-998-4552, 609-825-6800; www.wheaton village.org; 10th & G Streets, Millville; see also chapter 48). Wheaton Village's outstanding Museum of American Glass offers tribute to the artistry of the world's finest glass makers. The re-created glassworks features demonstrations and antique tools. The Down Jersey Folklife Center focuses on the cultural heritage of southern New Jersey. Crafts and Trades Row presents an opportunity to see many other artisans at work and the village's Main Street the chance to buy their wares. Open 10 to 5. Tuesday through Sunday, April through December; 10–5. Friday, Saturday and Sunday, January through March.

DARING YOUNG MEN (AND WOMEN) & FLYING MACHINES

THE SUSSEX AIR SHOW—SUSSEX

AS MY CHILDREN AND I DROVE around the bend, a DC-3 came into view. It sat on the short runway like a majestic bird, the verdant upland hills rising behind it. The workhorse of all airplanes, the DC-3 was the plane that changed the commercial airline business from a bizarre and daring novelty to a viable form of travel. It was also the airplane that did the grit and dirty work of World War II. You don't have to be an airplane buff to appreciate this machine. The plane is unmistakable—its nose sitting high off the ground—and beautiful. And here were not one but three DC-3 sparked on the Sussex County Airport's runway. It was the storied past come to life.

Watching the storied past come to life is the essence of the Sussex Air Show, subtitled "The Best Little Air Show in the Country."

Pardon the pun but, from the moment we arrived, we were aware of something special in the air. Folks arrived by car—and by air. The parking lot filled up early with every kind of motor transport imaginable, from minivans, SUVs, and motorcycles to motor homes outfitted with viewing platforms. In the air, small planes approached one by one from the south, executed two right turns, and made their final approach with a small mountain rising just behind them. It looked like an aerial parade.

Back on the ground, the usual festival atmosphere found at so many summertime events prevailed. But, this was different. For one thing, the

cost of a hot dog is $1.50, not $4.50; much of the money raised here
through admission tickets and booth sales goes to nonprofit causes; and a
sense of amused awe pervades the crowd. The spectators have come, just
like folks did 60 years ago, to see if these darned machines really can fly.
When the machines do—not only going up and staying up, but flying
upside down and in exotic spins or loops—folks are happily amazed. In
fact, those Stearman biplanes over there were the same planes that your
granddaddy and great-granddaddy marveled at when they left their farm
chores to gawk at the stunt flying show back in the 1920s and '30s. They
don't call it stunt flying any more. They call it aerobatics. But the pilots
must be just as nuts.

The PA announcer explained the moves and described the action, all
the while throwing in good old country-boy humor. Of one flyer he said,
"I'd fly with him anytime, anywhere—as long as it wasn't a commercial
flight." When two planes took off simultaneously, racing at each other
from opposite ends of the runway, he quipped, "I tried to get my sister-in-
law to do that; she's got a small car and I tried to pair her up against a big
truck." When the "world-renowned" pilot Jimmy Franklin buzzed the
runway upside down at an altitude of about 6 feet, he yelped, "He's flying
so low that even the worms will be looking up and ducking their heads!"

Sussex is not a grand military show. No Blue Angels circling the airport. The show evokes an old seat-of-the-pants sensibility. We watched a
guy named Oscar Boesch swoop his glider down in graceful silence, performing his "sailplane ballet," as the loudspeaker gargled the theme from
Born Free. We watched befuddled as a tractor-driving "farmer" suddenly
appeared, mowing the grass on the far side of the runway. He dismounted
to bum a ride in a classic Piper Cub—which he promptly "stole," and pro-
ceeded to fly in a manner that that small airplane was never designed for.

Oh, one thing is significantly different from the old Dust Bowl barnstorming days. It isn't all boys up there. The Misty Blues, an all-female
skydiving team, floated down from the clouds in precise spirals, and a
woman calling herself Patty Wagstaff showed why she owned the title
National Aerobatics Champion.

USAF (semi-retired), Sussex Air Show

The Sussex Air Show is the invention of a guy named Paul Styger. He manages this speck of an aerodrome and first staged this extravaganza in 1972. Now his show not only features three days of fantastic flying, but on the Thursday before the official opening, Styger hosts one of the Northeast's largest miniature airplane fly-arounds for model plane enthusiasts.

On show days, arrive early and leave plenty of time to wander among the booths. You'll find an enticing variety of goods. Two booths selling model planes were popular with the spectators; T-shirt collections empha-sized aircraft and military themes; a variety of aviation art could be pur-chased; and then there were plenty of parked aircraft to admire, including those DC-3s, and many antique, handmade, specialty, and military craft.

WINGS & WHEELS—MILLVILLE

In early May, another major air show is staged in southern New Jersey at the Millville Army Air Field Museum in Millville. The Millville Airport was part of the America's First Defense Airport system during World War

II and served as a gunnery school for fighter pilots, using primarily the Republic P-47 Thunderbolt. For three years during the war, some 1,500 pilots received advanced fighter training here. The museum preserves the airfield's history and focuses on the P-47 Thunderbolt's role. The air show features a huge lineup of flying marvels, including Air Force Thunderbirds, the AeroShell Aerobatic Team, a parachute jumping demonstration, Russian Aerobatic Aircraft, and many others. Plus, there's a classic car show, hot-air ballooning and a stunt motorcycle riding act.

DETAILS

The Sussex Air Show *takes place in late August. Information: 973-875-0783 or 973-875-7337; http://216.86.49.175/airshow.asp.* **Directions:** *From the New York City area, take NJ 23 north into Sussex, turn left onto CR 565, and drive until you see the airport.*

The Wings & Wheels Air Show *is held annually in early May. Information on the show and the museum: 856-327-2347; www.p47millville.org; Millville Army Air Field Museum, 1 Leddon Street, Millville Airport, Millville, NJ 08332.* **Directions:** *Take the New Jersey Turnpike to exit 2. Follow NJ 322 east to NJ 55 south. Take exit 29 (CR 552/Sherman Avenue), and drive on Sherman Avenue westbound 3.2 miles. Turn left onto CR 634 South (Nabb Avenue), and travel 1.7 miles to NJ 49 east. Follow the signs to CR 625 (Hogbin Road), and turn right on that to CR 670 (Buckshutem Road), where you turn left. At CR 555 (Dividing Creek Road) turn left into the airshow parking lot.*

Del Rosso's Blue Baron Tours, *Route 79, Marlboro, NJ 07746; www.bluebaronbiplane.com/home; 732-591-0588.*

NJBiplane, Inc., *300 Dahlia Avenue, Williamstown, NJ 08094; www.freefalladventures.com/nj_biplane/index.asp; 856-629-7553.*

TAKE FLIGHT

If watching isn't enough for you, and you'd like to experience the old-time thrill of flying, you can hop in a helicopter at the Millville show. Or, if you want the full antique plane treatment, get in touch with Del Rosso's Blue Baron Tours in Marlboro or, in the southern region, NJBiplane in Williamstown. NJBiplane offers scenic tours in a Stearman over South Jersey and Philadelphia. Blue Baron will take you over the shore and New York City's harbor. Sightseeing rides over northern New Jersey and southern New York are available at the Sussex County Airport.

ARTISTS AT WORK

Peters Valley Crafts Center—Layton

PETERS VALLEY JUST MIGHT be the ultimate summer camp for craftspeople. They gather at Peters Valley to ply their trades and learn new techniques in ceramics, blacksmithing, fine metal work, photography, fiber art, cloth work, woodworking, and jewelry-making by participating in three- to twelve-day workshops. They work and reside in buildings that range from a Greek Revival house, a Dutch Reformed Church, and various 19th-century barns to small cottages and rambling farmhouses. A quiet energy pervades the area, despite the fact that the grounds are spread over many hilly acres.

Indeed, that there are any buildings at all is no small bit of luck. In the late 1960s and early 1970s, the Army Corps of Engineers hatched a plan to dam the nearby Delaware River at a place called Tocks Island. Somewhere between three and five thousand buildings were bought and razed before the damming plan was permanently shelved. The lost buildings and resulting sparse development of the area has left an aura of early rural settlement. Consequently, this must be counted among the most bucolic and pleasant settings in New Jersey. Approaching over rolling hills and winding roads, the pastoral countryside perfectly sets the mood for viewing the work and workers of Peters Valley.

Your first stop should be the Craft Store and Gallery. Housed in a classic country store complete with covered veranda, this is the Peters

Valley nerve center. Inside, works from the various resident students and instructors are tastefully displayed. The imaginative nature and high quality of the work contrasts strongly to common commercial crafts-store fare. Upstairs, the center's gallery offers rotating exhibits, as well as a permanent collection of Peters Valley residents' work. Among the noteworthy gallery events are the Annual Summer Faculty Show and the Annual Studio Assistants' Show.

Come the end of September, Peters Valley mounts arguably the best crafts show in the state. After years at the Peters Valley grounds, the show moved a few years ago to the Sussex County Fair Grounds in Augusta, site of the Sussex County Horse & Farm Show/New Jersey State Fair (see chapter 18). The move may have sacrificed a bit of the craft show's down-home charm, but it affords the artists an improved venue in which to showcase their work and better accommodates visitors in rainy weather.

A major fund-raising event for the center, the juried show features the work of more than 160 professional craftspeople representing just about every discipline you can imagine. Music, demonstrations, and excellent food augment the festivities and lend a welcoming air to the already informal atmosphere. The annual Peters Valley Craft Auction & Benefit Dinner raises funds for the center's educational programs. If you've ever wanted to talk technique with an expert, select from an eclectic range of excellent works, or just find out "how they did that," this show is the time and the place. Don't get me wrong. The fair bustles. But, it bustles with the kind of appreciative excitement that inspires rather than tires.

Not all of us can schedule our visits to a single weekend's event. Luckily, through the Peters Valley Studio Interpretive Program, studios are open to the public on Saturday and Sunday afternoons throughout the summer. The opportunity to watch the artists at work, see works in progress, and perhaps to chat about their creations and techniques is delightful.

On non-festival weekends, Peters Valley offers soothing peacefulness. On our latest visit, Penny and I arrived at midday on Sunday. The center was as quiet as a church mouse. We wandered up and down the hills, browsed through the shop and gallery, and snapped photos. Meandering

Peters Valley Crafts Center

along the mown grass path from the parking area to the studios, we savored the surrounding wild, tangled vegetation, which at the bottom of the slope gave way to a brook that bubbled into a small wetland dotted with luxuriant weeping willows. Across the dirt-and-gravel drive up from the swamp stood a short row of cottages, each personalized in some way —a collection of hanging plants, a postage stamp–sized vegetable garden, a wicker love seat.

The dirt drive terminated at the ceramics studio, and as we approached an elderly, scraggly dog slowly rose from his rest in a shady spot to greet and inspect us with a creaky wag of his scruffy tail. Two young women stood out front affably engaged in an intense conversation. The object of their dialogue was a large, half-finished piece of clay artwork. We peeked into the long building behind them and found a large expanse filled with ceramists busily gabbing away over their work. Their creative energy filled the room, emanating a potent excitement. We were too early; the studio was not yet open to the public. We turned to stroll back up the road. As we passed the two women, they had literally taken a step back from the object of their attention, as if to view it neutrally, from a distance.

"You see it as a hanging piece, really?" said the work's creator. "I see it kind of—drooping down!" They laughed, high-spirited, enjoying the energy of creation and the ambiguity of interpretation.

For an artist, the ability to lose one's self in one's work in a calm, focused atmosphere complemented by colleagues' support is a treasure. A Peters Valley visit offers the privilege of peeking into their world.

DETAILS

Peters Valley Crafts Center's Studio Interpretive Program is in effect from mid-May through mid-September, Saturday and Sunday 2–4. One- to two-hour slide lectures and presentations open to the public are offered free throughout the summer. Call or check their web site for a schedule of classes and events. **Information:** *973-948-5200; www.pvcrafts.org.*

Directions: *Take I-80 to exit 34, then NJ 15 north approximately 26 miles. Turn right onto CR 560 west, through the blinking light in the center of Layton and continue straight onto CR 640; in approximately 1 mile turn right onto CR 615 and continue for 1 mile.*

GARDENS OF THE GARDEN STATE

THE NICKNAME "GARDEN STATE" was derived from the truck farms—small vegetable farms—that once abounded across New Jersey. Although some agriculture survives, a different kind of garden now thrives: We are blessed with some of the most picturesque and pleasant botanical gardens, arboretums, and formal public gardens to be found anywhere.

Here are just three I particularly like, one south, one mid-state, and one north.

LEAMING'S RUN—CAPE MAY COURT HOUSE

A woman sat at a wooden table, half hidden behind a pile of dried flowers and baskets that she was turning into artful arrangements. She hummed as she worked, and smiled graciously as she took my entrance fee.

"Do you have a brochure, or guide to the gardens?" I asked.

She shook her head. "Just follow the path."

Like follow the yellow brick road? Well, yes, there's a bit of Oz in Leaming's Run. The dirt path winds through the woods, connecting a series of clearings that reveal magnificent, colorful tableaux. The largest garden featuring annuals in the United States, Leaming's Run covers some 30 acres and holds 25 small gardens, each planted with a theme. A small sign explains each garden's composition and the plants that comprise it.

Leaming's Run

Periodically—and delightfully—you come upon a sign that says LOOK BACK! and reminds you that sometimes beauty is revealed behind.

After passing through the Yellow, Blue and White, and English Cottage Gardens, I encountered a Swedish Colonial Farmstead, with one-room log cabin, circa 1695. As I entered, a mother and daughter were fussing over a peacock that lolled in a deep, dusty hole it had dug for itself. The women, camera at the ready, were trying to coax it out to show its feathers. Like a somnambulant cat, it disdained their attentions.

Cameras are a must at Leaming's Run. The individual mini-vistas demand photographing, especially when you come into the Begonia Garden, Gazebo Garden, and Bridal Garden, all centered on a classic streamside gazebo and a nearby footbridge.

At path's end, the Cooperage Gift Shop sells pretty and reasonably priced dried flower arrangements and a book entitled *Gardening Without Work* by Jack Aprill, the man who is behind all this beauty.

DETAILS

Leaming's Run Gardens *(609-465-5871; www.leamingsrun gardens.com) is open daily 9:30–5 from May 15 through October 20; special hummingbird tours in August.*

Directions: *Leaming's Run is located on US 9 north of Cape May; take the Garden State Parkway to exit 13, go west on Avalon Boulevard, and turn north onto US 9.*

FRELINGHUYSEN ARBORETUM—MORRISTOWN

The oompah band was gathering on the portable stage, a crowd was gathering on the expansive lawn below the mansion house, and an ominous collection of thunderheads was gathering overhead. Did I have time to wander among the flowers and trees, and could the band commence playing, before the rain commenced falling?

Covering more than 125 acres, the Frelinghuysen Arboretum displays a unique collection of trees, flowers, and shrubs in an easily accessed, well-annotated fashion. The Haggerty Education Center offers a variety of horticultural learning opportunities for all ages, year-round, and houses a library, changing exhibits, and an engaging display of horse-drawn carriages from the late 19th and early 20th centuries. Adjacent to the center, the Cottage Gift Shop sells a variety of goods, ranging from trinkets to gardening implements to books. It's a pleasant place to browse.

I picked up a trail guide at the center and studied my choices. I opted to follow the Blue Trail, which seemed long enough to provide some mild exercise and short enough to allow me to sit through part of the concert and/or retreat from the impending storm. I was rewarded with an extremely pleasant walk through a variety of plants and terrain on a trail that was very clearly marked and well supported by the printed guide. From Chinese stranvaesia (an evergreen ground cover) to hardy rubber trees, with a detour through a wet meadow rife with wild grasses, the Blue Trail revealed a rich variety of flora.

About halfway through the walk, just as sounds of the band drifted over the hill, the clouds dissipated. Now I could stroll to a musical accompaniment under sunny skies.

The Blue Trail reascended the hill in front of the white, Colonial-revival mansion house (now serving as the Morris County Park System headquarters), but I diverted into the Knot Garden, a style of English Tudor origin. A brick path and a pond beautifully surrounded by large, white-flowering Japanese snowbell and oakleaf hydrangea proved just too tempting. I sat on a bench and let the band's pops sound float above, completing a classic, lazy summer Sunday afternoon.

DETAILS

The grounds at Frelinghuysen Arboretum *(973-326-7600; www.arboretumfriends.org) are open from 9:00 AM to dusk daily. The Haggerty Education Center is open 9:00–4:30 Monday through Saturday; noon–4:30 on Sunday, year-round. Closed holidays.*

Directions: *From I-287 northbound, take exit 36A and proceed on the center lane past Washington Headquarters. Bear left at the fork onto Whippany Road. Turn right onto E. Hanover Avenue at the second light. From I-287 southbound, take exit 36, turn right onto Ridgedale Avenue, and right at the first traffic light onto E. Hanover Avenue.*

NEW JERSEY STATE BOTANICAL GARDEN, RINGWOOD MANOR STATE PARK, RINGWOOD

Skylands and Ringwood Manor together transport you back to a genteel time—long before air-conditioning—when gentlemen and ladies lolled the summer away on estates where the cooler, high-country weather provided much needed relief from the city's heat.

An investment banker and trustee of the New York Botanical Garden, Clarence McKenzie Lewis, set out in 1922 to create at Skylands a botanical showplace. He built a magnificent Tudor mansion made of native granite

Skylands

and rich woods, then had the most prominent landscape architects of his time design a suitable setting for the extensive collection of plants he had gathered from around the world. The state of New Jersey purchased the property in 1966 and declared it the state's official Botanical Garden in 1984.

Today Skylands offers visitors a serene escape from the hectic megalopolis just half an hour's drive away. The house is not open to the public, so you'll have to content yourself with admiring it from the outside, but you can pick up a self-guided tour brochure at the carriage house.

Maple Avenue, the main road, is paralleled on the left by two lines of carmine crab apple trees that stretch for an impressive 1,600 feet through an expansive lawn called Swan Meadow. In front of these are the Annual and Perennial Gardens. Behind, to the east, several interweaving footpaths lead to informal displays of rhododendron, heather, and wildflowers. Continue back into the heavily wooded area at the base of a hill called Mount Defiance and you find a bog garden and, eventually, the picturesque Swan Pond.

Westward, across Maple Avenue, stand the formal gardens. Leaving the house's rear terrace, you come upon an octagonal pool surrounded by dwarf plants and evergreen shrubs from a variety of places. Next comes the Magnolia Walk, two parallel lines of southern sweet bay magnolias, planted where their fragrance could drift up to the nearby house; that's followed by the Azalea Garden, which features a rectangular reflecting pool lined by azaleas and rhododendrons with blooms of almost every conceivable color. Immediately below the azalea collection, the Summer Garden features daylilies. Next, you'll come to a collection of tree peonies that borders the Lilac Garden. Come May, Skylands' collection of nearly four hundred lilac varieties presents an array that nearly overwhelms the eye.

It's but a short drive to Ringwood Manor. The first section of the manor was built in 1765, and the building, purchased by the iron-magnate Abram Stevens Hewitt in 1807, was expanded section by section for many years. The final structure contains 78 rooms. The building is filled with marvelous paraphernalia dating from the early 1800s to the mid-1900s, and the free tour of the manor is well conducted. The manor also houses a small art gallery and magnificent formal gardens of its own.

Also a short drive within the state park is Shepherd's Lake. An over-sized pond, really, the lake offers swimming, small boating, fishing, picnicking, and a snack bar.

❋ ❋ ❋ ❋ ❋ ❋ ❋ ❋

DETAILS

New Jersey State Botanical Gardens *(Skylands Botanical Gardens) of Ringwood State Park (201-962-7031, 201-962-7527; Ringwood Manor, 201-962-9534 for recorded event information; www.njbg.org) are open 8–8 daily.*

Directions: *From I-80, take exit 53 to NJ 23 north. Drive about 15 miles to Butler and exit onto CR 511 north, and follow the signs to the botanical gardens.*

❋ ❋ ❋ ❋ ❋ ❋ ❋ ❋

OTHER NOTEWORTHY NEW JERSEY GARDENS

The Leonard J. Buck Garden, Far Hills (908-234-2677, www.park
.co.somerset.nj.us/activities/gardens/gardens_Buck.htm) This is among
the premier rock gardens in the eastern United States. Home to alpine
and woodland gardens on 33 acres, Buck Garden is operated by the
Somerset County Park Commission. Wooded trails lead to rare plants,
abundant wildflowers, a wide variety of ferns, azaleas, and rhododendrons. **Directions:** Take I-287 to exit 22B (northbound) or exit 22
(southbound) to US 202/206 north. Go through one traffic light and US
202/206 splits; bear right onto US 202 north and continue on that road
even as it merges with CR 523 east. Just before the railroad tracks, turn
right onto Liberty Corner Road (CR 512 east). Drive for 1 mile and turn
right onto Layton Road.

The Presby Memorial Iris Gardens, Upper Montclair (973-783-5974,
www.presbyiris.tripod.com/) Located in Mountainside Park, the gardens
are named for Frank H. Presby, the founder of the American Iris Society.
The collection, designated a National Historic Site, includes six species
with more than four thousand iris varieties, some of which date to the
1500s. **Directions:** Take US 46 east through Totowa and Little Falls to the
Clove Road/Montclair State University exit. Follow the road through the
back of the university and turn left at the stop sign onto Long Hill Road.
Pass through the traffic light at Normal Avenue (where road name
changes to Upper Mountain Avenue) and pass through the next intersection with Mt. Hebron Road. The gardens are on the right across from
public tennis courts.

Well-Sweep Herb Farm, Port Murray (908-852-5390, www.well
sweep.com) This Warren County farm is counted among the country's
premier herb farms. It covers 120 acres amid scenic hills and features a
half-acre display garden, 36 basil varieties, 60 lavenders, 80 thymes and
more than 100 scented geraniums. **Directions:** Take I-80 east to exit 19.
Turn left onto CR 517 south for approximately 5 miles to the second light.
Cross US 46 (Main Street) to Grand Avenue and follow it for 1 mile to a
one-lane train underpass where Grand Avenue becomes CR 629 south

and the name changes to Rockport Road. Continue for 4.4 miles. Turn right onto Mt. Bethel Road to the farm, 1 mile ahead on the left.

Sayen Gardens, Hamilton (609-587-7356; www.sayengardens.org) Mercer County's Sayen Gardens boasts more than 2,000 azaleas and more than 1,500 rhododendrons of hybrid and native species, some brought from as far away as China, Japan, and England by the late Fred Sayen. This is a brilliant color display in spring and all summer long. A pond holds water lilies and provides habitat for birds and wildlife. The gardens also represent New Jersey's largest collection of bulbs, with 500,000 daffodils, tulips, snowdrops, and many more. **Directions:** Take the New Jersey Turnpike south to exit 7A, west on I-195 toward Trenton. Take exit 3B and head north toward Hamilton Square. Bear right onto Yardville Hamilton Square Road, and turn left onto NJ 33. In less than 0.25 mile, turn right onto White Horse Hamilton Square Road, and in another 0.25 mile turn right onto CR 618 (Nottingham Way). Turn left onto Mercer Street, then left onto Hughes Drive. The gardens will be on the left.

The Gardens at Duke Farms, Hillsborough (908-243-3600, www.njskylands.com/atdukgar.htm) A childhood home of heiress Doris Duke, this enchanting, 700-acre estate of woodland, meadows, lakes, waterfalls, sculptures, and marvelous views can be toured by trolley from mid-June through mid-November. From October through May, thematic greenhouse gardens are opened to the public. Ms. Duke designed these gardens herself. Enclosing more than an acre, they represent the diverse flora and far-ranging cultures and places she visited worldwide—from the esoteric corners of Europe to Persia and the deserts and jungles of Africa. **Directions:** Take I-78 to exit 29, and then I-287 south to exit 17. Drive south on US 206; Duke Farms are 1.75 miles south of Somerville.

Camden Children's Garden, Camden (856-365-8733, www.camden childrensgarden.org, see also chapter 9) Four acres of delightful fantasy are adjacent to the New Jersey State Aquarium and just downriver from the Ben Franklin Bridge. The collection of themed gardens includes everything from fairy tales and history to dinosaurs and a maze, plus a carousel and ridable mini-train and a kid-friendly maze in which to wander. A great

place for kids to romp. Themed events are staged regularly. **Directions:**
Take the New Jersey Turnpike to exit 4, NJ 73 north. Follow signs to NJ 38
west toward Camden and bear right over the overpass to NJ 30 west.
Follow signs to Mickle Boulevard and the aquarium. You could also take I-
295 to exit 26 and follow I-676 north to exit 5A. Follow signs to the aquarium or the waterfront. The garden is also reachable by New Jersey Transit
buses and trains, Amtrak, SEPTA, PATCO, and the River Line, as well as
the RiverLink Ferry from Philadelphia.

PRIVATE GARDENS

Some of the state's most intriguing gardens are found in people's
backyards, developed by property owners with a love of horticulture. To
share the wealth, so to speak, and allow the public to see and appreciate
these marvelous creations, the Garden Conservancy (1-888-842-2442,
www.gardenconservancy.org), a national, nonprofit organization devoted
to preserving exceptional American gardens for the public's education and
enjoyment, created the Open Days program. Instituted in 1995, it allows
the public to be introduced to gardening and provides easy access to outstanding examples of design and horticultural practice. It's America's only
national private-garden-visiting program.

Gardens included in the Open Days program must show an "extra
something special," according to Laura Mumaw Palmer, director of the
program. Among the qualities sought: unity and harmony of design, with
strong and distinctive elements, plus aesthetic plant groupings and eco-
logically sound design and maintenance techniques.

The Conservancy publishes annual directories, paperbacks that list
the gardens to be displayed the dates the public can visit them, owner-
written descriptions, and detailed driving directions to each location. New
Jersey gardens are found in the northeast edition.

A Retreat Treat

Ocean Grove

Q UESTION: WHAT do Teddy Roosevelt, former New Jersey governor Christie Todd Whitman, John Philip Sousa, Glen Miller, Ulysses S. Grant, Guy Lombardo, Booker T. Washington, Jascha Heifitz, Billy Graham, Woodrow Wilson, and the Preservation Hall Jazz Band all have in common?

Answer: They've all graced the stage—to speak or perform—of the Great Auditorium in Ocean Grove.

Built in 1894, the magnificent hall remains Ocean Grove's centerpiece. Visitors still flock to hear speakers and concerts of all kinds and to attend religious services. Regardless of the event or occasion, the building itself is transfixing. It is, according to the Ocean Grove Camp Meeting Association, the largest all-wood auditorium in the country, covering nearly the length of a football field, seating 6,400 people, and housing an enormous Robert Hope Jones pipe organ. The roof is made of long, arched wooden planks and is said to have been conceived as Noah's ark upside down. That's impressive. But, when you learn that it was built in 92 days by 60 workers, and that the workers swore an oath not to drink, smoke, or curse while working on the construction, impressive turns into awesome.

Indeed, much about Ocean Grove is awesome. And curious. The town was founded in 1869 as a religious retreat for the Methodist Episcopal Church. It was not uncommon in those days for believers who sought spiritual uplift, as well as relief from daily cares and the summer's heat, to gather together, live in tents for several days or even weeks at a time, and listen to inspiring sermons and music. They called these gatherings Camp Meetings. Ocean Grove's Camp Meeting Association ranks as the nation's second-longest continually operating camp meeting organizations. The faithful no longer pitch tents, however. They set up canvases over wooden platforms that are attached to diminutive wood cabins, equipped with electricity, bathrooms, and kitchens; 114 of these canvas "front rooms" populate Ocean Grove today.

If the modern "tents" offer more creature comforts than their predecessors, the spirit that founded the town has not. Weekly concerts are performed on the auditorium's magnificent pipe organ, guest clerics from around the country lead Sunday morning services, the Tabernacle Bible Hour meets every weekday at 9 AM, and the mid-July camp meeting week still highlights the summer.

Time was when local blue laws closed the town off to worldly pleasures every Saturday at midnight. In fact, a chain blocked the road at the town's entry gates, and no wheeled vehicles were permitted to even be seen (no less operated) for 24 hours. Ocean Grove today can't be characterized as all-religion-and-no-fun. Yes, it remains a dry town, and the public bathhouse doesn't open until after noon on Sunday. But the engaging downtown is inviting and as active as any at the shore. Quaint galleries, singular gift shops, and several restaurants create an enjoyable browsing and strolling atmosphere. Try lunch at the Sampler Inn, which serves very affordable meals in an old-fashioned, cafeteria style.

As might be expected, Ocean Grove's boardwalk offers oceanfront serenity, not action. On the beach, volleyball tournaments, kite-flying contests, water races, and sand sculpture contests take place throughout the summer. The town's annual events include a Choir Festival, Giant Spring and Fall Flea Markets, House Tour, Boardwalk Art Show, Oktoberfest, the November Harvest Home Festival, the December Festival of Lights, and the Holiday House Tour.

Those who crave nightlife drive but 10 minutes north to find one of the Garden State's most famous nightspots—Asbury Park's Stone Pony, the venue that gave Bruce Springsteen his start. Chico's House of Jazz and Blues, featuring national artists, and Harry's Roadhouse, where classic rock rules, are both nearby. Naturally, if it's an evening immersed in the classic boardwalk cacophony of games, rides, and bright lights you're after, Asbury has long been famous for that.

Ocean Grove's combination of Victorian-rich architecture and religious retreat create a unique character. The little seaside town is on the National Register of Historic Places, and it contains the largest assemblage of Victorian architecture in an area of its size. Ocean Grove's collection of hotels, bed & breakfasts, and inns offer a beach holiday in an old-fashioned style that spans several eras. The Lilligard, for example, is a small hotel that has operated since 1871 and its prix fixe offering of afternoon tea complete with sandwiches, scones, fruit, desserts, and assorted teas is a real throwback. Meanwhile, Captain Jack's Restaurant & Cocktail Lounge is a modern spot with live music on Wednesday evenings.

It's the summer auditorium concerts that bring the most attention to Ocean Grove. And rightfully so. It is clearly a special space, one that bestows a special pride in the performers, preachers, and local children's theater club members who grace its stage; one in which an entire community has placed its identity and, indeed, its faith.

DETAILS

Information: *Ocean Grove Chamber of Commerce, P.O. Box 415, Ocean Grove, NJ 07756; www.neptunenj.com; 1-800-388-4768 or 732-774-1391. Ocean Grove Camp Meeting Association, 4 Pitman Avenue, P.O. Box 248, Ocean Grove, NJ 07756; www.oceangrove.org; 732-775-0035. Great Auditorium box office: 1-800-773-0097.*

Directions: *From the north or west, take the Garden State Parkway to exit 100B or the New Jersey Turnpike to exit 8 and follow NJ 33 west. From the south, take the New Jersey Turnpike to I-195 east to NJ 35 north.*

26

CABIN CAMPING

OUR TENT IS JINXED. Every time we pitch it, we're flooded out. We've spent most of our tenting trips at the laundromat running sleeping bags through the dryer.

Face it. When it comes to camping, we're not troopers.

That's why when cousin Vera asked us to join her family on a camping trip, we hesitated. Vera had two kids at the time — girls aged young and very young. The idea of suffering through a deluge with infants was daunting. Our own kids were seven and nine, and they already hated tenting because of the unfailing, unrelenting torrential rains.

"This will be different," cousin Vera assured us. "We'll rent a family cabin. You can do that at a lot of state parks." Rent a cabin? We remained skeptical, but Vera talked us into it. Two months later, as we drove to the mountains, we could only imagine the worst. We envisioned a dirty collection of rotting boards with a squeaky screen door, a cabin that had a musty reek and leaned precariously, ready to collapse with the first hard (and inevitable) rain. It probably had a dank privy out back.

We were right about the screen door squeaking. But, we were wrong about the rest. The cabin was an immaculately clean, roomy building made of sweet-smelling, rough-hewn pine, and it was downright comfortable. A path through the trees led to the lake just a few yards away, where we fished, hiked, and skipped stones. Small, electric motor–powered boats and canoes were available for rent.

The kids went ga-ga over fishing. The girls loved dangling their lines from shore. Many small fish were snagged; all were thrown back. Except one. And he was the biggest we caught. The poor guy swallowed the hook and died. Not knowing what else to do, we tossed it onto a rock next to a waiting water snake, then spent 15 minutes in rapt fascination as that skinny snake ingested that fat fish. No science class will ever make a stronger impression on those kids.

Yes, it rained. We didn't care. We had a real roof over our heads. We stayed dry.

We've become big fans of cabin camping. You get some of the comforts of home, some of the rough edges of camping, no backaches from sleeping on the ground, and never a wet sleeping bag.

A number of New Jersey state parks offer cabin camping. Most cabins have bunk beds, cold running water, kitchen facilities complete with refrigerator and stove, and flush toilets. Sizes range from four bunks to twenty-four. You must bring your own linens or sleeping bags, kitchen utensils, and towels. Cabins can be rented by the week or weekend. As you would expect, in the heart of summer, rentals are popular and reservations are a must—the further ahead, the better.

Up north, Stokes State Forest and nearby High Point are the places to go. Although both offer launch sites for small boats, neither of these parks provide rowboat or canoe rentals.

Toward the state's center, Wharton, Brendan Byrne, and Parvin State

❀ ❀ ❀ ❀ ❀ ❀ ❀ ❀

DETAILS

The Department of Environmental Protection, Division of Parks & Forestry *offers information on all state parks and forests, including a fee schedule for all park activities.* **Information:** *www.njparksandforests.org; 1-800-843-6420 or 609-984-0370.*

❀ ❀ ❀ ❀ ❀ ❀ ❀ ❀

High Point State Park

Forests offer cabin camping. Wharton and Parvin also have small boat rentals. A family trip to Wharton State Forest can combine a fantastic variety of activities—hiking, fishing, canoeing, mountain or road biking, and a visit to Batsto Village's living history exhibit (see chapter 21)—all for a very reasonable price without the discomfort of tent camping.

Along the south central shore, Bass River State Forest offers cabins. North of Dennisville, Belleplain State Forest offers yurts (think soft-sided cabin). Both offer great access to lake and river canoeing.

Incidentally, all these beautiful parks and forests offer tent camping as well, some with true wilderness campsites. You'll find plenty of places to pitch a tent. Just don't ask to borrow ours unless you like tenting in the rain.

PLAY BALL!
Minor League Baseball

WE ARRIVED AT THE BALLPARK EARLY. Not that there was a scarcity of tickets. We were, rather, seeking the full ambience—a chance to sit in the stands, absorb the smell of fresh-cut grass and hot dogs grilling, and watch the boys of summer go through their lazy rituals, whacking batting practice balls deep into the outfield and crisply running through fielding drills—as dusk darkened the sky.

It doesn't get much more Americana than this.

Some will tell you that baseball has slipped from its honored place as the Great American Pastime. But, how then do they explain the incredible and seemingly unlikely resurgence of minor-league baseball? Teams have sprung up in the past half-dozen years not only in New Jersey but across the country. Indeed, the Garden State now serves as home to at least eight professional minor-league clubs. Better still, each of these teams plays in a new ballpark. Best, just about anywhere you live or go in the state, there's a team playing near you.

Why attend a minor-league baseball game? Plenty of reasons. Many of these teams, like the Jersey Jackals and Newark Bears, are "unaffiliated" or "independent," which is to say they have no working agreement with a major-league team. The players are generally free-agent prospects, "on their way up" or so they hope, and are not being rewarded with huge money and celebrity. Untainted by trappings of wealth and fame, they hustle. They play with verve, desire, and a love of the game. Even if the skill level is a cut or two (okay, maybe three) below the big leaguers playing on the other sides of the Hudson and Delaware Rivers, the enthusiasm and sheer optimism is contagious.

Their enthusiasm spreads to the stands because the stadia are small, and the players are seen up-close-and-personal. You can hear their grunts as they swing the bat or dive for the ball. You can see 'em sweat.

But for my money, I like the presentation. No somber, overly serious approach here, born of the pretense that a world championship is at stake. No sir. In the minors, the games are peppered with humorous promotions and between-innings antics. I'm talking about fans brought onto the field dressed in ballooning rubber suits to "sumo wrestle;" shopping cart races; kids running the bases; T-shirts being tossed into the stands; prefabricated sounds of glass breaking when a foul ball heads toward the parking lot. It's fun. It's funny. It's like being at the proverbial community picnic, where a pickup game is always in progress and the kids run free with hot dogs in their hands.

And, for the true baseball afficionado, there's the kick of seeing a possible future major leaguer, a hall-of-famer perhaps (who knows?), at the beginning of his career. Years ago, my kids and I watched Mark Grace, who became a superb first baseman for the Chicago Cubs, and Jack Armstrong, who went on to be a twenty-game winner in the majors, play in a tiny Massachusetts stadium. In recent years, New Jersey Cardinals fans have had the satisfaction of seeing outfielder Covelli "Coco" Crisp move on to the St. Louis Cardinals. There's something magical, almost prescient, in being able to say "I saw him when . . ." On the flip side, Newark Bears fans have watched the likes of hall-of-famer Rickey Henderson finish out his remarkable career.

Here's a look at New Jersey's teams.

Trenton Thunder. The highest caliber team in the state, the Thunder are a New York Yankees' Double-A farm team. They play at Waterfront Park. Opened in 1994, Waterfront was among the first of the new generation of "old-fashioned" stadia. Views of the Delaware River add nicely to

A day game at Campbell's Field

the ambience. As an affiliated, higher-level team, the Thunder feature more players who may well play in "the bigs," but fun remains the operative word.

New Jersey Cardinals. This Class A affiliate of the St. Louis Cardinals plays at Skylands Park in Augusta. Surrounded by a cornfield in northern New Jersey farm country, the rural feel lends a nice "if you build it, they will come" feeling, augmented by architecture that mimics a red barn and farm buildings. The adjacent fun center lets kids and adults hit some in the batting cages or indulge in indoor mini-golf. Typically, St. Louis assigns its top college draft picks to this New Jersey affiliate.

Camden Riversharks. What a wonderful place to watch a ball game. Campbell's Field, so named because it sits on the site of a former Campbell's Soup factory, was designated Park of the Year in 2003 by both digitalball-parks.com and Baseball America. Sit on the first base side and fantastic views of Philadelphia are the backdrop, with the Ben Franklin Bridge arching over the scene just behind the outfield fences. Little ones who might not revel in cityscape views can retreat to a spot behind the right-field bull-pen fence, where a mini-amusement park keeps them entertained. Within walking distance to the New Jersey State Aquarium, the Battleship *New Jersey*, the Tweeter Center, and the RiverLink Ferry to Philadelphia's Penn's Landing, a visit to the ballpark is easily integrated into a mini-vacation at the Camden riverfront (see chapter 9). During my last visit, not only did the home team win, but one in-game promotion rewarded everyone in the stands with a free pizza if they visited the local pizzeria.

Lakewood BlueClaws. FirstEnergy Park is diminutive and puts you right in the action. It's outfitted with a conference center and a pub. The team plays in the South Atlantic League, a 100-year-old organization with competition in two divisions of eight teams each, including clubs hailing from as far away as West Virginia and South Carolina.

Jersey Jackals. What can you say about a team that plays at a place called Yogi Berra Stadium? It's enough to make a true fan sit in the stands and read one of Yogi's books, maybe *I Really Didn't Say Everything I Said or When You Come to a Fork in the Road, Take It!* My personal favorite Yogi expression? "Ninety percent of the game is half mental." The hall-of-fame catcher is a resident of Montclair and very active in the community. The Jackals play on the campus of Montclair State University. Hence, the stadium's name. The ballpark itself isn't architecturally monumental, but it does offer a pleasant, homey place to watch a game. I've ventured here with a friend and his elementary-school-aged kids, and we were able to let the kids roam free.

And there's a bonus: The Yogi Berra Museum & Learning Center. Located next to the ballpark, this small museum (which has announced plans to double in size in the near future) has been described as a mini-Cooperstown (site of the Baseball Hall of Fame). I suppose you don't have to be a Yankees fan—or a lifelong Yankees hater as I am —to enjoy the museum, but it certainly doesn't hurt. Permanent exhibits of Yogi and Yankees memorabilia include all of Yogi's World Series rings, plus photos of memorable moments in Berra's career. Changing exhibits are mounted regularly, with recent offerings such as the Negro Leagues; 19th-century baseball, and "Curses—Foiled Again," a look at the bad luck suffered by the Boston Red Sox and the Chicago Cubs. The Berra Center also hosts a steady stream of special events and celebrity appearances, but it's not all fun and games here. Its stated purpose: "Inspired by Yogi Berra's commitment to children, the museum leverages the historic and contemporary role of sports through programs that foster literacy, diversity, integrity, social justice, sportsmanship, hard work, and dedication in all aspects of life. Baseball, the National Pastime, and other sports teach many important social and cultural values that are as important off the field as they are on. The Yogi Berra Museum and Learning Center promotes these values in honor of, and as reflected in, the life of one of the greatest sports ambassadors in our time."

Somerset Patriots. It's the fully video-and-special effects-capable scoreboard at the 6,000-plus-seat Commerce Bank Park that takes center stage here. Somerset plays in the Atlantic League, along with the Camden Riversharks, the Atlantic City Surf, and the Newark Bears.Nicest feature: sitting on blankets on the lawn.

Newark Bears. Baseball in Newark has a long and glorious history that dates as far back as 1902. For years the city was home to the original Newark Bears, a Yankees' Triple-A farm team that was not only the class act of minor-league baseball, but the final proving ground for many Yankee stars just before they made the leap to the majors. Indeed, the 1937 Bears are considered by many to be the greatest minor-league team ever. Newark, too, was home to the Eagles, a premier Negro League team that boasted many greats on its rosters. So it was with great fanfare that the newest version of the Bears was reborn in 1999, when Bears & Eagles Riverfront Stadium was built. This is urban baseball at its best. A new 300-space parking garage eases earlier parking problems, and the way in which the stadium is tucked in among the oddly laid-out downtown streets gives it personality. On a clear day, you can see the Manhattan skyline in the distance. The team has, over the years, brought in some name players to fill out its roster—Rickey Henderson, Jose Canseco, and Bill Madlock among them. The city of Newark has devoted a lot of resources to this stadium, which combines with the adjacent New Jersey Performing Arts Center to form the backbone of the city's renaissance. Whether it can live up to that mandate remains to be seen, but the Bears' management has done an excellent job of connecting the modern team to the city's past historic ones, making this a baseball site worth visiting.

Atlantic City Surf. With the Atlantic City high-rise casinos sparkling in the background, the Sandcastle—the wonderfully named home to the equally well-monikered Surf—can be a dazzling spot for a night game. Yet another of New Jersey's Atlantic League entries, the Surf, like the Newark Bears, are carrying something of a heavy burden—the revitalization of a city hoping to rise to former glories. Attending a game is one of Atlantic City's nicer nongambling offerings, and the ballpark is a comfortable and welcoming as the others in the state. Whether the team can lure people away from the slots and tables is another question. But it's an intimate setting in which to watch a game, and that's essence of minor-league ball—up close and personal.

❀ ❀ ❀ ❀ ❀ ❀ ❀ ❀

DETAILS

Atlantic City Surf—*The Sandcastle: 609-344-8873; www.acsurf.com; 545 N. Albany Ave., Atlantic City, NJ 08401.*

Camden Riversharks—*Campbell's Field: 856-963-2600; www.riversharks.com; 401 N. Delaware Ave. Camden, NJ 08102.*

Lakewood BlueClaws—*FirstEnergy Park: 732-901-7000; www.lakewoodblueclaws.com; Lakewood, NJ 08701.*

New Jersey Cardinals—*Skylands Park: 973-579-7500; www.njcards.com; Augusta, NJ 07822.*

Jersey Jackals—*Yogi Berra Stadium: 973-746-3131; www.jackals.com; Little Falls, NJ 07424.*

Yogi Berra Museum & Learning Center *(on the campus of Montclair State University): 973-655-2378; www.yogiberra museum.org; 8 Quarry Road, Little Falls, NJ 07424.*

Newark Bears—*Bears & Eagles Riverfront Stadium: 973-483-6900; www.newarkbears.com; Newark, NJ 07102.*

Somerset Patriots—*Commerce Bank Ballpark: 908-252-0700; www.somersetpatriots.com; Bridgewater, NJ 08807.*

Trenton Thunder—*Mercer County Waterfront Park: 609-394-8326; www.trentonthunder.com; 1 Thunder Road, Trenton, NJ 08611*

❀ ❀ ❀ ❀ ❀ ❀ ❀ ❀

DARING DIVERSIONS

Amusement Parks & Water Playgrounds

THE GIRLS' EYES GREW BIG, opened wide like the saucers in the old cliché. Their necks craned; their mouths dropped open. Well, why not? It's hard, even for a crusty old parent, not to betray a sense of awe when you look at gigantic mechanical contraptions that stand dozens of stories high and are meant to whisk people into the air, whip them around loops, drop them like rag dolls and whiz them back to earth. Who thinks up these apparatuses? And why are people so keen on climbing aboard just to be scared half to death?

But, there you have it. Roller coasters and their brethren have always exuded an unnatural lure, a magnetic draw, that people can't seem to resist. In this case, my daughter and her friend—then 14 or so—were exulting in apoplectic joy over the skyscraping coasters at Six Flags Great Adventure. But, even I, the motion-sickness king, can remember doing the same at their age with the old Cyclone coaster at Palisades Park.

Palisades, long an icon in the amusement park world, is long gone, leaving not even a scratch on the collective memory of the younger generation. But its tradition of providing a day's thrills, arcade entertainment, and deliciously diverting excitement lives on throughout the state. Great Adventure is the "big kahuna" of the state's amusement parks, and each season its reputation is enhanced by the addition of a new monster ride. But, believe it or not, the last time I ventured to Six Flags, in the company of a young guy named Neal, my friend's 10-year-old, we never set foot in the amusement park. There were wild animals to visit and a waterpark in which to splash about.

Tell the uninitiated that New Jersey has a drive-through wildlife park and they snicker, "What Exit?" Until they drive through Wild Safari. Up-close encounters with more than 1,200 land animals—many of them endangered species—turns the laughter to awe. Where else do baboons climb on your windshield and hang from your side-view mirrors? A narrative that can be piped in through your car radio guides you as you pass within arm's length of magnificent beasts. Lions, tigers, elephants, rhinos, hippos—the list seems to match the Ark's roster. Even Neal, who is not known for being an animal guy, loved it. Especially when the baboons were staring at us upside down through the windshield. And he'll remember those apes—not to mention the baby tiger we met—more vividly than any roller coasters.

We drove out of the safari and sought relief from the heat at Six Flags' waterpark, Hurricane Harbor. I quickly lost Neal. I bent over to put on my shoes and somehow he was gone. Luckily, we had agreed on a meeting place, and after I'd indulged in some frantic searching, we managed to find each other. As waterparks go, this isn't gargantuan. It happily entertains children under 12; teens may be disappointed with the dearth of death-defying slides. My buddy and I found thrills enough, however, on Cannonball, Wahini, and Jurahnimo Falls, slides that were not too steep, not too scary, not too tame, but just right. (I was also happy for the park's relative diminutiveness when I was hunting for the kid.)

Great Adventure, on the other hand, *is* big. It houses 13 coasters, two areas designated for specifically families, and regularly stages concerts, fireworks displays, and other special events. My 14-year-old confreres were in seventh heaven, dashing from one ride to the next. I was content to watch, browse the carnie-like midway where "games of skill" were constantly underway, and check out the more laid-back attractions, like the SpongeBob SquarePants 3-D Ride Simulator and Blackbeard's Lost Treasure Train Ride. Even though there are "family" areas here, Great

Adventure might be too much for little ones, especially when compared with attractions at parks particularly aimed at young children (see listings below). Still, for those who crave the amusement park major leagues, Great Adventure is the answer.

MAKING A BIG SPLASH

Water parks are growing in popularity across the state, and Mountain Creek, a ski area in Sussex County, has one of the best. Ten-year-old Neal, his nearly 13-year-old brother, Scott, and their dad, Mark, all joined me for a day. Here we found some seriously steep slides and adventurous water elements—like ropes and cliffs from which to jump. And the kids spent inordinate amounts of time splashing in the sizeable wave pool.

Mountain Creek's water park required a goodly measure of uphill walking to get from one attraction to the next (this is a ski hill, after all), but the mountain ambience is pleasant and, because it's a stand-alone operation (no other amusements, save a mountain biking park and, way down the hill all by itself, a skate park), crowds weren't problematic, even when some of the lines grew long.

We stayed away from the more extreme aqua adventures, like Bombs Away, which finishes with an 18-foot drop into a pool, and something called Cannonball Falls, whose name alone scared the kids off. But the name High Anxiety didn't faze them a bit, and the Colorado River ride proved a favorite, as it has with everyone I've visited this park with. It's a tube-riding affair that has just the right number of drop-offs and general pitch of descent keep riders laughing between screams. The park provides tame areas that work well for smaller children—I mean how can you not be attracted to a place called Half Pint Harbor?—and all ages are drawn to a series of special events, including Hydrofest, a gathering of bands and special vendors, and assemblages like wave pool dance parties and model search contests.

THEY'RE EVERYWHERE!

No part of the state lies unserved by amusement parks and water emporia. Here's an alphabetical roundup of the various offerings.

Splash down!

Bowcraft Amusement Park (908-233-0675; www.bowcraft.com; Route 22 W, Scotch Plains) Bowcraft features 19 rides, an arcade, a "speedway," and an 18-hole miniature golf course. This is a smaller park and probably a better choice for families with younger children. It's been around a long time and is a quality operation.

Casino Pier/Breakwater Beach Water Park (908-793-6488; www.casinopier-waterworks.com; 800 Ocean Terrace, Seaside Heights) Seaside is "where it's at" for active beachgoers, and this big amusement park, set above the ocean on a boardwalk pier, is one reason why. You'll find 35 rides, including a carousel, roller coaster, water rides, Ferris wheel, a famous sky ride. And, of course, there's the beach. If its honky-tonk and arcades you're after, few do it bigger than Casino Pier. They have games of chance galore, innumerable food stands, and mini-golf, too. Carousel afficionados appreciate the Dr. Floyd L. Moreland Historic Dentzel/Looff Carousel. Pushing 100 years old, it's not only a museum piece, it's one of just two surviving American-made classic carousels in the state.

The Breakwater Beach waterpark is a renovation of the old Water

Works. Attractions are aimed all age groups. The Toddler Area takes care of the littlest ones, and the Family Play Area presents a variety of ways in which all ages can get wet. In addition to the expected slides, chutes, and giant barrels dumping water on heads, a pair of Hot Springs adds a different dimension on cool evenings.

Clementon Amusement Park/Waterpark (609-783-0263; www.clementonpark.com; 144 Berlin Road, Clementon) Clementon goes way back—all the way to 1907. This is a family-oriented place. It holds 25 rides, but adds some unique, old-timey aspects, like a petting zoo, strolling bands, clowns, face-painters, and jugglers. Recently they've added Big Cat Encounter—African lions and Royal Bengal tigers are presented to both entertain and educate. You'll find some roller coasters and some new, more daring rides with scary names like Thunderbolt and Chaos. The enclosed Kiddie Land is a nice touch, offering gentle rides for the little ones in a setting that's protected from the hot sun. The waterpark presents something for everyone, from the exhilarating Sky River Rapids to head-first mat racing to a Lazy River.

Fantasy Island Amusement Park (609-492-4000; www.fantasyisland park.com; 320 W. Seventh Street, Beach Haven) Located toward the southern end of Long Beach Island, Fantasy Island effects a Victorian atmosphere through the use of Z-brick walkways, oak benches, ornate lamp posts, and Tiffany glass chandeliers. It's a longstanding landmark on the island, and here you'll find the full range of rides—carousel, roller coaster, kiddy rides, and some adult zingers—along with the usual arcade, food stands, and midway. Animals come into play with reptile shows, and acts featuring magic and illusion are regularly scheduled live entertainment. Rounding out the offerings are an adult casino arcade and an old-fashioned ice cream parlor.

Funtown Amusement Pier (732-830-7437; www.funtownpier.com; 1930 Boardwalk, Seaside Park) Here's another old-timer that's also a beachside fixture. Funtown's been in action for more than 75 years, offering beach-goers an amusement break in a setting that yields pretty fine ocean views. One nice feature here is the family-friendliness: more than

35 kiddie rides and a roller coaster built with families in mind. Adrenalin junkies need not panic. Rides like the 225-foot Tower of Fear (said to be the state's tallest ride) and the Kamikaze provide thrills. There's also a go-cart track and bumper cars. The latest addition is a Haunted Manor walk-through in which the frights are delivered by both live actors and animatronic beings. Another nice aspect: the ability to purchase individual tickets or pay one price. Arcade and games fans find all they want right out the exit along the hustle-bustle Seaside boardwalk.

Gillian's Wonderland Pier Theme Park & Waterpark (609-399-0483; www.gillians.com; P.O. Box 1186, Ocean City 08226) A pay-as-you-go park, Gillian's is a South Jersey shore fixture, having been around in one form or another since 1930. You'll find more than 35 thrills of all degrees, including the 138-foot Ferris wheel and such gentile undertakings as an antique carousel and a monorail. Other highlights include a NASCAR Speedway, a full slate of water slides, mini-golf, picnic grounds, and indoor rides for those less-than-perfect days. Ocean City is all about families (see chapter 5), and Gillian's is part of the reason why.

Jenkinson's Boardwalk (732-892-0600; www.jenkinsons.com; 300 Ocean Avenue, Point Pleasant Beach, NJ) In addition to having one of the cooler small aquariums around (see chapter 43), Jenkinson's is a large, classic boardwalk amusement park. Of the 27 rides, 13 are for the kiddies, and there are innumerable games of chance, arcades, novelty shops, and food outlets, plus a fun house and live music and special events on the beach all summer long. Speaking of food, from sushi to peanut butter and jelly, there's little you can't find here. Come nighttime, adults can get in on a pretty hot nightclub scene.

Keansburg Amusement Park and Waterpark (1-800-805-4386 or 732-495-1400; www.keansburgamusementpark.com; 275 Beachway, Keansburg) Keansburg is another boardwalk amusement park, this time at the northern reaches of the Jersey Shore. Here you'll find more than 45 rides that cover the full range of challenge to your heartbeat. One of the newest is something called the Double Shot; it propels riders 100 feet straight up and then drops them back to earth. Chaos is a swirling disk thing that looks like it would surely make me throw up, and then there's this Gravitron thing that uses centrifugal force to float passengers aloft in simulated weightlessness. Oy. Here, too, you'll find alternative amusements: two go-cart tracks—one for adults and one for children; a rock-climbing wall, batting cages, games of chance, arcades, and a carousel. On their web site, the park rates their rides K (Kiddie), F (Family), T (Thrill). More than a dozen water slides and the Kiddie Lagoon make up the waterplay area. And, of course, there's plenty of boardwalk-style food.

Land of Make Believe Amusement Park & Pirate's Cove Waterpark (908-459-9000; www.lomb.com; Route 611, Great Meadows Road, Hope) The Land of Make Believe and Pirate's Cove just might be the best little kids' amusement destination my family's ever encountered. We went there when the kids were small. My friends took their kids. And my neighbors who now have small children are all taking theirs. Both parks are aimed at younger children and families on an outing. Even the so-called thrill rides and slides are toned down to the point where a 10-year-old can love 'em without intimidation. You can also do things like take an old-fashioned hayride drawn by a farm tractor, take a train ride around the park on a Civil War locomotive, watch a kid-friendly show at the Middle Earth Theatre, make your way through a maze, sit in the cockpit of a World War II plane, or pet farm animals at (you guessed it) Old McDonald's Farm. The picnic grove allows you to keep the costs down by bringing your own food, and the Pirate's Cove waterpark is just as small-thrill oriented. No big time, monster thrill rides or slides scare small kids or make them feel like they're just babies. If little ones are in your entourage, this is the place.

Morey's Piers Amusement Park & Raging Waters Waterpark (609-522-3900 or 609-729-0586; www.moreyspiers.com; Wildwood Pier, 3501 Boardwalk, Wildwood) The classic boardwalk emporium on *the* classic Wildwood boardwalk. This one is big. Only Six Flags is bigger. We're talking some 150 rides and attractions spread over three amusement piers and a pair of oceanfront waterparks. Whatever your tastes in scaring or amusing yourself, you'll find it here. Locally, the Skeeball is legendary (although hardly unique), but for me the highlight is the Sea Serpent, a roller coaster that begins 12 stories above the piers. Morey's also hosts many free events and concerts throughout the summer. And, as you'd expect, the boardwalk food and trinket shopping goes on endlessly.

Playland's Castaway Cove (609-399-4751; www.boardwalkfun.com; 1020 Boardwalk, Ocean City) Another Ocean City park, Playland stands right on the boardwalk at 10th Street and, in keeping with this town's family-friendly orientation (see chapter 5), it provides for all ages. You can chose among 30 or so rides, including four roller coasters that range from small to big and looping (the aptly named Python). There are bumper cars large and small, and tame rides like the Antique Cars and the Old Fashioned Train, as well as a pair of mini-golf courses. Good stuff.

Six Flags Great Adventure Theme Park, Wild Safari Park, and Hurricane Harbor Waterpark (908-928-2000; www.sixflags.com/parks/greatadventure/index.asp; Route 537, Jackson) More than 100 rides and attractions, a drive-through safari, a waterpark, some of the most monster roller coasters in the country, live entertainment—you name it. Be aware, however: the joint really gets to jumping, and if you'd like to avoid the crowds, go early or late in the season, go midweek whenever possible, and arrive early in the day.

Steel Pier (609-345-4893; www.steelpier.com; 1000 Boardwalk, Atlantic City) Originally opened in 1898 and destroyed in a 1982 fire, Atlantic City's famous Steel Pier came back to life in 1993. Here, directly across from the beachfront casinos, you'll find 24 rides, plus prize wheels, games, a double-decker carousel, and a food court. Rides include bumper cars, bumper boats, a giant slide, go-carts, a kiddie coaster, kiddie go-carts, a climbing wall, and a Ferris wheel.

Storybook Land (609-641-7847 or 609-646-0103; www.storybook land.com; 6415 Black Horse Pike, Cardiff, Egg Harbor Township) Located on US 40 and US 322 in Cardiff, this is a relatively small, little-kid-oriented park that follows a nursery rhyme theme. The rides are augmented by seasonal activities and special events. The live animals are always a hit, the picnic area is a nice, money-saving touch, and the pay-one-price admission keeps things simple, always a good thing when dealing with small children.

Wild West City (973-347-8900; www.wildwestcity.com; US 206 and Lackawanna Drive, Netcong) Yee-ha! Here's a chance to head up to North Jersey and find yourself in the Wild, Wild West. The theme: Dodge City, Kansas, circa the 1880s. This Western heritage theme park portends to "bring the Old West to life through portrayals of real-life Western characters, legendary events, and a frontier town re-creation." They perform no fewer than 22 different live-action shows on any given day and supplement the performances with rides on a miniature train, stagecoach, or ponies. Along the way you can meet up with and talk to costumed reenactors and learn about the lives of everyday folks, even some famous ones. The opportunity to pan for gold, pet some animals, or play mini-golf round out the action. It's all a bit hokey, but fun.

PARKS DEVOTED STRICTLY TO WATER

Crystal Springs Family Aquatic Center (732-390-6981; www.eastbrunswick.org; Dunhams Corner Road, East Brunswick) Crystal Springs might be characterized as something like an over-grown community swim center. Owned and operated by the town of East Brunswick, it presents a chance to play on a handful of small slides, roll down a lazy river tube ride, frolic with your tot in splash pools, or swim in three different pools. The facility includes a sand beach, a kids' area, volleyball and basketball courts, and grill-equipped picnic sites. There's a hamburger stand as well. Even though Crystal Springs is a municipal facility, it's open to nonresidents. Nice idea.

Mountain Creek (973-827-2000; www.mountaincreekwaterpark.com; 200 Route 94, Vernon) Mountain Creek is roughly divided into four sections, each with unique activities and rides, and each appealing to different ages or adventure quotients. You'll encounter everything from the 99-foot drop at OH-NO to a wading pool, and everything in-between. Add some beach volleyball courts, a 12,000-square-foot skate park, and the Diablo Freeride Mountain Bike Park and it all adds up to one busy, happy day.

DOO-WOPPIN' AT THE BEACH

Wildwood by the Sea

HIGH SCHOOL AND WILDWOOD: they're synonymous for so many of us. For many others, the synonyms would be childhood and Wildwood. But, when you stop to consider this place, which has been characterized as the Doo-Wop Capital of the World, I think high school is most apt.

I was a little too young and a touch too late to catch the doo-wop generation at its height. Still, my friends and I came to Wildwood not to dance at the famous clubs, nor to listen to famous or near-famous rock'n' roll performers, but to burn our skins to a crisp on the beach and to lose ourselves in boardwalk hyperactivity. And what a boardwalk it was. Three miles long, bustling end-to-end with arcades, amusements, food emporia, clubs, rides, and just about anything else a boardwalk could have— including the famous tram that chugged along, ferrying beachgoers who just couldn't walk one more step.

This beach haven, so popular among Philadelphians because it's so accessible to them, remains well-rooted in its 1950s and early '60s prime. On my last venture to Wildwood, I arrived just in time to witness the World Marble Championships. Heck, I didn't even know kids played marbles anymore. But, there it was, a series of platforms spread out on the sand, each painted bright blue and yellow and accented by a overarching banners, a small grandstand, and not much else in the way of pomp or

National Marble Championships, Wildwood

circumstance. A few dozen kids milled around waiting their chance to shoot, while a band of parents and well-wishers looked on anxiously.

I was blown away. I knew Wildwood was a throwback town, but if ever there was a throwback, this marbles thing was it. A kind of low-key intensity pervaded the playing platforms. The kids played hard, but no overt demonstrations of emotion erupted. (At least I think they played hard. In my playground marble-playing days, external indications of intensity meant games that were punctuated by a lot of yelling, accusations, and sometimes the odd punch.) I stuck around for an hour or so, by which time I'd seen the culmination of several matches. The sun was too intense, and I had to retreat to some air-conditioned shelter. I never did find who won. Too bad. Part of the victors' crowning ceremony is the exchange of a kiss by the male and female winners. It would've been cute to see it.

"Cutely nostalgic" is perhaps the best description for Wildwood. One simply must drive down the commercial streets and ogle the 1950s and '60s architecture. They call it doo-wop architecture, these days. It's a sight to see, and there are people down there who are fighting to preserve it. They call themselves the Doo-Wop Preservation League. On their web site, they describe the architecture's roots: "The Wildwoods' motels sprang up like weeds in the '50s as a result of the auto vacation boom. . . . Since these motels were primarily built and are still owned by individual entrepreneurs, they have always been very individual in their expression."

All of these buildings make you smile—some make you laugh—but it's all because you remember when (as the '60s hit had it: "Re-mem-mem, Re-mem-mem, Remember when when, Remember when"). Buildings like the Satellite Motel, circa-1955, with a boomerang roof and neon Sputniks; Casa Bahama Motel, an overgrown A-frame with bright yellow trim; the aqua-green Bel Air Motel, named after the Chevrolet; the Wildwood Diner, just one of three diners in the country manufactured by the Superior Diner Company still standing; and Laura's Fudge, a genuine Wildwood landmark done in bright pink accented by dazzling neon.

In describing the town's motel architecture in interviews for a New Jersey Network (public broadcasting) special on Wildwood, lifetime locals remarked "mystique was the idea behind it all," "here you could vacation in an exotic place and you don't even have to leave New Jersey," and "Wildwood was like our version of Las Vegas—the lights, the colors, the plastic palm trees." Indeed, Wildwood is the home of the plastic palm tree. It was named the Official Tree of Wildwood by Christine Todd Whitman when she was governor. And the plastic palm just about says it all: with modern materials, be they neon lights or malleable plastics, you could create a fantasy wonderland anywhere. Even in South Jersey.

Or, maybe the plastic tree doesn't say it all. For the Wildwood tradition is also deeply grounded in the advent of rock 'n' roll. It was here that *American Bandstand*, based in Philadelphia, rocked in the summers before it became a national TV show. In fact, even after Dick Clark became its MC, the show—and Clark with it—moved to Wildwood in summer to play at the Starlight Ballroom. Clark has related how he first "tested" at the Starlight in the summer of 1957 a new song by an unknown band—"That'll Be the Day" by Buddy Holly and the Crickets. The town back then spilled over with clubs playing cutting edge rock performed by stars. Clubs with names like the Hurricane, Club Avalon, and the Rip Tide. Major performers, including Bill Haley and the Comets, Fats Domino, the Shirelles, Gary "U.S." Bonds, Bobby Darin, Brenda Lee, the Chantelles, and Bobby Rydell.

Rydell's "Wildwood Days" was not only a summertime hit, it became the town's anthem. And, here too, a guy named Chubby Checker got his start fresh out of high school, singing a song called "The Twist" that, as he said when interviewed, "changed dancing in America forever."

Said one local, "This was the entertainment Mecca of the Jersey Shore through the early '70s."

And yet, there was still more. There was that boardwalk. It rocked late into the night, hawkers calling in the rubes to play games of skill and games of chance. It's been said that before there was Disneyland or Six Flags there was the Wildwood boardwalk. Hunt's Pier dominated the amusement scene with rides like the Flyer, a roller coaster. There were bumper cars, cotton candy, and Skeeball. The tram car was constantly on the go, announcing its presence repeatedly with the recorded proclamation "Watch the tram car, please," to the point where vacationers heard it in their sleep.

Later, the Morley brothers took the amusements and rides to the next level, meeting the expectations of the 1990s and now the new century. In fact, it's claimed that there are more rides here than at Disneyland. And, the kids working the boardwalk now come from all over the world—some 600 of them each summer hailing from 30 different countries.

All that "history," those eras, is caught time-capsule fashion in the Wildwood buildings that remain. And in the boardwalk, which remains 3 miles long, filled with activity, action, and artifice. And in the beach, which itself can stretch to a mile wide. Wildwood sits on a 5-mile-long island and is primarily comprised of three towns: Wildwood, Wildwood Crest, and North Wildwood.

North Wildwood began life as a fishing village in the 1890s. So wide is the beach here that a beach tram transports folks from the street to the shoreline. At midisland stands Wildwood, where the boardwalk provides the heartbeat. Here, you can get the greatest overview with a ride on the East Coast's tallest Ferris wheel, or shop, dine, and listen to live music at the Holly Beach Station Mall. Wildwood Crest, occupying the southern end of the island, presents a more modern collection of accommodations and a lower-key atmosphere. Water sports junkies head west to Sunset Lake, where they can Jet Ski, waterski, or drive a boat.

Among the must-do activities at Wildwood by the Sea:

• Take a Doo-Wop Trolley Tour. They last 45 minutes and includes a visit to the Doo-Wop Museum.

• Visit the Wildwood Historical Society's George F. Boyer Historical Museum at 3907 Pacific Avenue. It holds a collection of vintage photos, artifacts, and memorabilia depicting Wildwood's history. It also holds the National Marbles Hall of Fame.

• Get in on some live music and dancing at the area's clubs. Yes, Wildwood is synonymous with doo-wop, but just about any musical taste is accommodated these days, from hip-hop, oldies, and Motown to alternative rock and Top 40. There's a collection of Irish pubs, too. Many clubs stay open until the small hours. The best spots have decks overlooking the water or offer a high-energy ambience with dance floors, disc jockeys, and entertainment catering to the 21-to-40-year-old crowd.

• Visit the Hereford Inlet Lighthouse in North Wildwood. Built in 1874, it features some startling Swiss Gothic architecture.

• Bike the boardwalk before 10:30 AM on weekends or 11 AM on weekdays.

• Ride the boardwalk tram. It's just one of those must-do things.

• Try to be there for one of the annual special events. The most famous, perhaps, are the Baby Parade in July, and the National Marbles Tournament in early June. But, others include: Wildwoods Classic Pinball Challenge (April), the Thunder on the Beach Series (Motorcross, Monster Trucks on various dates), Pirates Weekend (May), International Kite Festival (Memorial Day), Classic Car Show (September). This list is by no means inclusive; more than 100 events are staged annually.

• Bicycle the bike trail. It runs nearly the length of the entire the island, beginning in the south at Rambler Road in Wildwood Crest and heads north to the start of the boardwalk at Cresse Avenue (which is bikeable in the morning); after the boardwalk, the bike path connects to a beachside path up to 3rd Avenue in North Wildwood and, moving ever northward, a bicycle lane then runs on Surf Avenue up to 26th Avenue.

• Attend an on-beach, Captain Ocean ecological program on a

Monday at Rambler Road in Wildwood Crest at 8 AM, July through Labor Day. The Captain makes marine ecology fun and informative for all ages.

• Get yourself to a free concert. There's one nearly every evening during summer somewhere in the Wildwoods, including: Monday at the Crest Pier Recreation Center in Wildwood Crest, Wednesday at the Sunset Lake Gazebo at Miami and New Jersey Avenues in Wildwood Crest, Thursday on the Wildwood Boardwalk at Cedar Avenue, beginning at 7 PM, or at the Lou Booth Amphitheater at Second and Ocean Avenues in North Wildwood.

• Have a ball at the Thursday evening Family Fun Nights on the Wildwood Boardwalk. You'll find parades, strolling, clowns and musicians.

• Watch the Friday night fireworks show at Pine Avenue in Wildwood.

• Be entertained by young dancers and singers at the free Wildwood Talent Showcase on Monday, Wednesday, Thursday, and Friday at the Wildwoods Band Shell (Schellenger Avenue at the boardwalk) at 7:30 PM.

• Peruse the 220-foot long, 30-foot high Whaling Wall mural. Painted by the world-renowned environmental artist Wyland, you'll find it at Garfield Avenue and the boardwalk.

• And, of course, loll on the free beach (no beach tags necessary here).

❀ ❀ ❀ ❀ ❀ ❀ ❀ ❀

DETAILS

General Information: *Greater Wildwoods Tourism Improvement & Development Authority (1-800-992-9732 or 609-729-9000, www.wildwoodsnj.com); Greater Wildwood Chamber of Commerce (1-888-729-0033 or 609-729-4000, www.gwcoc.com); City of Wildwood (609-522-2444, www.wildwoodnj.org); Doo-Wop Preservation League (609-729-4000, www.doowopusa.org); the Wildwoods Resort web site is www.the-wildwoods.com.*

Directions: *Take the Garden State Parkway to exit 4B. New Jersey Transit provides bus transportation to the Wildwoods with departures from New York City's Penn Station, Jersey City, Newark's Penn Station, and Atlantic City (1-800-626-RIDE; www.njtransit.com).*

❀ ❀ ❀ ❀ ❀ ❀ ❀ ❀

UP, UP & AWAY!
The New Jersey Festival of Ballooning—
Readington

WHEN THE CLOUDS BURST, I found myself standing just outside the Quick Chek food tent. A propitious position, to say the least. I ducked the deluge and the good folks in the tent sold me a nice ham-and-cheese sub. While at least an inch of rain fell in a half an hour, I sat at a table and enjoyed lunch.

The skies opening can put a damper on an outdoor event like the Quick Chek New Jersey Festival of Ballooning, but everyone took this downpour with good humor. Well, except maybe the guys in the Hewlett-Packard tent, where flooding knocked out their electricity. I never did get inside to learn all about print-your-own digital photography. But, over in the PSE&G Energy tent they were contriving footbridges for crossing the flooded ground out of long, rectangular, folding tables. The rain would stop soon, the fun could continue, and the balloons would later fly. We hoped.

Awesome. There's no other word for these bursting-with-color, lighter-than-air flying machines we call hot-air balloons. They rise from the ground like sleeping giants coming slowly awake. When, over the course of perhaps half an hour, some 125 balloons stand tall and rise, they change the landscape. What was a clearing in the woods has become something akin to a lollipop jungle as thickly overgrown as the Amazon. Only here, the lollipops stand 60–120 feet high. And they can fly.

"I liken hot-air balloons to pelicans," said the pilot of the United Van

Lines balloon. "They're ungainly and awkward on the ground but elegant in the air."

The Quick Chek New Jersey Festival of Ballooning turns a remote, private airfield into a hotbed of activity each year during a late-July weekend. The fest's highlight, of course, is when the balloonists take their gear out beyond the crowds for inflation and ascension. One by one the balloons fill out like flowers opening to the sun. The familiar tear-drop shapes are so resplendent one is hard pressed to know where to look first. Or which looks best. The shiny nylon fabric makes the most of the fluorescent greens, deep purples, and fireball oranges and reds. When each new color combination reaches to the sky, it instantly becomes your new favorite.

Then the special shapes arise. The Energizer Bunny. A giant house built by Re/Max. An Oriental chef from Benihana. A giant Pepsi can. Enough "ooohs" and "ahhs" fill the air to match the clatter of the enormous inflation fans that force air into the balloons and the fiery whoosh of the propane tanks that heat the canopies and send them aloft. Up they go. Like a flock, the balloons rise and drift downwind toward the horizon until the sky resembles a flying polka-dot circus.

The mass ascensions, staged at 6:30 in the morning and again at 6:30 in the evening, may highlight this event, but the remainder of its three-day duration must be filled with other distractions. So dozens upon dozens of country-fair-style booths invite exploration. Climbing walls can be ascended, assorted games of skill can be played, there is music to be heard, and tons of food to be eaten. The special Quick Chek Sports Center offers amusements like finger painting, jewelry making, and cute carnival games just for the little ones, while any number of food booths allow adults to relax with a refreshing "adult beverage" and the *Star-Ledger* Shade Tent provides just that—refuge from the sun.

One stumbles upon a lot of expected junk among the tents: magnetic jewelry, hot tub displays, balloon festival T-shirts and other assorted trinkets. But one also uncovers some unusual and pleasant surprises. "Free book!" came the cry from one booth. They were giving away a novel entitled *Wild Animus*. "Guerilla marketing," they called it—put thousands of

Aloft

books into people's hands by way of fairs and festivals nationwide, before actual publication date, and create word-of-mouth excitement. I took one, naturally. Moving on, I engaged in a long conversation with Gary Schlegel, who actually makes a living running a company he calls Balloon-A-Tics. Basically, he goes to balloon festivals and crafts fairs selling miniature balloons that are made of a handcrafted hardwood frame covered with designer fabrics mounted atop commercial wind chime sets. They were eye-catching and gorgeous. And then there were the two guys selling hand-hewn wooden airplane sculptures.

All the while, a small circus of entertainments are being staged. The Nestlé Purina Incredible Dog Challenge team presents a dog lover's gala of tricks and unbearably cute behaviors. Directly adjacent, watching gator rassling at the Kachunga and the Alligator Show satisfies something in people, although I'm not sure what. And, naturally, everyone loves magic, so the tent advertising Belmont—A Special Kind of Magic! attracts quite a crowd.

There's music aplenty, too. The main stage booms each evening with a

Saturday-evening balloon glow

name group, albeit sometimes the names, like Herman's Hermits, drift in, as if out of the fog of your distant past. But, throughout the day the stage is alive with everything from the New Jersey Jazz Society Youth Quarter to the Whitehouse Wind Symphony, while over in the Family Fun Pavilion some guy named Dr. Planet most amusingly entertains kids with bound-less energy and participatory songfests.

I don't know about you, but I'll never look at a hot-air balloon rising, its basket dangling below, without thinking of Dorothy left forlornly behind by the erstwhile Wizard of Oz. At the Soldberg-Hunterdon County Airfield, however, you needn't be left standing on the ground. Just buy a ride. They're not cheap, but if you've never experienced the serenity of silently riding on the wind, it's well worth it.

Balloons aren't the only flying machines here. Twice a day on the weekend, the Barnstorming Air Show takes off, highlighted (for me, at least) by the Red Baron Pizza Squadron flying classic Stearman biplanes. I could watch those beautiful machines forever. (See chapter 22 for more on flying machines.)

Friday and Saturday evenings highlight the festival. In addition to the main-stage concerts, Friday evening visitors are treated to a fireworks spectacular. Better, for me anyway, is the Saturday evening balloon glow. Come dusk, the balloonists reappear and reinflate on the runway infield. Staying tethered to the ground, all the pilots simultaneously fire their propane burners, and the field is ablaze with iridescent glowing jewels. Dazzling, to say the least. I don't know that I've ever seen anything quite like it. Fireworks are fine. But the glow left me with an ever-lasting imprint.

DETAILS

Quick Chek New Jersey Festival of Ballooning *takes place in late July at the Soldberg-Hunterdon County Airport in Readington. Admission is charged. Information: 1-800-468-2479; www.balloonfestival.com.*

Directions: *From the north, take I-287 or the Garden State Parkway to I-78 west to exit 26, and turn left onto CR 665 (Rattlesnake Bridge Road). Travel south past Raritan Valley Community College and turn left onto CR 614; turn right onto CR 637 (Readington Road/Raritan Valley College Drive). Cross US 22, and follow signs to balloon festival parking. From the south: Take US 1, the Garden State Parkway, or the New Jersey Turnpike to I-287 north to US 22 west. Go past the Somerville area and Bridgewater Commons Mall, enter the township of Branchburg, and exit at Readington Road/Raritan Valley College Drive. Turn left onto CR 637 (Readington Road), cross US 22, and follow signs to balloon festival parking.*

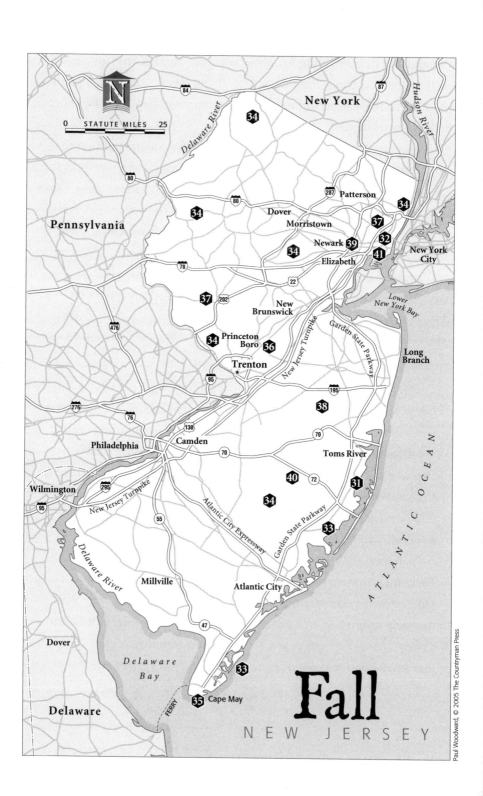

Fall

TOE TAPPIN' IN THE PINES

The Albert Music Hall—Waretown
Plus Other Music Performance Venues

Of course my brother said exactly what you'd expect a member of our generation to say when I asked him if he wanted to come along to the Albert Hall. "Sure," he quipped, "we'll finally know how many holes it takes to fill the Albert Hall."

The Beatles this is not, however. Not even the Rolling Stones. Flat & Scruggs, perhaps. A bit of Johnny Cash, certainly. And a touch of Doc Watson, too, and Woody Guthrie.

The Albert Music Hall in Waretown is about as unpretentious a place as can be imagined. Every Saturday night, year-round, it provides a marvelous venue for simple, good-old country music for the princely entrance fee of $5. The Albert Music Hall is operated by the Pinelands Cultural Society, an organization devoted to sustaining, furthering, and promulgating the cultural traditions of the New Jersey Pinelands. Here, they do it primarily through music.

We arrived at about seven, a half-hour before the music begins, and I spent some time trying to absorb the setting's ambiguous ambience. You're but a few minutes drive from the ocean, so it has that sandy, saltwater, flatlands feel. But this is the edge of the Pinelands, and a marshy, forested, somewhat semitropical aura could be felt. Adding to the strange mix was the large public school that stands next door, lending a completely suburban sensibility. Still, all those elements were overridden by a small crowd gathered on the front porch listening to a pick-up group

The front porch of the Albert Music Hall

strum tunes. Standing among them, the mood was all local and down-home, toe-tapping and warmly welcoming.

A relatively small building for a public gathering place, the hall's facade resembles a demure country house with a nice-sized front porch. The lobby continues the simplicity theme. It's a relatively modest, rectangular space, carpeted in an industrial strength, dirt-hiding mud-brown. The walls are adorned with blow-up reprints of a typed history of the hall. Take a few more steps and you're in the main hall, a larger rectangle with rows of folding chairs standing on a concrete floor facing a stage that sports a painted backdrop to look like, you guessed it, a front porch. Where better to pick banjos, guitars, and mandolins than on the front porch, eh, Granny? One white wall is adorned with antique farm implements; old-time musical instruments decorate the other.

A small gift shop is housed at the back of the auditorium on one side, mirrored by an equally small snack bar on the other. The prices there mirror the ticket fee. I quickly bought a T-shirt for $10. My brother scarfed up a large piece of homemade cake (passing up some damned fine-looking brownies and pie slices) for $1.25. The last two seating rows on the snack bar side have been reserved for picnic tables, complete with red-and-white checkered tablecloths.

But it was the music we'd come to hear, and at 7:30 on the dot, a big guy in large glasses appeared at the podium to get things rolling. This was Tom, who fills the role of host and master of ceremonies. This is an entirely volunteer operation, and everyone functions on a first-name basis, from Roy, the president, to Marion and Emily, the snack-bar operators. Tom made a few announcements. We all had a chance to buy 50-50 tickets, he informed us, or to secure one of the half-dozen seats still available on the fund-raiser bus trip to Pigeon Forge, Tennessee. The national anthem was played. And, without further ado, a slow-moving group of six musicians took the stage.

The on-stage music goes on for four hours, each group playing a half-hour set. Sometimes a group will perform early in the program, then reappear later to play some more. The quality ranges significantly. A few folks we heard were clearly well-intentioned, fairly talented amateurs. Others seemed to be groups put together on the fly. Lonnie La Cour, first on the bill, put on a laconic air, told silly jokes between numbers, like the ones we used to hear on *Hee-Haw*, and sang heartfelt tunes like "Drunken Ira Hayes," a ballad that relates the story of the Native American who helped raise the flag at Iwo Jima and later drowned, drunk, in a ditch containing 3 inches of water.

A group calling themselves the Wooldlot Howlers pressed through "Comin' Through the Rye," annotating it with the comment that, south of the Mason-Dixon Line, the title was said to be "Whiskey Before Breakfast." The Sunday River Gang introduced one song with a question to the audience: "Is Roy here tonight? I wrote this song for Roy." The song apparently chronicled Roy's backyard miniature train. I never did figure out if Roy was present.

Just when I thought we'd come all this way to hear the Amateur Hour—good natured and very pleasant, but still a bit too homey for such a long trip, along came Past Times. Suddenly the audience came to life, the pickin' got intense, and everyone was a-hootin' and a-hollerin'. These guys were good, displaying some superb banjo work and slide guitar picking that would move any foot to tapping. They were good enough for me to run out to the front porch at intermission and buy one of their CDs.

Following intermission the full house was half-empty. Some of the audience had stayed outside to listen to the informal playing at the adjacent Pickin' Shed and on the porch. Many, since it was already 10 o'clock, had headed home. I had a two-hour drive ahead of me and was thinking of making an exit after the first post-intermission act. But after they'd taken their bows, something held me in my seat. "We'll just stick around to see who comes on next," I said. One song later, I knew we'd be there through the entire half-hour. Three guys calling themselves Evening Hours—a vibrant, balding, middle-aged gent on the mandolin; a large, silent man of middle years on the acoustic guitar; and an older, humorously cantankerous, fat fella who had to sit down to play the stand-up bass—took over with high energy and some superb instrumental versions of songs ranging from bluegrass to classic pop to gospel. They rendered songs like "Please Don't Talk about Me When I'm Gone" and "It's a Sin to Tell a Lie" in a unique, high-stylin' fashion, and exited with an instrumental version of "Amazing Grace" that was truly inspiring.

So, why, I know you're wondering, is this place called the Albert Music Hall? Something to do with London's Royal Albert Hall? No. It comes from the brothers Albert, George and Joe, a pair of guys who grew up in Sayreville but who would come down to Waretown each year to duck hunt. Seems the Albert boys had a backwoods cabin—no electricity—in the Pinelands woods, and each Saturday night when they were around, a bunch of friends and locals would make their way to the cabin to join fiddle-playing George, playing local folk tunes, so-called Piney music. They called the cabin the Home Place. Soon enough these Saturday evening get-togethers were drawing hundreds of people, musicians and listeners alike. By 1974, things had grown to the point where the Pinelands Cultural Society was formed, a big room was rented at the

Waretown Auction, and the Saturday night gatherings became Sounds of the Jersey Pines. The auction building burned in 1992, and after five years of fund-raising and temporary digs, the current building opened, named for the Albert brothers who'd started it all.

As we drove out of the parking lot, the picking was still going on—in the shed, on the porch, and inside onstage. A person gets a lot of music for five bucks. But, more importantly, a lot of good fellowship, plus local tradition and history shared. You can't put a price on that.

DETAILS

The Albert Music Hall *is located on 131 Wells Mill Road (CR 532). For information contact the Pinelands Cultural Society (609-971-1593; www.alberthall.org; P.O. Box 657, Waretown, NJ 08758). Music every Saturday, except for some holidays, from 7:30 PM, doors open at 6:30; admission $5 adults, $1 children under 12, listening at the Pickin' Shed or front porch is free.*

Directions: *From the north, take the Garden State Parkway south to exit 74. Turn east onto Lacey Road. Turn right onto US 9 south for 3 miles, then right onto CR 532 for 0.25 mile. From the south, take the Garden State Parkway north to exit 69 and follow CR 532 for 2 miles.*

OTHER MUSIC VENUES

Here's a sampling of some of the other New Jersey places that host concerts, music festivals, and musical events. For general information on what's happening around the state, visit New Jersey Arts at www.jersey arts.com/links/links_centers.html.

Appel Farm Arts and Music Center (1-800-394-1211; www.appel farm.org; 457 Shirley Road, P.O. Box 888, Elmer, NJ 08318) This is really a farm, and they do a lot of arts workshops, camps, and other programs. The Clare Rostan Appel Theatre is a 250-seat venue where concerts by well-known folksingers and family concerts are staged all year.

Blockbuster–Sony Entertainment Centre a.k.a the Tweeter Center (856-365-1300; www.tweetercenter.com/philadelphia/; 1 Harbour Boulevard, Camden, NJ 08103) A major Philadelphia-area venue for concerts and performances of all kinds, open year-round.

Count Basie Theater (732-842-9000; www.countbasietheatre.org; 99 Monmouth Street, Red Bank, NJ 07701) This 1500-seat theater, built in 1926 in the heart of downtown Red Bank features major performers and performances, ranging from Spyro Gyra, Def Poetry Jam, and the Count Basie Orchestra to Neil Sedaka, LeAnn Rimes, and Bob Newhart.

Bergen Performing Arts Center and the John Harms Theater (201-227-1030; www.bergenpac.org; 30 North Van Brunt Street, Englewood, NJ 07631) Closed a short while back and recently reopened, the center presents a full range of musical genres and performers from classical (New Jersey Symphony Orchestra and the Venice Baroque Orchestra) to jazz (Wynton Marsalis) to the blues (B.B. King) to stand-up comedy (Richard Lewis) and everything in between.

New Jersey Performing Arts Center (1-888-GO-NJPAC or 973-642-0404; www.njpac.org; 36 Park Place, Newark, NJ 07102) The gem of downtown Newark and New Jersey's performing venues, NJPAC presents a bit of everything, from the New Jersey Symphony Orchestra to children's theater and major name performers (see also chapter 39).

Watchung Arts Center (908-753-0190; www.watchungarts.org; 18 Stirling Road on the Circle, Watchung, NJ 07069) Presents acoustic folk concerts on the second and fourth Saturday of every month, with additional performances by local artists as well. Styles cover most every form of acoustic music.

PNC Bank Arts Center (732-335-0400; www.artscenter.com; P.O. Box 144, Holmdel, NJ 07733) Located at exit 116 off the Garden State Parkway, the center presents approximately 50 performances by artists of every musical style including rock, pop, country, jazz, rhythm and blues, and oldies, from late May through September. Special events and festivals are also staged. The center can be reached via New Jersey Transit by taking a train to the Matawan station from which free shuttle buses are operated (1-800-626-RIDE; www.njtransit.com).

Six Flags Great Adventure (732-928-1821 or 732-928-2000; www.sixflags.com/parks/greatadventure/index.asp; Route 537, P.O. Box 120, Jackson, NJ 08527-0120) The state's largest amusement park presents national performers in a variety of disciplines during the summer.

Sovereign Bank Arena (609-656-3200; www.sovereignbankarena.com; 81 Hamilton Avenue at NJ 129, Trenton 08611) A full range of presentations, including festivals like the Marley Roots Rock Reggae Festival, and the Trenton Jazz Festival.

The Starland Ballroom (732-238-5500; www.starlandballroom.com; 570 Jernee Mill Road, Sayreville NJ 08872) The old Club Hunka Bunka has been converted into the Starland Ballroom concert hall, featuring local acts, national recording artists, and Teen Night Tuesdays.

The Historic Strand Theater (732-367-7789; www.strandlakewood .com; 400 Clifton Avenue, Lakewood, NJ 08701). Built in 1922, the theater boasts superb acoustics. Performances range from concerts by national and regional performers to children's theater.

THE SQUARE CITY THAT'S REALLY COOL

Hoboken

SOME CALL HOBOKEN "THE SQUARE-MILE CITY"; from 1st to 13th Streets covers almost exactly a square mile. Some think of it as "the train place"; many of North Jersey's commuter railroads end (or begin) here. Others think of Hoboken as the birthplace of Frank Sinatra and professional baseball. Still others—some 33,000 of them—think of Hoboken as home. I think of Hoboken as the phoenix of New Jersey: the small city that rose from semi-squalor and neglect to become a vital, vibrant, stimulating town.

Hoboken is happening.

It was the artists who brought vitality back to this dormant city. Priced out of New York City's Greenwich Village and SoHo, they began drifting across the river. Why not? Hoboken townhouses rivaled Manhattan's. Unused industrial spaces were waiting to be transformed into lofts and studios. Not only did Hoboken offer easy Manhattan access, the cost of living and taxes were far lower. The artists came. The financial workers, the young yuppie couples, and the recent college grads followed. They bought and renovated the houses and rejuvenated the town. Today the tale of the young couple who bought their home for $25,000 and could now sell it for upward of $1 million is common.

For visitors, this rejuvenation brings other benefits. Consider Washington Street, the town's main drag. The street bustles with an eclectic collection of restaurants, shops, bars, and clubs. Maxwell's, at 1039 Washington Street, is the best-known of the music spots. Often frequented by major rock bands and performers on their way to and from gigs in the Big Apple or Giants Stadium, this small bar has developed a large reputation as the place for great rock. But it's just one of many hot spots—there were at least a dozen clubs at my last count—for music and libations along Washington Street.

Washington Street shopping ranges from art and artifacts to scuba gear, snowboards, and skateboards. At Schnackenerg's Confectionery—a true old-time soda fountain—you can sip a phosphate the way Mom and Dad did when they dated. Big Fun Toys is a down-home store that'll remind you of the time before chains stores along the highway.

And there are plenty of other nightspots, eateries, shops, and bars off the main avenue. One can find at least 16 Irish pubs in this town. If you prefer your dining and entertainment with a view, Hudson Street's restaurants whet the appetite with classic Manhattan vistas. The Guitar Bar buys, sells, trades, and repairs 'em—and they rent guitars, too. Lepore's Homemade Chocolates is a chocaholics' delight. Hoboken Pottery creates handmade pieces and tiles. The list goes on.

As might be expected in a town revitalized by creative types, the arts thrive here. The Hudson Shakespeare Company performs Shakespeare in the Park during summer months and in winter, their Second Stage series offers modern and classic plays. The Hudson Theatre Ensemble is a local company that employs Hudson County artists and technicians. The Mile Square Theatre produces new and classic works; their annual *7th Inning Stretch*, performed in June, celebrates Hoboken heritage by commissioning and performing seven 10-minute plays about baseball. The Monroe Center for the Arts presents First Sundays, in which visitors can enjoy artists' work in their studios. And the city holds at least half a dozen private art galleries.

In addition to the above-mentioned Shakespeare in the Park, summertime brings outdoor performances and showings. Free outdoor movie screenings take place on Wednesday evenings in Pier A Park, which overlooks the Hudson River. Free Concerts in the Park are offered on Thursday at Frank Sinatra Park, also along the river, and on Tuesday at Shipyard Park on 13th Street.

Hoboken stages a plethora of annual events. Among the longest standing are the Feast of St. Anthony and the Children's Festival in June, and St. Ann's Feast in July. Another major event is the Hoboken Street Art & Music Festival, held in May, in which the main thoroughfare is transformed into a fair, the express purpose of which is to show off local talent—performers, musicians, and visual artists—and display the town's family spirit.

One of Hoboken's oldest annual events may also be one of its best-kept secrets. Let's call it "The Night Before Macy's" celebration. It goes like this: At Hoboken's northern end, just south of the entrance to the Lincoln Tunnel, stands a nondescript warehouse. Inside this warehouse are built and stored all the great floats for the annual Macy's Thanksgiving Day Parade—arguably among the country's two or three best-known parades. During the evening preceding the parade, the warehouse is open to the public, and if you get there early (oh, say, just around dinnertime), you can often catch the artists at work, finishing up with last-minute adjustments. If they're not too frazzled, you can catch their ear and get them talking about their work.

DETAILS

A weekly newspaper, the *Hudson Reporter*, lists Hoboken events and entertainment (www.hudsonreporter.com). Useful Web sites include www.hobokennj.org, www.hoboken.com, and www.hoboken-bar.net.

Directions: Hoboken can be reached by New Jersey Transit (1-800-626-RIDE; www.njtransit.com) commuter trains or buses, PATH trains from New York City, Jersey City, or Newark, or by car from the Lincoln and Holland Tunnel access roads. Be aware that on Thursday, Friday, and Saturday nights, on-street parking can be very tight; public parking lots are located on the south end of town and along Frank Sinatra Drive.

Shortly after that, about 8:30, the floats that will dazzle the nation the next day on television emerge onto Willow Street. In a three-block-long procession, this "parade preview" travels into the Lincoln Tunnel and on into Manhattan. The Night Before Macy's is an informal event. It was described to me by one local as "totally disorganized, but we want it that way." Which just goes to show you that even though Hoboken has been gentrified, it hasn't lost its sense of fun.

SEPTEMBER FESTIVALS AT THE SHORE

Stone Harbor and Tuckerton

THE WINGS 'N' WATER FESTIVAL

A SERIES OF LARGE POSTERS adorned the back wall of the Wetlands Institute's meeting room. They documented the Save the Terrapin Project. Each year female adult turtles seek high ground to lay their eggs. Many of them become roadkill. Wetlands Institute volunteers collect the unhatched eggs, incubate them, and nurse the newborn turtles until they're large enough to venture off on their own. Partial funding for this noble project is generated by turtle-shaped cookies baked and sold by Avalon-Stone School kindergarten students, who also earn the right to help release the young turtles into the wild. As many as 900 infant terrapins are given a good start in life every year. But, more importantly, an attitude becomes instilled in young humans. And, it's that attitude that best describes the mission of the Wetlands Institute.

The Wetlands Institute sits on 6,000 acres of salt marsh just west of Stone Harbor. It works to advance research and educate the public on tidal wetlands and their inhabitants. For one glorious weekend in September, the institute erupts into a beehive of activity that spills into Stone Harbor, Avalon, and Middle Township. They call it the Wings 'n' Water Festival.

The festival starts with an auction and VIP cocktail party on Friday evening; items for sale have included vacations, Broadway show tickets, and works of art. Come Saturday morning, the joint really starts rocking,

The Wetlands Institute

with something for just about everyone. Naturalists conduct dune walks in Avalon. Live folk music plays throughout the weekend. The North American Shorebird Carving Championships are judged at Avalon Community Hall. Care for a cruise? The good ship *Miss Avalon* sets off for a series of Back Bay Cruises. Other options include "marsh bingo" for the kids, duck painting, air-sea rescue demonstrations by the U.S. Coast Guard, salt marsh safaris, and my favorite, the annual Battle of the Bisques cook-off. (You can go to New England, but you won't find better clam chowder, I promise.)

Of course, most visitors want more to eat than just clam chowder, and delicious food is available in great quantity. A variety of choices are available at the Civic Center, and a full array of South Jersey cuisine—beef barbecue, crabcakes, and shrimp—is offered at a food court at the institute.

Between bites, you'll find ample opportunity to explore the marshlands and oceanfront and to learn how vital these delicate and changeable environments can be. You'll also be helping to support an important institution do its indispensable work.

TUCKERTON SEAPORT AND THE DECOY & GUNNING SHOW

Tuckerton, sited just south of Long Beach Island on US 9, was settled in 1698 and known as Clamtown. The name changed in 1789 to honor Ebenezer Tucker, who had been the official collector at Clamtown, the country's third authorized port of entry (behind New York and Philadelphia). But clamming remained the town's raison d'etre for many years. Some 60,000 clams were shipped out daily at the turn of the 20th century. An active trade in oystering, fishing, hunting, boatbuilding, and decoy making was carried out here as well. Tuckerton Seaport today is a re-creation of that old maritime village. Within it, the Barnegat Bay Decoy & Baymen's Museum pays tribute to tiny Tuckerton's rich history with rotating and permanent displays, research, and continued restoration of the old seaport along the banks of Tuckerton Creek.

Each year, Ocean County salutes this history, along with the traditions of Barnegat Bay, life in the Pinelands, and the skills of the region's outdoorsmen and boatmen, with its Old Time Barnegat Bay Decoy & Gunning Show.

The show sets up in three locations: indoor exhibits and presentations are mounted at Pinelands middle and high schools, and tent exhibitions, local food concessions (featuring more remarkable clam chowder), and demonstrations take place along the tree-lined shores of Lake Pohatcong. How popular is the Decoy & Gunning Show? In the words of my friend Bob—hunter, fisherman, and Long Beach Island homeowner—"Basically, I think all of Ocean County turns out."

The show educates and entertains with displays by dozens of woodcarvers, naturalist artists, and jewelers; the unique sounds of Pinelands musicians; and with talks and presentations on everything from Lyme disease and Ghosts of the Pines to hypothermia and Backyard Birds in Winter. But, to me, it's the contests that make this event special.

It starts with a preliminary round of skeet shooting from a singular boat called a "sneakbox." Then the puppies show their stuff in the puppy retrieving contest. Kids get into the act at the kids' duck- and goose-calling seminar, and the boatmakers have their moment at the gunning boats accessories contest and the working shorebird rigs demo. The last time I attended, the show program listed 34 of these events spanning most of the weekend.

Come Saturday evening everyone sashays over to the high-school cafeteria for the big spaghetti dinner, proceeds of which benefit the school's student organizations. After dinner, bidding opens at the Annual Decoy & Related Items Auction in the school's auditorium. The auction, which according to the show's official program features "decoys by many old-time Barnegat Bay carvers," benefits the Baymen's Museum Building Fund.

The Baymen's Museum is at the center of it all. The museum contains artifacts and thousands of photographs chronicling the Barnegat Bay area's culture. In there you'll find everything there is to know about sneakboxes: 12-foot-long, shallow-draft wooden boats designed specifically to handle the rough Barnegat Bay winters. The original one, built in 1836, is displayed. You'll also find Barnegat Bay–style wildfowl decoys and fishery items (such as eeling baskets and oyster tongs), and a changing displays of prize-winning local carvers.

Together, these festivals add up to fascinating fun.

DETAILS

The Wetlands Institute *(609-368-1211, www.wetlands institute.org) is located on Stone Harbor Boulevard in Stone Harbor. The Wings 'n' Water Festival takes place in mid-September, admission fee. Directions: Take the Garden State Parkway to exit 10, then drive 4 miles east; the institute is on the right.*

Tuckerton Seaport and the Barnegat Bay Decoy & Baymen's Museum *(609-296-8868, www.tuckertonseaport.org) is located at 137 West Main Street (US 9) in Tuckerton. Admission to the Decoy & Gunning Show is free; it takes place toward the end of September. For additional information, check www.ocean.nj.us/parks.*

A Cacaphony of Color

Fall Foliage

A VERMONT FRIEND CALLS THEM "LEAF PEEPERS," the tourists who drive past her house at 5 miles per hour gawking at the fall colors. But you needn't journey to New England to see spectacular foliage. In the mountains and rural parts of the state, the show ranks with the best in the East. Indeed, when the leaf display is at its most radiant, a drive on almost any nonurban street or highway dazzles the eye; even my daily car pool to gymnastics along well-developed I-80 or a quick jaunt to the veterinarian up NJ 208 becomes an eye-dazzler in mid- to late-October.

New Jersey's length from north to south means that peak foliage season stretches for two to three weeks. If your schedule causes you to miss the prime array up north, you can still take it in down south.

It's impossible, of course, to list all the great places to go leaf-peeping, but here are a few that stand out.

High Point State Park. Can there be a better place to witness the colorful splendor than the state's highest point? A climb up the park's 220-foot obelisk-style tower seems the obvious thing to do. But the small, barren concrete chamber at the zenith contains only tiny, barred windows. The best views are found at the monument's base, sitting or standing on its stone retaining wall. The panorama expands for miles in all directions, taking in lakes, rivers, and the hills of Pennsylvania and southern New

York. The visual reward is worth the trip. High Point offers plenty of picnicking sites and hiking trails, too. **Directions:** Follow NJ 23 almost as far north as it goes.

Palisades Interstate Park. Once upon a time the Palisades along the Hudson River supplied New York City and Hoboken with tons of brownstone from which their famous townhouses were constructed. Palisades Interstate Park was created to preserve what remained unspoiled—spectacular cliffs and riverside lands—and today the park provides a marvelously mixed visual delight.

The Palisades' hiking trails follow the river's shoreline from Fort Lee, just south of the George Washington Bridge, north to Hastings-on-Hudson in New York. Side trails along the way ascend and descend the bluffs.

Start under the G.W. Bridge, especially if you retain any of a typical three-year-olds' wonder at elaborate constructions. Heading north, the riverside route reveals splendid and powerful views of the cliffs, made honey-sweet and tea-time warm by the Candyland colors. When you round the bend and the Tappan Zee Bridge comes into view, spanning the Hudson at its widest point, the combination of manmade and natural spectacle stops you in your tracks. Although the Tappan Zee is generally a nightmare to drive, its curved roadway exudes a majestic grace that somehow contrasts to and blends strikingly with the land- and riverscape.

Turn back south now, and you'll be rewarded by another unique combination of manmade and natural spectacle—the Manhattan skyline, the wide river, and the high cliffs that loom over your right shoulder. Talk about power. **Directions:** From NJ 4, US 46, I-80, and I-95, take the exit for Fort Lee/Palisades Interstate Parkway. Continue straight on Bridge Plaza South through several traffic lights. At the last light, a T intersection, turn right onto Bigler Street. At the stop sign, turn left (east) onto Main Street, then stay in the right lane to bear right (south) at River Road. The southern park entrance will be on the left. Follow Henry Hudson Drive. Park either at the Fort Lee Historic Park (to walk under the bridge), or drive about 1 mile (under the bridge) to the Ross Dock circle and follow the signs.

The Delaware Water Gap. The gap is spectacular any time of the year (see chapter 11). Add abundant splashes of color and the effect is dizzying. Hike, float, or just sit and stare. Take the riverside drive along Old Mine Road, or ogle the gap from the back porch of the Kittatinny Visitors Center, just off I-80.

Jenny Jump State Forest. One of New Jersey's smaller state reserves, Jenny Jump offers easy-to-get-to views from its main drive, Vista East Road, and fine visual rewards for hikers along the Summit Trail. Jenny Jump is just outside the town of Hope, and is accessible from CR 519 (exit 12 off I-80).

Autumn leaves at Batsto Village

The Great Swamp/Lord Stirling Park. Here's an excellent opportunity to see fall foliage, wetlands style. The park, located not far from I-287 in Basking Ridge, contains some 8½ miles of wide, flat trails, including a special interpretive nature trail for wheelchair hikers and the blind. This is true swamp and wetland, so many of the trails are actually raised boardwalks that make the going as easy as it is intriguing; the hickory, beech, and oak trees blend with the native grasses to put on one of the state's more complex color shows. The park's interpretive center sells trail maps.

Wharton State Forest. Start with a visit to the historical re-creation at Batsto Village (on CR 542; see chapter 21) and pay a visit to the little nature center there. The naturalist on duty is delighted to share insights about the natural treasures of the area. Nearby you'll find the Batsto Natural Area nature trail. The center prints a trail guide and sometimes offers guided hikes.

When you're ready for more prolonged exploration, join the Batona Trail (see chapter 8), a 50-mile wilderness path that traverses the Pine Barrens and roams through Wharton, Byrne, and Bass River State Forests; most of it is relatively easy walking.

Washington's Crossing State Park. Although Washington crossed the Delaware in the dead of winter, and his voyage is re-created each Christmas, dedicated leaf-peepers will enjoy this riverside site, off NJ 29 north of Trenton, during late October. Another option in the area is to visit nearby Lambertville and walk or bike the path that parallels the Delaware River and the Delaware & Raritan Canal.

DETAILS

New Jersey foliage generally peaks in mid-October. A toll-free phone number is maintained by the National Forest Service to supply peak viewing times and spots throughout the state: 1-800-354-4595. See also www.leafpeepers.com.

VICTORIAN WEEK & WHALE-WATCHING

Cape May

VICTORIAN WEEK

I DROPPED ONTO THE BED IN MY ROOM at the Virginia Hotel, too tired to take off my shoes, but craving a massage for my aching feet. Exploring Cape May—trying to see every last bit of Victoriana, to examine all the gingerbread latticework, and to admire each exquisite restoration—I'd walked myself into a state of exhaustion.

The name *Cape May* and the term *Victorian* have become synonymous. More than 600 authentic Victorian buildings stand within the town, and many modern homes have been built in the Victorian style. There is, indeed, more Victoriana than the eye can absorb, and the plethora of marvelous structures that line the quaint, narrow backstreets and broad, oceanfront boulevard create a walker's paradise. Armed with a good pair of shoes and a sunny day, a visitor can stroll here for hours, marveling at the grand scale of the homes with their romantic pastel paint jobs, and studying the dazzling architectural details, another one popping into your view just when you'd thought you'd studied it all.

Cape May bills itself as America's Oldest Seashore Resort; its vacationing tradition can be traced to a June 1766, advertisement placed in the *Pennsylvania Gazette* by Robert Parsons, a local farmer, extolling the wonders of Cape May's ocean bathing and offering to accept paying guests at his large farmhouse. It was a crude and rudimentary beginning, and it didn't take immediately. But, after the War of 1812, the Cape began to come into its own.

The Emlen Physick House

In midcentury, the advent of train access helped Cape May grow. Still, it was—as the realtors say—location, location, location that engendered the town's visitor-attracting advantage. Sited at the very southern tip of New Jersey, folks were readily drawn from Philadelphia, Baltimore, and most importantly, from Washington, D.C. Indeed (and this my favorite bit of New Jersey trivia), Cape May and the nation's capitol reside at the same latitude! Fashionable Washingtonians could readily get here by boat. Plus, the Cape has the "twenty-degree advantage." Since the town is set on a peninsula, with the benefit of ocean and bay breezes—a sort of natural cross-ventilation—summertime temperatures stay considerably cooler than those on the mainland.

The little city gets its current character not from its natural blessings but from calamity. An 1878 fire destroyed almost everything in the 30-acre heart of town. Landowners took the opportunity to rebuild in the fashionable style, but did so with superior quality and a close attention to detail. The result? The rich cache of Victorian houses we so admire today.

During early October the town celebrates this wealth with Victorian Week. The celebration includes events of all kinds. But, fittingly, walking tours are among the most abundant of the special offerings. Some of the tour possibilities include the Cape May Homes and Collections Tour, which travels to inns and private homes, focusing on the owners' personal collections; the In Search of . . . Victoriana Tour, in which a scavenger hunt is staged in the historic district and through the interiors of five Victorian homes; a Champagne Brunch Walk, which culminates with mimosas and a southern-style breakfast; and the Private Homes Tour, which looks at homes and gardens not normally open to the public.

Victorian Week isn't all walking. You can tour the town by trolley and the surrounding waters by boat, or you can attend any number of special programs, including an antiques lecture and appraisal, a brass band musical gala, a Victorian fashion show, a Tea and Temperance debate, a number of lectures and demonstrations, and a Victorian mystery dinner.

One tour that is offered year-round and should not be missed is the guided exploration of the Emlen Physick House. Designed by architect Frank Furness (best known for his work on Philadelphia's Academy of Fine Arts), the 18-room mansion was built in the 1870s, and for years it was Cape May's architectural centerpiece. But time and neglect eventually brought it to such disrepair that by 1970 its fame stemmed not from its lineage but from its reputation for being haunted. The Mid-Atlantic Center for the Arts (MAC) was formed and the building was saved.

The Emlen Physick House tour is led by remarkably well-informed volunteers who mix a vibrant and lively collection of historical fact, fiction, and insight with personal perspective, experience, and anecdotes—all delivered in a personable manner that holds the entire group's attention. Even the children who toured with in my group remained fascinated throughout.

Cape May offers more than Victoriana, of course. In addition to a delightful beach, the area holds Cape May State Park, fantastic birding, a nice collection of museums (the Cape May County Historical Museum, Cape May Firemen's Museum, Cape May Point Lighthouse, and the Dollhouse and Miniature Museum of Cape May among them), excellent regional bicycling, fine golf, and a superb collection of restaurants. Among the destination's noteworthy special events are the Cape May Jazz Festival (staged in two installments, April and November); Strawberry, Tomato, and Lima Bean Festivals; and a Dickens Christmas Extravaganza.

Once I'd gotten my feet back in working order, I set out on another Cape May odyssey—seeking the great whales.

DETAILS

The Cape May Chamber of Commerce *(609-884-5508; www.capemaychamber.com; P.O. Box 556, Cape May, NJ 08204) sponsors special events year-round and publishes an avalanche of literature offering general and events information and lodging help. Overnight accommodations run the gamut from large hotels, to small motels, bed & breakfasts, and campgrounds. I count the Virginia Hotel among the best small hotels I've ever experienced (1-800-732-4236 or 609-884-5700; www.virginiahotel.com). Another useful Web site: www.cape may.com.*

The Mid-Atlantic Center for the Arts *(800-275-4278 or 609-884-5404, www.capemaymac.org) conducts house tours of the Emlen Physick Estate and town trolley tours, as well as a plethora of special events ranging from Victorian Week and dine-arounds to the Cape May Music Festival and a Holiday Crafts Show.*

Whale-watching is best done in the early spring or fall. In Cape May, tours are operated by the Cape May Whale Watch and Research Center (609-898-0055; www.capemaywhalewatch.com) and by Cape May Whale Watcher (800-786-5445 or 609-884-5445; www.capemay whalewatcher.com). Whale-watching can also be done from a number of shore locations. The New Jersey Division of Travel and Tourism's "Travel Guide" contains information on other whale-watching companies; visit www.visitnj.org or call 1-800-847-4865 to obtain a copy.

The Virginia Hotel

WHALE-WATCHING

The fog rolled in as the boat rolled out. Quietly, we slipped under Cape May Island Bridge, traveling through water droplets suspended in midair and over those that comprised the ocean. I conjured visions of Gregory Peck in the Hollywood version of Herman Melville's epic, *Moby-Dick*.

A true landlubber, I prepared for the journey quite differently from the way Ahab might, with a motion-sickness pill for breakfast and a vow to avoid the ship's snack bar, except perhaps to purchase popcorn. Popcorn, it turns out, is a favorite among gulls. All we need do, Captain Ron informed us over the loudspeaker, was stand at the side rail with a morsel held lightly between thumb and forefinger. The birds would eat right from our hands.

Chugging along, we received instructions to scan the horizon "that's just where the sky meets the water, folks." (Although the fog rendered the sky and sea indistinguishable from each other.) Look, we were told, for grand plumes of water. That would be whales spouting. Search, we were admonished, for enormous black blobs flopping against the blue-gray background. That would be whales breaching. Scan constantly, we were beseeched, because whales are not particularly trackable by radar or sonar. For the longest time, no luck. Then I saw it! A big, black . . . Or did I? Guess not. Just a wave catching a little light at just the wrong angle. But wait! A shout from the kids on the bow! Oops. Not a whale. A commercial fishing boat approaching in the mist.

Three hours passed. Our chances of seeing whales grew as dim as the visibility. Captain Ron and his assistant, a naturalist named Kelly, did their best to keep us from giving up, educating us nonstop over the loud-speaker about whales and seabirds. We searched to the very end. To quote Melville's narrator, Ishmael, "Not till her skysail-poles sail in among the spires of the port, does she altogether relinquish the hope of capturing one whale more." Or, in our case, seeing one whale at all. Alas, it was to no avail. In seeking the whale we got skunked. But we received coupons to try again another day at half-price, and—even without whales—we had a good time.

36

A CLASSIC COLLEGE TOWN

Princeton

T WAS A BRILLIANTLY SUNNY NOVEMBER SATURDAY. Penny and I strolled across the Princeton University campus, arching our necks to admire the Gothic architecture. At a place where several walkways crossed, our path intersected that of a professorial-looking gentleman, perhaps in his early sixties, dressed in a Harris tweed coat and tie, smiling amiably to himself. Had he been carrying books or a briefcase, we could have assumed he was on his way to or from an important lecture. But this was Saturday, and under his arm he held a pair of stadium seat cushions, brightly decorated in Princeton Tigers' black and orange. Our professor had apparently come from today's game at Palmer Stadium. He was smiling, no doubt, over the final score: Princeton 20, Dartmouth 13.

A fall football-weekend visit to Princeton, a pretty, prestigious town along the Delaware and Raritan Canal, is the stuff of classic Hollywood imagery. Ivy League football is played with the perfect combination of prowess and perspective; the athletes are good, but there are no scholarship players or academic hardship cases, so the true spirit of amateur athletics prevails. The kids play hard and for the love of the game. The pep and pageantry stem from true school spirit, not the hope of filling the school coffers by winning a major bowl appearance or a mythical national championship. Kick-off is at 1 PM, but if you arrive early and join the alumni and other faithful for a tailgate picnic in the parking lot, you'll get the full flavor of the day. It's Americana at its best.

After the game, tour the campus. Stop first at either the University Bookstore or Stanhope Hall and pick up a guidebook. It will not only fill you in on all the sculpture, art, and architecture you'll see, but it'll prove indispensable when trying to locate a specific building. Believe me—we tried getting around without one and learned what it meant to be like lost sheep. Maybe like a lost freshman. Formal tours, dubbed Orange Key Tours, are conducted by gregarious and enthusiastic university students. The kids give an insider's insight into the institution's history and what's going on there today.

We exchanged "hellos" with the cheerful professor and entered Nassau Hall, the oldest building on campus. The entry hall—a stark, marble-walled war memorial—somberly displayed engraved listings of Princetonians who had given their lives in wars dating back to the Revolution. Sobered, we encountered a student who entered as we exited. His long hair flowing out from under a 1910 straw skimmer hat, he sported a striped blazer and carried an all-in-one, pep-band bass-drum-and-noisemaker set strapped to his chest. An orange and black striped tiger tail flopped from his hat's rear brim. The building and the student created a vivid picture: heritage, modernity, and tradition all rolled into one.

We walked to the university chapel. Built in the 1920s, it is a classic piece of Gothic Revival architecture. A descriptive pamphlet is available at the building's entrance. It points out such particulars as the figure of James Madison (class of 1771) depicted in one of the tall stained-glass windows. Madison championed Article I of the Bill of Rights, establishing religious freedom a basic American tenet and making his a particularly appropriate image for this church. The booklet notes, as well, that the oak pews were constructed from wood originally intended to make gun carriages during the Civil War.

Next door, in the Firestone Library's Rare Books section, the impressive collection is complemented by a rotating exhibit that explores the historical uses of books. We saw a display on Islamic Culture and Quar'an (Koran), featuring handwritten books dating to ancient times. Upstairs and to the rear is hidden the Leonard L. Millberg Gallery; you may have to ask for directions to find it, but it's worth the effort. We discovered a fascinating exhibit of children's book illustrations there.

The Princeton University Art Museum in McCormick Hall houses an eyeball-wrenching collection of classic paintings. The works of great Impressionists, great portrait artists, and classic landscape painters adorn nearly every square inch of wall space; impressive but overwhelming.

Beyond the campus, Princeton offers a number of historical sites. These include two houses once occupied by Woodrow Wilson, one that was the childhood residence of singer-actor Paul Robeson, and another where Albert Einstein lived. At the corner of Nassau Street and Washington Road, you'll find the historical society, housed in a classic Georgian home. The society offers a wealth of information and guided tours on Sunday afternoons.

Downtown Princeton is defined by Nassau Street, Witherspoon Street, and Palmer Square. Not so long ago, this area was pretty sleepy. But the influx and expansion of major corporations, including Merrill Lynch and Johnson & Johnson, along the US 1 corridor has led to a downtown renaissance. The place bustles, especially on sunny weekends. Most of the Nassau Street and Palmer Square shopping leans to well-known, upscale chains, plus a few local retailers, selling clothes and jewelry. There's a sprinkling of art galleries, bookstores, and music shops. And, of course, you can purchase almost any kind of Princeton University paraphernalia. A swing down Witherspoon Street takes you to an amusing selection of arty shops—crafts, galleries, and similar stores.

This renewed liveliness shows itself best perhaps in the increasing number, and increasingly quality, of restaurants. Where not so long ago, it seems to me, just a few average eateries could be found here, the choices now run the gamut: seafood specialists, Thai, Indian, fine French, Italian (of course, New Jersey's favorite type of restaurant), bistro, and naturally, American fare make for fun and interesting choices. Two small specialty stores we like, both located on Palmer Square are Bucks County Coffee Company, where all manner of coffee drinks and sinfully good baked goods are served; and the Bent Spoon, purveyor of the homemade Italian-style ice creams.

The performing arts, too, flourish in Princeton. The McCarter Theatre Center can be counted among the finer regional theaters in the country (see chapter 44), and professional and collegiate music, theater, and dance performances are plentiful. We wandered, lost, for half an hour in search of an auditorium that nobody seemed to have heard of (yes, we should have bought that campus guide first). When we finally located the place, we enjoyed a pleasant free concert of works by Bartók, Ives, Hayden, and Copland performed by an ensemble comprised largely of freshmen and sophomores. After each piece the performers' friends and roommates literally cheered for their musician schoolmates—not unlike many of them had no doubt done for their athlete schoolmates that very afternoon at the stadium. But, in the concert hall, few wore black and orange, and nobody carried a tiger's tail.

DETAILS

General information and the "Princeton Visitor's Guide" *are available by calling 609-520-1776 or from the Web site, www.prince ton.edu.* U.S. 1 Newspaper *(609-452-0038; www.princetoninfo.com) publishes a useful seasonal guide to the Princeton area, which can be obtained at area hotels and at the news kiosk in Palmer Square. The* Princeton Packet *is another local newspaper whose Web site can prove useful: www.pacpub.com.*

Other useful Web sites: *Princeton Chamber of Commerce, www.princetonchamber.org; Princeton Historical Society, www.prince tonhistory.org; Princeton Online, www.princetonol.com.*

For football and other game tickets: *call 609-258-3538, or click on http://goprincetontigers.collegesports.com.*

Directions: *Princeton is located just off US 1 on US 206, which can be accessed from the Garden State Parkway, the New Jersey Turnpike, or I-295. The town can be reached by bus and train via New Jersey Transit (1-800-626-RIDE; www.njtransit.com).*

Outlet Shopping

Secaucus and Flemington

Secaucus

SECAUCUS WAS ONCE THE BUTT of many pejorative New Jersey jokes. No wonder. The town stood at the edge of an expansive swamp (more politically correctly known today as a wetland) and was the site of several large pig stockyards and slaughterhouses. Between the mosquitoes and the smell, Secaucus never had a chance.

That changed when warehouses began popping up in the town. A number of big-name Manhattan fashion and garment houses took to storing their goods in New Jersey. These fashion trendsetters soon discovered that they could unload their unsold or slightly blemished goods right from their warehouses. It seemed that the same adventurous spirit that will drive some to compulsively scour for bargains among Manhattan lofts would also drive them to explore the industrial back roads of New Jersey. Secaucus, after all, lies only a few minutes' drive from the Lincoln Tunnel. And more importantly *there is no sales tax on clothing in New Jersey!* Thus was warehouse outlet shopping born.

Secaucus discount shopping isn't quite what it once was. The "presentation" has grown more mall-like and pleasant, many of the original warehouses no longer sell, and a tribe of low-end, chainlike dollar stores have moved in. But some warehouses open for special events, and the shopping here does remain a viable adventure among the huge buildings and trucking depots.

To thrive in Secaucus—indeed, to even survive here—you must: a) have a car, and b) stop at the first available shopping site and grab the area guides, either "Secaucus Guide Book," or "Secaucus Outlet Centre." Take both; not every shop is listed in each. Without these maps, you may be doomed to wander aimlessly for hours.

My friend Alison—a real shopaholic—and I started at a place called Outlets at the Cove on Meadowlands Parkway. Careful—it's easily missed. We picked up the magazines here, and we found two stores offering excellent name-brand bargains: Bugle Boy and Van Heusen. I bought my extra-large-sized, ultra-picky teenager a collared Bugle Boy polo shirt for five dollars, and myself a Van Heusen broadcloth dress shirt for twelve. We were both happy. But by the time of this writing, Bugle Boy was gone. That's the way it is with this outlet business.

A few blocks south, on the left, another super find awaits—A Real New York Bargain. Ten dollars is the highest price you'll pay for almost anything among the store's hodgepodge collection of clothing that includes everything from pure silk blouses and Izod shirts to real junk. It takes a sharp shopper's eye to get the most from "the ten-dollar store" (plus timing, since the stock can turn over daily), but the bargains make it worthwhile. You say that a ten-dollar outlet isn't inexpensive enough? Well, A Real New York Bargain has its own outlet's outlet several doors down, in which most items sell for five bucks.

If name brands are more your style, there's hardly one you can't find somewhere in the Secaucus labyrinth. Several vendors offer more than one location. Among the visitors' musts: London Fog, Gucci, Sango, Jones New York, HE-RO Group Outlet, Syms, and Perry Ellis for clothes; Marty's Shoes; Enterprise Golf; the Door Store for furniture; and a number of spots for leather, kids' clothes, handbags, and, well you name it. Before heading home, we ventured into the Mikasa Warehouse and came away with an armful of glassware that made perfect gifts.

Okay, so maybe Secaucus outlet shopping isn't as funky as it once was. Maybe it's been sanitized and made more like outlet mall shopping nationwide. But there's a lot to be found here, many treasures to be discovered. Just one caution: Expect to get lost. It helps to turn the shopping guide map upside down as you navigate. I'm not sure why.

FLEMINGTON

While Secaucus sits right next door to Manhattan, Flemington is located in the middle of nowhere. What could make Flemington a discount shopping center?

I don't know.

I drove into town on a day heavy with rain, accompanied by two expert shopping consultants—my 13-year-old daughter, Laina, and her pal Megan. We approached from the north via NJ 31, a far more scenic and pleasant approach than that afforded by commercially cluttered US 202. By approaching from the road less traveled, our first impression of the village came from its downtown. Main Street in Flemington has character. An imposing, old-fashioned hotel demands your eye's attention, and one of the state's more pleasant bed & breakfasts—the Queen Anne–style Main Street Manor—graces the heart of town. Alas, I was not allowed to linger. My traveling companions were impatient to get to the meat of the matter. We followed the signs to Liberty Village.

Liberty Village, its management proudly declares, was "the first 'outlet village' of its kind." Exactly what kind of outlet village is it? Well, even a shopping crumudgeon like me will admit, a very pleasant one. Done in neo-colonial architecture with rich, redbrick walkways, there really is a village feeling. There are more than 60 stores here, ranging from Brooks Brothers to Royal Doulton to LL Bean (for the outdoorsman in me). The kids gravitated toward the Bass Clothing Outlet. Somehow they weren't moved by the Brooks Brothers or Jones New York offerings. We peeked in on the required big names—Anne Klein, Ellen Tracy, and Calvin Klein—and stopped in at the Who Wants Coffee! Café & Panini Grill for some scrumptious munchies.

When the rain made it too awkward to ramble outdoors, we scooted next door to Feed Mill Plaza. It really was an old feed mill—although you have to approach it from the rear to fully appreciate that fact. Now, with a classy glass facade and entryway, it has been converted into two upscale-looking floors of shops.

Time and weather prevented us from stopping in at Turntable Junction (where perfume and chocolate might have caught my companions' interest) or Heritage Place (where the Jockey Store, Levi's Outlet, Reebok, and Rockport might've captured me), but we finished our tour with a stop Flemington's most famous store, Flemington Fur. We came only to see the shrine, not to shop it. Good thing. They'd just closed for the day.

Altogether, Flemington offers some 120 outlet stores. As in Secaucus, a magazine-like guide is published. Pick one up almost anywhere in town. You can break up your shopping spree with an 1½-hour-long scenic ride on the restored steam train of the Black River & Western Railroad. Or just go ahead and shop till you drop.

DETAILS

Many of the outlets *in both Secaucus and Flemington are closed in the evenings; those that do stay open most likely only do so on Thursday. For general Secaucus information and store listings click on www.secaucus.org or www.secaucusoutlets.com. For general Flemington information call the Flemington Business Association at 908-284-8118 or visit the following sites: www.flemingtonoutlets.com; www.shopflem ington.com; www.mainstreetflemington.com.*

Secaucus Directions: *From the east or west, take NJ 3 to the Meadowlands Parkway exit. From the north or south, take the New Jersey Turnpike or Garden State Parkway to NJ 3 east and exit at Meadowlands Parkway. New Jersey Transit operates buses to the outlets from New York City, Newark, and Jersey City (1-800-626-RIDE or www.njtransit.com for schedules and fares).*

Flemington Directions: *From the north, take I-80 west to I-287 south and exit onto US 202 south. From the south, take I-295 and exit onto NJ 31 north to US 202 north.*

Canoeing in the Pinelands

Jackson

E D MASON DROPPED THE CANOE into the murky water. Not 10 feet above us and 20 feet away, vehicles rushed over a highway viaduct. But down here among the thick brambles and knotted trees, we were in another world.

We climbed aboard, gently pushed off, passed under the highway, and began to ease on down the stream. After a few bends in the river, we passed the last houses of a nearby development, and we entered the timeless wilderness of the northern Pinelands.

The north branch of the Toms River runs parallel to CR 527 out of Jackson and eventually empties into Barnegat Bay at the town of Toms River. We were paddling a section that Ed described as "winding and narrow, but safe enough." The current flowed at a deceptive 5 knots. The river seemed placid, but when we negotiated its many hairpin turns, we required quick reactions to keep the canoe from hanging up in the weeds, grounding on a rock, or getting snared by the dense thicket that overruns the riverbanks.

"Duck!" Ed called. I looked up, expecting to see a mallard flying overhead. Instead, I came within a hair's breadth of smacking my forehead on a tree trunk. The water was also half-bridged by many low-clearance, overhanging tree trunks.

The Toms' shores are dense with river beech, holly, oak, and maple.

On the Toms River

Here and there you find stands of pine. You're never really far from development, but the woods are dense enough to create a wilderness feeling, which the lack of other river travelers reinforces. "There's canoeing down in Wharton State Park, but on the weekends it's as busy as Disney World," Ed commented.

Among the animals to look for, Ed listed beaver, river otters, and ducks. Blue heron frequent the river in the spring, and owls are a common sight. "Some people claim that they've been attacked by the owls," Ed told me. "But, actually the owl needs to dive to pick up enough air speed to fly off. It's really trying to get out of the way."

Ed Mason, 66 years of age when I paddled with him, had been canoeing these parts for nearly six decades. A retired schoolteacher, he operated a canoe rental business. And, typical of the rental services down here, he did no guiding. Indeed, Ed claimed nobody runs guided canoe trips in the Pines. "The insurance costs too damned much," he muttered. For a reasonable fee, a rental service will rent you a canoe, take you to the drop-off point, point you in the right direction, and pick you up at a designated takeout. "On this section of the Toms, you're not likely to get disoriented." Ed said. Further south in the Pinelands, he cautioned, the rivers and streams meander, fork, and cross, and you can become dangerously lost.

Typical trips run from two hours to two days. If you want to camp overnight along the Toms, he recommended Riverwood Park in Dover Township. You need a permit to camp in Riverwood, but you can pitch your tent for free. As we approached a wide, left-turning bend, he decided to show me the campsites. We beached, disembarked, and followed a well-worn path that first paralleled the river, then turned sharply into the woods, and finally opened into a small clearing with two or three wilderness-style sites. "This is were you'd spend the night," Ed announced. It would make a very pleasant place to camp. If camping is your cup of tea.

Back on the river, Ed talked about growing up in Trenton and paddling with his older brother from near here to the ocean when he was about 10 years old. "My father was a builder," he said, "and he did a lot of work in Seaside Park. When we got to the mouth of the Toms, we had to paddle across Barnegat Bay. We made it, too."

We encountered no such challenge on this trip. Too soon we reached our "takeout point"—another highway overpass. We'd paddled about 5 miles in just over two hours. A very pleasant trip, indeed, that could probably be handled by paddlers with only basic canoeing skills and experience.

DETAILS

The New Jersey Pinelands Commission *posts a list of canoe liveries on its web site: www.state.nj.us/pinelands/canoe.htm. Several New Jersey state parks offer canoeing; a list can be found at www.state.nj .us/dep/parksandforests/parks/parkactivity.html#boat. For a comprehensive guide, read* Canoeing the Jersey Pine Barrens, 4th Edition *by Robert Parnes (Globe Pequot, 1998).*

WORLD CLASS

Newark

AN EXCITED BUZZ RUNS THROUGH THE AUDIENCE, an electric undercurrent rippling beneath the usual pre-performance chatter. The house lights dim, the stage lights rise, and with the appearance of dancer Savion Glover, the buzz transforms into a palpable, eager energy. Sure, the full house has come to see one of its own—a star born and raised right here in Newark—display his internationally renowned, ingenious, and revolutionary approach to tap. But enthusiastic full houses are not unusual here. A veritable who's who from all disciplines of the performing arts regularly graces the New Jersey Performing Arts Center (NJPAC) main stage, and much to the surprise of some, people are coming in record numbers to see them.

Less than 20 years ago such a building seemed unimaginable. Newark in the 1980s was ailing. Still reeling from civil unrest, it was vilified by Harper's as "the worst city in America." Thus, when Governor Thomas Kean revealed plans in 1987 to create a major performing arts center in downtown Newark, it left many New Jerseyans in disbelief. Few argued that New Jersey was entitled to its own first-class center. No existing facilities could adequately house the New Jersey Symphony Orchestra, the New Jersey State Opera, and the growing number of New Jersey–based dance and theater companies, not to mention national and international touring companies. But Newark? Desolate Newark? To build here seemed a supreme act of foolishness. Or faith.

Yet Newark boasts a long, vibrant cultural history. It was always a major stop on the jazz circuit. The city's Symphony Hall has hosted many great performers and is considered an architectural and acoustical gem. The Newark Museum holds the country's most important Tibetan art collection. Cathedral Basilica of the Sacred Heart ranks among the nation's most magnificent churches and often hosts classical concerts. The city's nearby Portugese neighborhood, the Ironbound, flourishes. The New Jersey Historical Society is here, too, as are a Rutgers University campus and Seton Hall University. So, why not a world-class performance facility?

Today, NJPAC stands on Newark's Passaic River waterfront, positioned formidably as the cornerstone of the city's slowly burgeoning renaissance. It's an airy, grand-but-understated building of brick and glass. The brick connects to Newark's traditional Victorian brick architecture, the glass to an open future. Inside, the lobby rises five stories, balancing its lofty scale with warmth. Terra cotta pillars complement balconies and facades of rich wood. A bright, multi-hued carpet of African design enlivens the floor.

Prudential Hall, the 2,750-seat main theater, rises in four elegant tiers, faced in red-brown, cherry-stained mahogany, to create, again, a space both grand and comfortable. The hall is not only beautiful but a consummate performance venue. Artists from rock stars and rappers to classical musicians and dancers sing its praises.

"It's a performance space that doesn't have to work for 'warmth.' It comes with the architecture. It is a theater that comes with an attitude, a personality that resonates as if it's been here forever!" Judith Jamison, artistic director of the Alvin Ailey American Dance Theater, has stated.

Famed cellist Yo Yo Ma commented, "The sound of Prudential Hall has both warmth and clarity. The hall is aurally and visually enveloping, like being inside of a great string instrument."

Or, as rock star Meatloaf put it, "Cool place."

And there's more. A second theater, the 540-seat Victoria, provides a venue for off-Broadway–style productions, children's plays, and more intimate music presentations. Off the lobby, the Theater Square Grill serves truly gourmet cuisine in an atmosphere of casual elegance. Out front, Theater Square, a tree-lined, brick courtyard, hosts weekly, summer-evening music fests and its own café.

Meanwhile, Symphony Hall remains the setting for many other concerts. Considered an acoustical masterpiece, the hall is a wonderful place to listen to any kind of music. More musical performance in a rich acoustic setting can be found at the Cathedral Basilica of the Sacred Heart, a National Historic Landmark and home to a very active music ministry. Organ and choral concerts are performed here regularly.

Functioning in another world-class realm, there's the Newark Museum, ranked among the premier institutions of its type in the country. The museum houses 66 galleries and 60,000 square feet of exhibition space. It holds one of the world's outstanding collections of American art, ranging from colonial times to the present. The Asian collection features an internationally renowned assemblage of Tibetan works, and the classical collection contains some of the most remarkable pieces of ancient glasswork anywhere. The adjacent, 21-room, Ballantine House is the only landmark, urban, Victorian mansion in the state open to the public. In addition to providing a unique study in and collection of Victoriana, Ballantine House also holds the museum's extensive decorative arts collection.

The Junior Museum conducts a series of weekend workshops for kids ages 6–16. Activities range from constructing building models in the architecture workshop to drawing and painting sessions. A series of free special events for children is also offered. For adults, the museum offers subject-specific guided tours and a travel program. Come Thursday in summer, the midday Jazz in the Garden series is a real treat.

If you're going to visit Newark, you'd better want to eat. Newark's Ironbound section has become famous for its array of Spanish, Portuguese, and Italian restaurants. I'm not talking about the latest "hot spot," or the current "johnny-come-lately" darling of the nouveau cuisine set. I'm talking about places like the Spanish Tavern, which opened for business in 1932; the Iberia Tavern, in business for nearly 80 years; or even such "newcomers" as Tony Da Caneca or Rogue & Rebelo, both of which opened in the 1960s.

And, speaking of longstanding traditions, let's talk baseball. Newark was for years home to the Newark Eagles, one of the best Negro Leagues franchises, and to the Newark Bears, the Yankees' Triple-A farm team that helped to develop many of the Yanks' hall of famers. Now, just around the corner from NJPAC, a new incarnation of the Newark Bears has revitalized that tradition, playing at the stylish, 6,000-seat Bears & Eagles Riverfront Stadium (see chapter 27).

Newark holds one countrified surprise: the cherry trees of Branch Brook Park. While the cherry blossoms of Washington, D.C., garner much more attention, Branch Brook's display is actually larger, and the annual Cherry Blossom Festival in April celebrates that in a colorful fashion.

Call it a renaissance if you will, or tradition carried froward. Either way, Newark is alive, well, and artistically flourishing.

DETAILS

General Information: *Newark Municipal web site, www.ci .newark.nj.us; Newark Downtown District, 973-733-9333, www.down townnewark.com; general info, www.gonewark.com.*

Specific Venue Information: *New Jersey Performing Arts Center, 1-888-466-5722; Newark Museum, 973-596-6550, www.newarkmuseum .org; Newark Bears, 973-848-1000, www.newarkbears.com; New Jersey Historical Society, 973-596-8500,www.newjerseyhistory.org; Cathedral Basilica of the Sacred Heart, 973-484-4600, www.cathedralbasilica.org; Newark Symphony Hall, 973-643-4550, www.newarksymphonyhall.org.*

Directions: *To get to downtown Newark from the Garden State Parkway, take exit 145 to I-280 east. From the New Jersey Turnpike, take exit 15W to I-280 west. New Jersey Transit trains and buses service Newark (1-800-626-RIDE, www.njtransit.com), as does the PATH subway system.*

CRANBERRY FESTIVAL

Chatsworth

L ET US NOW PRAISE THE GREAT RED BERRY. The cranberry, that is, a fruit that flourishes in the Pinelands. The berries grow in great sloughy bogs and are harvested by knocking them afloat from their perches, then raking them downstream for collection in waist-deep water. In Chatsworth, home of an Ocean Spray juice factory, the cranberry harvest has long been an autumn tradition. At the turn of the twentieth century, pickers migrated to these fields on chartered trains out of Philadelphia to harvest the berries by hand. Today, the picking process is mechanized, and the harvest has become a wonderful excuse for this town of 200 souls to stage a festival.

The festival starts even before you get into town. For several miles to the east, CR 532 is lined with makeshift roadside stands selling everything but the kitchen sink. Well, you just might find the kitchen sink, too. But, don't tarry too long, for the show is just beginning.

In town, the festivities center around the landmark White Horse Inn, and everything turns berry, berry red: the clothes, candy, ornaments, hats, decorations, and even the ice-cream cones. Well, you might see the odd exception, like a clown sporting bright green or yellow hair. But rest assured, he'll boast a bright red nose. The mythical Jersey Devil will be there, dressed in a red jacket.

Just when you think you've been seeing red long enough, you'll begin to

Harvesting cranberries

discover that honoring the cranberry goes deeper than mere surface color. The fest presents an array of remarkably clever uses of the honored berry.

Cranberry crafts, anyone? How about bouquets, dolls, wreaths, and decorations of all kinds.

Even though we know that the cranberry is edible, the scope of food-stuffs into which it can be cooked will still surprise you. Jelly, yes, and pies, of course. Cookies, too, and jam, chutney, ices, tea, and . . . oh yes, I almost forgot—sauce. Do try the cranberry-topped funnel cakes. But, the jury's still out on the cranberry pizza and the cranberry fudge. Me? I'll recommend any of the muffin offerings.

If you arrive early enough—between 6 and 11 AM—you can catch breakfast at the Chatsworth Volunteer Fire House. Catered by the White Horse Café, you can munch on jams, jellies, breads, other baked goods, and, why not? cranberry ice cream.

If you've any doubt about modern Chatsworthians' devotion to the cranberry, take a look at the biggest and smallest berries cultivated this year. You may need a magnifying glass to admire the smallest.

For the full background on this cranberry mania, stop in at the history tent. The festival is organized and mounted by something called the Chatsworth Club II. The club was founded to help restore the White Horse Inn, and it uses the proceeds from the festival to do that. But the original Chatsworth Club, established in 1900 or so, was something quite different. With a membership role that included such names as Astor, Du Pont, and Vanderbilt, the club was dedicated to hunting, fishing, hiking, and no doubt, riding to the hunt. The inn is the sole remaining building of many that club members erected.

Since you've traveled all this way, please don't bypass the bog tour. You must make advance reservations, but it's worth the commitment. It takes 10 acres of water storage to farm 1 acre of cranberries. While flooding the bog is the preferred commercial harvesting method for juice and sauce berries, the locals will tell you that the finest eating berries are dry-picked by hand. The difference was explained to me, but I'll not pretend I understood. Regardless, the wet-harvesting process is fascinating—the bog turns into a deep red lake from the millions of berries bobbing around in the water as the men, legs encased in long rubber boots, herd the fruit to capture and transport to the factory. The color must be seen to be believed. (Note: Bog tours were unavailable during the 2004 festival, but it was expected that would be just a one-year suspension; check ahead to see if the tours are running.)

While the harvest may be the pièce de résistance of the festival, it's hardly the finale. Make sure to catch some of the impromptu country music that's performed daily. And then there's the antique car parade, with the requisite award for the car wearing the best cranberry-colored coat of paint. The storytelling contest reveals much about local folkways. And the flea market behind the inn is a testament to the notion that one person's junk is another's treasure. Nearly three dozen antiques dealers will be selling their own treasures, and more than 150 vendors offer the chance to obtain just about anything in the way of arts, crafts, or what-have-you.

Just one more stop before you leave: Buzby's General Store. Built in

1865, Buzby's long served the region as a feed store, grocery, and candy shop. Newly renovated and now listed on the New Jersey Register of Historic Places, it functions as a kind of modern-day general store, gift shop, bookstore, and informal resource center venerating the art, history, and folkways of the Pine Barrens. The simple, pleasant feeling of a time long past generated here will make you appreciate that something personal and wonderful has been lost in our fast-paced, shopping-mall world.

Now, pick up a quart or two of cranberries and a copy of the festival's cookbook, and you're ready to take the Chatsworth tradition home. It's the berries.

DETAILS

The Cranberry Fest *runs over two weekends in early October. For schedule and event information: www.cranfest.org.*

Directions: From the south, take I-295 north to NJ 70 east to NJ 72 east. Drive 3 miles to CR 563 and follow the signs. From the north, take the New Jersey Turnpike south to exit 7, then follow US 206 south to CR 532 east into downtown Chatsworth. You could also take the Garden State Parkway south to exit 69 and follow NJ 72 west to CR 563.

ARTISTS STUDIO TOUR, LIBERTY STATE PARK, AND ELLIS ISLAND

Jersey City

ARTISTS STUDIO TOUR

A RECENT SURVEY OFFERS A TELLING SNAPSHOT of Jersey City. In the homes of Jersey City schoolchildren, some 90 different languages are spoken. Talk about diversity.

That survey illustrates Jersey City's traditional place as a haven for new arrivals from foreign lands. It started with the Dutch, who first settled here not long after Henry Hudson sailed into New York Harbor and founded the state's first city of European origin. Later, in the boom immigration years of the late 19th and early 20th centuries, Jersey City became the pivot point for tens of thousands who came from Europe. They disembarked from boats, were processed for immigration at Ellis Island, and then had two choices: take the ferry to New York City or the ferry to Jersey City's Grand Central Railroad Station. Of those who chose the latter, many boarded trains for points inland where relatives or friends awaited them. The others made Jersey City their new home.

Goods as well as people moved into and out of the country through Jersey City. First, oceangoing cargo traveled through on the Morris Canal. Later, the great railway lines transported goods to and from Jersey City's docks. But time brought changes and decline—container shipping caused the large docks to move to more modern Bayonne, and companies sought new sites where labor was cheaper.

Despite the decline, Jersey City today ranks as New Jersey's third

Ellis Island exhibit

largest city, and it has begun a comeback. Like Hoboken before it, the Jersey City renaissance can be found in the growing arts community.

Artists—be they visual or performance—often represent the vanguard of a return to urban health. They are cleverly adept at converting old industrial habitats into magnificent living and work spaces. With its myriad antiquated factory buildings and warehouses, easy access to Manhattan, and low cost of living, Jersey City makes sense for artists. According to an article in the *New York Times*, the city is home to "the largest concentration of artists in the state," some 1,600 or more of them.

Each October, Jersey City celebrates its burgeoning arts community with an Artists Studio Tour. For one weekend, professional artists throughout the community open their studios to the public to show their work, answer questions, share ideas, and maybe even to sell a piece or two. Performers and musicians participate, too, at more than 40 public and private sites. A free shuttle bus transports visitors to key spots along the route.

The collection of studios at 111 First Street, an old P. Lorrilard

New Jersey Central Railroad Terminal

Tobacco Company warehouse, typifies an industrial building adapted for artists' use. The labyrinthine halls of this five-story, brick edifice contain a sensational variety of media, styles, and artistic statements that represent a vibrant and eclectic mix. Not all of it may be to your personal taste, but the work provides wonderful surprises and constant stimulation.

A few blocks away at Grace Church, everything from photography to oil painting to Lego sculpture might be on display, and performances include dance, storytelling, and poetry readings. In a small pocket park, a jazz ensemble plays. The Jersey City Museum offers free admission and displays art with Jersey City themes, artists with Jersey City roots, and live music and performance. Performance art (theater, stilt-walking, spoken word, and who-knows what-all), is staged on the City Hall steps. Inside City Hall, the Rotunda Gallery shows the work of Hispanic artists in celebration of Hispanic Heritage Month. Acoustic bands play outside the Grove Street PATH station.

An Artist Studio Tour Block Party can be found on Grove Street between Newark Avenue and First Street on Saturday evening. Live jazz highlights that gathering, and a collection of the city's restaurants open their doors to feature their culinary skills.

And for kids? Try Art in the Park, an event held in Van Vorst Park that includes children's activities like kite-making, origami, and wind chime creation, plus dance and puppet shows.

The studio tour is compelling and fascinating—and plenty of wine and hors d'oeuvres are available along the way.

LIBERTY STATE PARK AND ELLIS ISLAND

Liberty State Park sits on the water's edge along Upper New York Bay. The park is an expansive urban greenspace of 1,114 acres and home to the Liberty Science Center (see chapter 43). Views from the waterside promenade take in the Statue of Liberty, Ellis Island, and Manhattan—a superb cityscape. Access to the Statue of Liberty and Ellis Island is far easier from here than from downtown Manhattan.

Tickets for the ferry to Ellis Island and the Statue of Liberty are sold in the old Jersey Central Railroad Terminal. Often overlooked, it was the site that began the last stage of the immigrants' journey. Beautifully restored, and now home to a variety of special events and festivals, the terminal completes for us today the best picture of those times.

While a visit to the Statue of Liberty is probably a must-do for most visitors, for me the Ellis Island Immigration Museum is particularly special. The restoration of the main building and the presentation of the arriving immigrants' stories are beautifully rendered and extremely powerful. Many come to Ellis Island thinking that they'll spend an hour. Don't. Come early and be prepared to spend the better part of a day. Do rent a tape player and listen to the audio tour as you explore the three floors of exhibits. Do, without question, view the short but compelling introductory film that describes what it was like to arrive here from a faraway land, and the agony of those who were detained or turned away.

In some ways, the newly restored building is a bit too sanitized. Yet it takes only a smidgeon of imagination to look at the entrance hall's large display of antique luggage, or to view of the main hall's benches, and put yourself into an immigrant's shoes. Ellis Island, simply put, represents some of the National Park Service's best work.

Return to Liberty State Park, and take the 15-minute walk along the riverside promenade. The Manhattan views are spectacular. At the other

DETAILS

The Artists Studio Tour, *sponsored by Pro Arts and the city of Jersey City, is staged in early October. For information, contact the Jersey City Department of Cultural Affairs, 973-547-4333.*

Liberty State Park *(201-915-3403; www.state.nj.us/dep/park sandforests/parks/liberty.html) hosts a number of festivals throughout the year, the most spectacular of which is the American Heritage Festival, an enormous, gala celebration of American history that is staged in October. The park is open daily from 6 AM to 10 PM; its office is open from 6 to 6. For Liberty State Park Interpretive Center Information call 201-915-3409.*

Directions: *Take the New Jersey Turnpike to exit 14-B. At the bottom of the ramp, turn left and follow the signs. The park can also be reached by New Jersey Transit bus (1-800-626-RIDE, www.nj transit.com).*

Ellis Island and the Statue of Liberty *are open daily from 9 to 6:30. Both are accessible from Liberty State Park by the Circle Line Ferry (201-435-9499; www.circlelineferry.com). Information on Ellis Island, 212-363-7620, www.nps.gov/elis; on the Statue of Liberty, 212-363-3200, www.nps.gov/stli.*

The Central Railroad Terminal *(201-915-3400) is open during daylight hours and offers special exhibits during summer. In September it hosts the Jersey Central Railroad Heritage Festival (www.cnj festival.com).*

end of the walk, near the park's main reception building, stands sculptor Natan Rapoport's statue *Liberation*. Here, with Lady Liberty and lower Manhattan as a backdrop, is depicted an American soldier carrying a concentration camp survivor to rescue. Joined at the shoulder to represent them as one, as fellow members of the human race, the sculpture offers tribute to what we can only hope is the best and true meaning of military action—to protect and deliver the oppressed to freedom.

The environmental and historical exhibits at Liberty State Park Interpretive Center, set in mid-park along Freedom Way, focus on the Hudson River and the surrounding area.

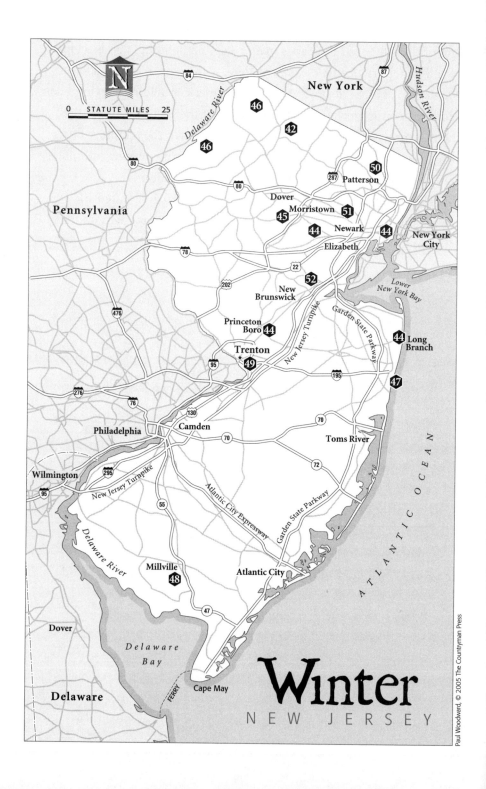

❄42❄

YES, YOU CAN SKI HERE

Mountain Creek, Hidden Valley, and Campgaw

THE OLDER GENTLEMAN JOINED ME on the chairlift, and we rode together toward the snowfields that rested 10,000 feet up in the Wyoming sky. We exchanged the usual skier-to-skier pleasantries—the weather, the wonderful snow conditions, and eventually, where we each lived. An Idaho Falls, Idaho, native, he did a startled double-take when I said, "New Jersey."

"Jersey, eh? No skiing there, I reckon."

"Oh sure there is," I answered, as I had with so many westerners so many times before. "I learned to ski in New Jersey."

It's not unusual to find denizens of the Rocky Mountain states, or even New England, who find it hard to believe there could be real alpine skiing in New Jersey. I can remember being equally as surprised at the notion plans to build the first large ski area were announced. Some entrepreneurial types cut ski runs and installed lifts in McAfee, a small town in Sussex County. They called their "resort" Great Gorge. Soon a rival, Vernon Valley, appeared next door. Several years later, when I was 16, two friends took me to Great Gorge, and I began a pastime that quickly developed into a passion.

With modern snowmaking and snow grooming technology, skiing in New Jersey has become more than viable. Although the state houses but three ski areas, it's major area—the now merged Vernon Valley and Great

222

Fresh snow in New Jersey

Gorge, renamed Mountain Creek—can be called a true resort. Owned and operated by Intrawest Corporation, the same folks who handle world-class resorts like Whistler/Blackcomb in British Columbia and Copper Mountain and Winter Park in Colorado, Mountain Creek is fast becoming a significant recreation destination and indeed, a place where people own vacation homes and condominiums. The resort has 46 trails, 11 lifts, 170 skiable acres, a 7-lane snowtubing park, the mid-Atlantic states' only SuperPipe, and one of the country's most extensive collections of snow terrain parks.

Before Intrawest entered the scene, the resort area had a nice compliment of condominiums, restaurants, and a health spa. But now a new hotel is under construction, as are a pair of Intrawest's signature, state-of-the-art vacation home developments.

Skiing at Mountain Creek isn't sylvan, like skiing in the remote wilds of Colorado or northern New England. An obtrusive high-tension power line cuts right down the middle of the hill, and many trails are bordered by amusement park equipment waiting for summer. But from the top you look over miles of rolling Appalachian hills and valleys, and you can still gain the sense of freedom that comes from standing on top of the world. A few of the resort's trails are truly challenging, and some wind through the woods in an old-fashioned way. And the skiing, like skiing almost anywhere, frees your spirit and makes your adrenalin flow.

It's in the development of terrain parks and that SuperPipe, combined with an incredibly powerful snowmaking system and a collection of newly installed high-speed lifts, that has in recent years created Mountain Creek's identity. Among snowboarders and freeskiers, the parks and half-pipes have given this place a reputation among the best in the East, if not the entire country. National half-pipe competitions are staged here, in addition to seemingly unnumberable local and regional events. Clinics

DETAILS

Mountain Creek information: *973-827-2000, www.mountain creek.com;lodging, 973-209-3300.*

Directions: *Take I-80 to NJ 23 north to CR 515 north to NJ 94 south. New Jersey Transit provides bus service directly to the ski area (1-800-626-RIDE, www.njtransit.com).*

Hidden Valley information: *973-764-4200, www.hidden valleynj.com.*

Directions: *Take I-80 west to NJ 23 north to CR 515 north for 8 miles; at the bottom of the steep hill, turn right onto Breakneck Road.*

Campgaw information: *201-327-7800, www.skicampgaw.com.*

Directions: *Take NJ 208 north to the Ewing Avenue exit; follow signs for the Police and Fire Academy and turn left onto Franklin Avenue, then right on Pulis Avenue. Drive approximately 3 miles and turn left onto Campgaw Road; the county park entrance is 1.2 miles up on the left; enter the park and make the first right through the yellow gates.*

taught by pro snowboarders happen regularly, and events featuring live bands are common. For the young, and perhaps even the young at heart, this is one happening place.

Just down the road a piece, Hidden Valley offers a much less frenetic and more personalized atmosphere. Originally a private club, Hidden Valley has been open to the public for many years, but it retains a quiet, peaceful, out-of-the-way ambience. Most of the skiing is fairly easy, and the trails short, but the area does boast one run that is steep enough to have met international racing standards. The area's base lodge is home to Bonnie's Angus Grill and the Breakneck Bar, pleasant places to relax and dine. Their Wednesday Learn-to-Ski package, priced at just $25, can't be beat.

Beginners can be introduced to skiing at Mountain Creek, as I was, or at Hidden Valley, but northern New Jersey's other alpine ski center presents the perfect introductory setting. Campgaw, owned by the Bergen County Parks Department, offers a touch of alpine country in the heart of suburbia. Having caught the growing snowboarding trend early, Campgaw offers a surprisingly long half-pipe and an extremely popular snowboard park, and has become a mecca for young riders. After-school programs offer a great way to get kids started, and their tubing park is quite popular.

So, yes indeed, you can ski New Jersey. Ski quite well, actually.

HANDS-ON SCIENCE

LIBERTY SCIENCE CENTER—JERSEY CITY

"HE WANTS US TO DO WHAT!?!" 12-year-old Stephanie screeched. She crinkled her nose like an old candy wrapper and curled her lips like burning newspaper.

"He wants you to pet the giant cockroach," I said innocently. "You're not afraid of a li'l ole cockroach, are you?" Judging by the sound that came out of her, I guess she was. She settled for staring at a "disgusting" tarantula. At least it was held safely behind glass.

The Liberty Science Center in Liberty State Park brings science to life, up close and personal. You don't come here to see, you come to do. Even if some of the displays curl your lip. The museum is divided by topics, one to each of the three exhibition floors: the environment, health, and inventions; it also holds an auditorium and one of the world's largest OmniMax film theaters.

The guy with the pet cockroach was on the top floor—the environment. I wasn't squeamish. What's a roach feel like? Uh, well, you'll just have to go find out for yourself.

Down a flight, the kids lined up for a 3-D movie. Yep, they even wore those silly glasses. This was the health floor, site of the museum's most popular exhibit, the Touch Tunnel. It's totally dark in that tunnel. You get through by your sense of feel. But here we ran into the museum's major problem—too crowded. The wait was an hour. No thank you.

On the invention floor you could move lasers around, make a miniature

The Liberty Science Center

suspension bridge respond to the forces of your own weight, and work with mechanical puzzles. This floor also houses the visiting exhibits, some of which—like that season's Whodunit, a murder-mystery-solving challenge that explores how police use science to solve crimes—are sophisticated and impressive.

With the Liberty Science Center, New Jersey has a hands-on science center that ranks with the best. Just watch those crowds. Go early in the day on a weekend, when there are no school groups.

❋ ❋ ❋ ❋ ❋ ❋ ❋ ❋

DETAILS

Information: *201-200-1000, www.lsc.org*

Directions: *Take the New Jersey Turnpike to exit 14C, staying in right-hand lanes at the toll. Drive past the exit to Liberty State Park and take the first right, then make an immediate left to enter the science center parking lot. New Jersey Transit buses connect to the Hudson-Bergen Light Rail and PATH trains (1-800-626-RIDE, www.njtransit.com).*

❋ ❋ ❋ ❋ ❋ ❋ ❋ ❋

NEW JERSEY STATE AQUARIUM—CAMDEN

The kids had a hard time deciding which was more exciting and scary—seeing the shark swim past right in front of your face or actually touching the shark. True, the sharks in the large tank were safely behind glass, but they sure loomed large and dangerous! And, yes, the sharks in the touch pool were small and harmless, but (yuck! wow!) you could actually pet them!

The New Jersey State Aquarium represents a cornerstone of the effort to revitalize Camden's downtown and waterfront (see also chapter 9). It certainly represents a wonderful start. The facility's major attraction is a 760,000 gallon, open-ocean tank in which live more than fifty fish species. An outdoor, 170,000-gallon tank houses harbor and gray seals, which are always fun to watch. The adjacent penguin habitat is also very cute.

The two-floor aquarium building is undergoing a major expansion. Closed for the winter of 2004–05, it will reopen in the spring of '05 having doubled in size and with a 4-D Imax Theater. Already a fun and wondrous place to visit (after all, underwater life is endlessly fascinating and sometimes bizarre), the new aquarium should be more than twice the fun.

Adjacent to the aquarium stands the Camden Children's Garden (see chapters 9 and 24). Outdoors and open year-round, its plants make a wonderful complement to the indoors fish experience.

DETAILS

Information: 609-365-3300, www.njaquarium.org

Directions: Take the New Jersey Turnpike to exit 4 onto NJ 73 north; follow signs to NJ 38 west toward Camden and bear right over the overpass to NJ 30 west. Follow signs to Mickle Boulevard and the aquarium. You could also take I-295 to exit 26 into I-676 north to exit 5A and follow signs to the aquarium or waterfront. The aquarium is also reachable by New Jersey Transit buses and trains (1-800-626-RIDE, www.njtransit.com), as well as by AMTRAK, SEPTA, PATCO and the River Line trains. You could also take the RiverLink Ferry from Philadelphia.

MORE HANDS-ON OPPORTUNITIES

JCP&L's Energy Spectrum, Forked River (609-971-2100) Jersey Central Power & Light's Oyster Creek Plant, off exit 74 of the Garden State Parkway, is the site for this hands-on learning center that focuses on almost all aspects of electricity. The building's stone facade is warm and welcoming, and inside you get to do everything from generate your own power to play computer games.

Jenkinson's Aquarium, Point Pleasant (908-899-1659, www.jenkin sons.com) Take any of the great aquariums from around the country—like the one in Camden—and shrink it. Now, you've got Jenkinson's. Located on the boardwalk in Point Pleasant, this collection of sea life contains a bit of everything, all very well displayed and made family friendly through its design and its emphasis on programs for both kids and seniors. The actual sailing ship *HMS Bounty*, from the film *Mutiny on the Bounty*, provides the decor's centerpiece (surprise! it's not full sized); seal training is the major animal-oriented attraction. A must for all ages when at the north-central shore.

Directions: From the north, take the Garden State Parkway south to exit 98 onto NJ 34 south to NJ 35 south. Cross the Manasquan Inlet Bridge, staying in the left lane, and follow the left jug-handle turn a quarter-mile after the Exxon station. Complete the turn onto NJ 35 north and turn right onto Broadway. Take Broadway to its end, turn right onto Ocean Avenue, and drive 0.5 mile to the aquarium. From the south, take the Garden State Parkway north to exit 90 onto NJ 70 east to NJ 88 east. NJ 88 leads into NJ 35 north. Turn right onto Arnold Avenue and later left onto Ocean Avenue and drive 2 blocks.

New Jersey State Museum, Trenton (609-292-6308 or 609-292-6464, www.newjerseystatemuseum.org) The New Jersey State Museum does everything well—the graphic arts, the performing arts, and the sciences. The science highlight of the year comes in late January with Super Science Weekend. That's when visitors can get together with staff and guest scientists for a hands-on exploration of many disciplines. The museum's planetarium presents shows and events on most weekends, including laser concerts. The Kaleidoscope Kids program explores science, art, and history, and there are teen programs in science and the arts—even a Young Astronaut Program. For adults, there's an ongoing lecture series. The State Museum is simply a great resource.

Directions: Take the New Jersey Turnpike to exit 7A to I-195 west and follow the 195/29/129 signs. Stay left and when road divides and follow NJ 29 north through the tunnel and onto the Memorial Drive exit; proceed through light at the bottom of the exit ramp and take the first right, following the jug-handle turn and signs to Capitol Complex Parking. You could also take US 1 south, exiting at Market Street; turn left at the light and stay in the far right lane to a right at the next light onto Market Street. Follow Market through five traffic lights and stay in left lane, following signs to NJ 29 north. Exit NJ 29 almost immediately at Memorial Drive. Go through light and take the first right following the jug-handle turn and signs to Capitol Complex Parking.

Newark Museum, Newark (201-596-6550, www.newarkmuseum.org) Cute, indoor mini-zoo and a planetarium highlight the Newark Museum's hands-on science facilities.

Directions to downtown Newark: Take the Garden State Parkway to exit 145, to I-280 east. You could also take the New Jersey Turnpike to exit 15W, I-280 west. From I-280, take exit 15A. Stay right toward Broad Street, following purple signs to The Newark Museum. Turn left onto Broad Street. Stay to the right, and make the third right onto Washington Place. Turn left onto Halsey Street. Turn right onto Central Avenue. Turn right onto Washington Street, stay to the left, and quickly turn left into Museum parking lot. New Jersey Transit trains and buses and the PATH subway system all service Newark (1-800-626-RIDE; www.njtransit.com).

Bergen Museum of Art & Science, Paramus (201-291-8848; www.thebergenmuseum.com) A small but dynamic museum in the heart of suburbia. Before you look in on the Hackensack Mastodon and visit the science wing, call ahead for the extensive schedule of science and cultural programs for kids and adults.

Directions: The museum is located on the lower level of the Bergen

Mall Shopping Center off NJ 4 eastbound, about 2 miles past the intersection with NJ 17.

Meadowlands Environment Center, Lyndhurst (201-460-8300; www.hmdc.state.nj.us/ec/) Onced dubbed "The Trash Museum," the Environment Center now focuses on Meadowlands ecology, offering an up-close-and-personal look at life in a wetland. The Interactive Learning Center presents a variety of hands-on activities, and the park trails and wetlands cruises offer another way to get next to, and to gain understanding of, this ecosystem. The birding here, by the way, is terrific. And they offer a cool lineup of special events.

Directions: Take the New Jersey Turnpike to exit 16W to NJ 3 west to NJ 17 south (Lyndhurst exit). Follow the ramp around to the traffic light and turn left onto Polito Avenue to the stop sign at Valley Brook Avenue. Turn left and drive to the end, about 1.5 miles, cross railroad tracks, and bear left to the first building. Or take the Garden State Parkway north to exit 153A (or south to exit 153) to NJ 3 east to the second NJ 17 south exit (signed Rt. 17 south/Lyndhurst—Service Road), and follow the directions given above.

Monmouth Museum, Lincroft (732-747-2266, www.monmouth museum.org) Constantly changing exhibits are combined with participatory activities on the campus of Brookdale Community College.

Directions: Take the Garden State Parkway to exit 109 and head west on CR 520 (Newman Springs Road) to the Monmouth College entrance on left; make the first right turn and follow signs to parking area #1.

Morris Museum, Morristown (201-538-0454; www.morrismuseum.org) Special events and learning opportunities abound, and there's even a live animal gallery. Request a class and event schedule for this one.

Directions: From the north, take I-287 south to exit 35 and turn left onto CR124 east (Madison Avenue). At the third traffic light turn left onto Normandy Heights Road, drive through the next light to the first driveway on your left. From the south, take I-287 north to exit 36A, turning right onto Morris Avenue. Bear right at the fork, following signs for CR 510 as Morris Avenue turns into the Columbia Turnpike. Turn left at the first traffic light onto Normandy Heights Road, and follow the directions above.

Sea Life Museum, Brigantine (609-266-0538, www.marinemammal strandingcenter.org) The Sea Life Museum houses many life-sized replicas of water animals and fish. It is also the home of the Marine Mammal Stranding Center, and the story of how stranded sea life can be saved and returned to the wild makes this a compelling place to visit.

Directions: Take the Atlantic City Expressway, US 30, or US 40/US322 east into Atlantic City, then follow the signs for Trump Casino and State Marina. Take the Brigantine Bridge (between Harrah's and Trump's Casinos) into Brigantine, and travel on Brigantine Boulevard 2 miles from the top of the bridge; the museum is 100 yards before Lighthouse Circle.

Robert J. Novins Planetarium, Toms River (732-255-0342 (recording) or 732-255-0343, www.ocean.edu) A full-fledged planetarium on the Ocean County College campus. For directions, contact the college.

Six Flags Great Adventure Safari, Jackson (see also chapter 28, 732-928-1821, www.sixflags.com/parks/greatadventure) Call this a "car-top wildlife experience." Located next to the amusement park, the safari offers a realistic drive-through visit to Africa. Some 1,200 animals of 60 different species—giraffes, antelopes, tigers, camels, birds, elephants, rhinos, and more—live in this 350-acre preserve. You observe all of them from the comfort of your own car while you listen to an informative narrative on your radio. The hit of the ride? When the baboons use your car as a jungle gym.

Directions: Take the New Jersey Turnpike to exit 7A and then I-195 east to exit 16A. Or take the Garden State Parkway to exit 98 and then I-195 west to exit 16. The park is 1 mile west on CR 537.

TREADING THE BOARDS

Theater in New Jersey

OLD MEETS NEW

WE STEPPED OUT OF THE CAR, and I was immediately transported to another time. Same place, but another time. High school, in fact. I, a member in good standing of the Drama Club, had come on a class trip to see Shakespeare performed at Princeton's McCarter Theatre Center. The ornately semi-Gothic building yawned up in front of us, at once forbidding and inviting, regal and seductive, suggesting that those who entered would experience something special. And, that something was special—live theater.

Now, here we were, my wife, Penny, and I, some 35 years later, coming to McCarter to watch a revival of *My Fair Lady*, and nothing had changed. Well, no, actually, that's not true. The feeling remained, and the building holding the main stage remained. But we were heading for a completely new building, the Roger S. Berlind Theatre, housing a completely new venue.

My contrasting feelings when arriving at McCarter reflect the state of theater across New Jersey. It's the same old sensibility—live performance is special and always has been—but many old venues have expanded and new venues have been added. Indeed, in the last 10 years alone, the New Jersey theater scene has begun to blossom into a flower that's unrecognizable when compared to its meager bloom in earlier years.

"We have a quality and diverse professional theater [scene] right here in New Jersey," John McKuen told me on the phone. John is the executive director of the New Jersey Theatre Alliance (NJTA), an organization that assists the state's professional theaters with marketing, promotion, technical assistance, staffing, strategic planning, and collaborative opportunities. When the alliance began, it had just six members. Now it has 32 in all— 20 full member theaters and 12 associate members, theaters that are moving toward full professional status.

Why the growth? "In New Jersey there is a supportive and forward-thinking State Arts Council, and there's a great opportunity there for support," McKuen counseled. "This is a very collaborative and cooperative arts community. The fact that NJTA is here is attractive and helps theaters make a go of it. It is more challenging to try to start a theater in a place like Manhattan. People are looking for alternatives and New Jersey isn't as saturated [with theaters] as are other areas in the region."

McCarter's Berlind Theatre exemplifies those assertions. A smaller house than the main stage, it provides an excellent venue for less elaborate productions and longer runs. The version of *My Fair Lady* that we'd come to see had been pared down to its essentials: one set, minimal costumes, double- and triple-casting. The result was a delightful production that emphasized characters, songs, and the performances themselves, not elaborate production values. And that's what the Berlind is all about. "If we didn't have the Berlind Theatre, we wouldn't have done this production of *My Fair Lady*," I was told by Mara Isaacs, McCarter's producing director.

McCarter represents theatrical tradition in this state, as well. It dates back to 1929, and has seen the full gamut of performances, from Vaudeville to the 1930s Broadway shows of Thornton Wilder, George S. Kaufman and Moss Hart, and James Thurber. Along the way almost every major name in the performance worlds—theater, dance, music, and comedy—has graced the stage. But now, the organization's focus takes in both producing and presenting. "There's no formula for how we put a season together," Isaacs explained. "We tend to be director-driven, but we have a strong play development program, and we also partner with other producing organizations. We're looking for first-rate artists and text to create a performance experience that will engage the audience."

Like most New Jersey theaters, McCarter's audience is generated locally, from within a 50-mile radius. But the organization is a leader in the New Jersey theatrical world, and it extends a strong influence in many directions. A Tony Award winner, it rates among the country's top regional theaters; it has created school outreach programs that include residencies, productions of works by high-school playwrights, and—just like when I was in high school—special matinees for students.

The final product at McCarter reflects that reach. Since 1991, more than 20 new plays and adaptations have had their world or American premieres here, with plenty of Shakespeare and other classics to be seen as well. Between shows produced and other forms of entertainment presented, a theatergoer witnesses the best that live performance has to offer in McCarter's two venues.

NEW PLAYS NOTHING BUT NEW PLAYS

Downtown Long Branch appears a bit worn at the seams. Don't be fooled. There's a rebirth happening here and, at the heart of this budding renewal, stands the New Jersey Repertory Company.

Operating out of a renovated industrial building now called the Lumia Theatre, New Jersey Rep devotes itself to producing new plays, first American performances of foreign plays, and plays being presented in the region for the first time. "Our mission is to do new works, mostly because we feel there is a need for it," the company's artistic director, SuzAnne Barabas, said when I telephoned her. "Not many theaters take the chance on presenting new works; it's a risky business. We need to give new playwrights a voice, to give playwrights an opportunity to work in a protective creative environment where they can fine-tune their plays."

New Jersey Rep is succeeding. Several of their premiers have had productions in other regional theaters, or have been picked up elsewhere in showcases, readings, or workshops, according to Ms. Barabas. And several have been published. The theater is a member of the National New Play Network, a nationwide organization whose mission is to perform new works and second or third productions of new works. "A good play might be done in Kalamazoo and may not be Broadway material, but is perfect for a regional production," SuzAnne said. "We help get the word out."

Then she added, "About six theaters in New Jersey are dedicated to doing new works to some extent. It's a remarkable thing to see that."

On a Sunday in late July, Penny and I contended with the shore-bound Garden State Parkway traffic to see New Jersey Rep's production of *Old Clown Wanted*, an American premier by Romanian playwright Matei Visniec. Conceived in the best Eastern European absurdist tradition, the play was enjoyable. But it was the direction and the performances that made a true impact. Three veteran actors with enough national, Broadway, and television credits to fill a book, delivered a most impressive afternoon. Here in this tiny, 65-seat house, we were watching world-class talent. It's a remarkable thing to see *that*.

THE BARD AND OTHER CLASSICS

On the Drew University campus, we walked footpaths set under a thick, forest-like canopy en route to watching the Shakespeare Theatre of New Jersey. This group has put in more than 40 years of performing the Bard and other classical theater, and has gained national recognition for its efforts. The "Who's Who in the Cast," and in the company, for that matter, lists artists with experience on Broadway, Off-Broadway, at major regional theaters, and in television and film.

The festival currently occupies the F. M. Kirby Shakespeare Theatre on Drew University's campus. The building started life as a gymnasium, was converted to a theater in the 1970s, and was completely renovated, reopening as a first-rate theatrical facility in 1998. A comfortable and charismatic little theater, the house seats 308, and it really is a great place to watch a play—large enough to allow some spectacle, small enough to lend an intimate feeling. Arriving early in nice weather, you can purchase a soft drink from the rolling cart positioned outside the theater's front door, stroll the campus grounds, or picnic at the tables on the grass nearby.

The company shows a lively willingness to experiment, often responding to the classics with imagination and creative interpretation. On our first visit some years ago, for example, we saw a production of *The Merry Wives of Windsor* set in the 1950s at a Catskills resort. The result was a fast-paced, clever show that simultaneously bridged the gap between the distant past (Elizabethan England) and relative modernity (1950s America), enhancing the audience's appreciation of both eras.

The company debuted their new summertime venue, the Other Stage at the College of Saint Elizabeth in Morristown, in 2002. An open-air Greek amphitheater inspired by Athens' Theater of Dionysus, it's a unique venue that gives play-going an entirely different dimension. Also in summertime, the company's actors-in-training—called the Other Stage Ensemble—perform on specific evenings abridged versions of the classics as part of the Picnic Series. Shows are staged on the lawn outside the Kirby Theatre, and audiences are encouraged to bring along a picnic supper.

The Shakespeare Theatre of New Jersey, too, extends its reach through school programs and special events in the community. Few theaters in the country are giving life to the classics as effectively as these Jerseyans.

PLAY BALL

It was a perfect summer evening for baseball—not too hot or humid, a few scattered clouds promising a spectacular sunset over the Manhattan skyline. Near the Hoboken waterfront, Little Leaguers were embroiled in a game while, just across the street, we entered the DeBaum Auditorium on the Stevens Institute of Technology campus. While we weren't there to play ball, we had come to watch plays about the national pastime.

Hoboken is the recognized birthplace of baseball, and the nascent Mile Square Theatre, a Hoboken troupe, honors that historical footnote by annually staging a baseball-themed fund-raiser. Entitled *Seventh Inning Stretch*, the evening consists of seven 10-minute plays about baseball specifically penned for the event. The evening's proceeds go toward supporting the company's yearly Shakespeare production, staged outdoors right on the waterfront. Of that evening's seven plays, two proved top-notch, a few fell short, and all were fun. It was, in fact, as much fun as being at the old ball game and, at times, a lot funnier.

But more importantly, Mile Square, as one of the state's many small, budding groups, represents yet another aspect of New Jersey theater's vibrancy and growth.

"People underestimate what's in New Jersey in the theater," New Jersey Rep's Barabas commented. "Other than New York City, Los Angeles, and Chicago, we might have the most professional theaters in the country ... People in New Jersey can see anything—musicals, new works, readings—anything."

The NJTA's John McKuen echoed that sentiment. "Our theaters range from budgets of $50,000 to $22 million. Their missions are very different, as is the work that they do," he said. "New Jersey theater has made a national impact. McCarter has won a Tony Award. The Paper Mill Playhouse for many years had the largest subscription audience in the country. Many theaters are contributing to the American repertoire and shows are moving across the river [to New York City]. The Crossroads Theatre won a Tony and has sent plays to Kennedy Center. There continues to be much excitement."

❋ ❋ ❋ ❋ ❋ ❋ ❋ ❋

DETAILS

New Jersey Theatre Alliance *(973-540-0515; www.njtheatre alliance.org, 163 Madison Avenue, Suite 500, Morristown, NJ 07960) NJTA's current membership is comprised of 20 member theatres and 12 associate Members. They are:*

MEMBERS

12 Miles West Theatre Company *(973-746-7181; www.12miles west.org; 488 Bloomfield Avenue, Clairidge Cinema (Lower Level), Montclair, NJ 07042)*

Bickford Theatre *(973-971-3706; www.morrismuseum.org; 6 Normandy Heights Road, Morristown, NJ 07960)*

Cape May Stage *(609 884-1341; www.capemaystage.com; 31 Perry Street, Cape May, NJ 08204)*

Centenary Stage Company *(908-979-0900; www.centenarystage co.org; Centenary College, 400 Jefferson Street, Hackettstown, NJ 07840)*

Forum Theatre Company *(732-548-4670; www.forumtheatre company.com; 314 Main Street, Metuchen, NJ 08840)*

George Street Playhouse *(732-846-2895; www.gsponline.org; 9 Livingston Avenue, New Brunswick, NJ 08901)*

Growing Stage Theatre for Young Audiences, Historic Palace Theatre *(973-347-4946; www.growingstage.com; Route 183, Netcong, NJ 07857)*

Luna Stage Company *(973-744-3309; www.lunastage.org; 695 Bloomfield Avenue, Montclair, NJ 07042)*

McCarter Theatre Center *(609-258-6500; www.mccarter.org; 91 University Place, Princeton, NJ 08540)*

New Jersey Repertory Company, Lumia Theatre *(732-229-3166; www.njrep.org; 179 Broadway, Long Branch, NJ 07740)*

Paper Mill Playhouse *(973-379-3636; www.papermill.org; Brookside Drive, Millburn, NJ 07041)*

Passage Theatre Company, Mill Hill Playhouse *(609-392-0766; www.passagetheatre.org; Front and Montgomery Streets, Trenton, NJ 08611)*

Playwrights Theatre of New Jersey *(973-514-1787; www.ptnj.org; 33 Green Village Road, Madison, NJ 07940)*

Pushcart Players *(973-857-1115; www.pushcartplayers.org; 197 Bloomfield Avenue, Verona, NJ 07044)*

Surflight Theatre *(609-492-9477; www.surflight.org; Engleside and Beach Avenues, Beach Haven, NJ 08008)*

The East Lynne Theater Company, First Presbyterian Church of Cape May *(609-884-5898; www.eastlynnetheater.org; 500 Hughes Street, Cape May, NJ 08024)*

The Shakespeare Theatre of New Jersey *(973-408-3278; www.shakespearenj.org; 36 Madison Avenue, Madison, NJ 07940)*

TheatreFest *(973-655-7071; www.montclair.edu; Montclair State University, Montclair, NJ 07043)*

Two River Theatre Company, Algonquin Arts Theatre *(732-345-1400; www.tworivertheatre.org; 171 Main Street, Manasquan, NJ 08736)*

Women's Theater Company, Theatre at the Y *(973-316-3033; www.womenstheatercompany.org; One Pike Drive, Wayne, NJ 07470)*

Associate Members

Actors Shakespeare Company *(201-459-1117, 201-216 -8937 for the box office; www.ascnj.org; P.O. Box 311, Hoboken, NJ 07030)*

African Globe TheatreWorks *(973-624-1584; www.african globe.com; 1028 Broad Street, Symphony Hall, Newark, NJ 07102)*

Alliance Repertory Theatre Company, Liberty Theatre *(973-566-0066; www.alliancerep.org; 252 Liberty Street, 2nd Floor, Bloomfield, NJ 07003)*

Celtic Theatre Company *(973-761-9790; http://artsci.shu.edu/ celtic; Seton Hall University, P.O. Box 857, South Orange, NJ 07079)*

Crossroads Theatre Company *(732-545-8100; 7 Livingston Avenue, New Brunswick, NJ 08901)*

Dreamcatcher Repertory Theatre, The Baird Center *(973-378-7754; www.dreamcatcherrep.org; 5 Mead Street, South Orange, NJ 07079)*

New Jersey Dramatists & Waterfront Ensemble *(201-708-6535; www.njdramatists.org; P.O. Box 1486, Hoboken, NJ 07030)*

The Garage Theatre Group, Becton Theatre at Faisrleigh Dickinson University *(201-569-7710; www.garagetheatre.org; 960 River Road, Teaneck, NJ 07666)*

The Theater Project *(908-659-5189; Union County College, 1033 Springfield Avenue, Cranford, NJ 07016)*

Theater Under the Stars, Oskar Schindler Performing Arts Center *(973-325-0795; www.theaterunderthestars.org; Parish House, 662 Eagle Rock Avenue (winter); 4 Boland Drive (summer), West Orange, NJ 07052)*

Tri State Actors Theater *(973-875-2950 www.tristateactors theater.org; P.O. Box 7225, 74 Fountain Square, Sussex, NJ 07461)*

What Exit? Theatre Company, Burgdorff Cultural Center *(973-378-2133; www.whatexittheatre.com; 10 Durand Road, Maplewood, NJ 07040)*

The Holly Walk and Other Seasonal Events

Morristown

"**G**eorge Washington slept here!"
The phrase is heard so often in New Jersey it has become a cliché. But, in Morristown, George Washington actually spent many a night. His most famous stays took place during Christmas and the weeks that follow. Morristown was also the longtime residence of Thomas Nast, the artist and caricaturist who created the image of Santa Claus we use today. No wonder Christmas is such a good season to go back in time at Morristown.

But, beware. Christmas arrives early here. The season officially gets under way when Santa comes to town at the end of November. He rides in accompanied not just by a crew of reindeer or elves, but by everybody. The entire population gathers in town square, the large Christmas tree is lighted, and the season to be jolly has officially begun. After that, it's one event after another right through the end of the year.

George Washington set up shop at Morristown in January, 1777, shortly after the American victories at Trenton and Princeton. Here, strategically stationed between New York and Philadelphia, the army spent the winter regrouping. After two more years of bitter fighting, they were back for the winter of 1779–80. That winter brought 28 blizzards and was declared the worst of the century. The troops, who had little to eat, barely endured. By 1781, a rebellion among the underfed and underclothed troops began in Morristown. It spilled headlong into Philadelphia, where the men marched on their own Congress demanding pay, food, and supplies.

Today, during the first weekend in December, the annual Holly Walk allows Morristown visitors to imagine those long Revolutionary winters, and voyage through the Christmas celebration styles from colonial times through the Victorian era and into the early 20th century.

Start at the Ford Mansion and Museum, part of the National Historic Park. In addition to the colonial-era seasonal decorations, the permanent displays offer a glance at military hardware and other Revolutionary period artifacts; the museum also presents a gem of a film that realistically depicts the ordeal of one common solider during the Continental Army's second Morristown winter.

Drive next to the Wick Farm, a prosperous and spacious homesite for its time, where General St. Clair headquartered during the winter of 1779–80.

Move ahead in time at Macculloch Hall, a Federal-style mansion circa 1810 (with later improvements), and notice not only the architectural and lifestyle changes, but the changes in the way in which Christmas was celebrated. Note, too, the noteworthy collection of Thomas Nast's works. A recent Macculloch Hall Christmas display featured sleighs and other over-the-snow conveyances used in the 19th century.

Next, travel to the turn of the 20th century at Fosterfields, a living history farmstead, and move on to the height of the industrial age at Historic Speedwell, the place where Samuel Morse perfected the telegraph. A few weeks prior to the Holly Walk, Speedwell Village operates a holiday crafts boutique, offering for sale an impressive variety of pieces from nearly 100 artists. The collection is good enough to merit a separate trip.

All this—the parade, the historical re-creations—is but the beginning of Christmas in Morristown.

Christmas 1920s style was a recent theme at the Morris Museum's Geraldine R. Dodge Room annual exhibit. An eye-delighting display of mannequins attending a Jazz Age, Roaring Twenties, holiday party

Morristown National Historical Park

created the scene. The display of costumes, jewelry, and Christmas ornaments was dazzling. A Victorian Christmas lantern exhibition made up
another museum exhibit.

Blooming flowers may be out of season, but the Frelinghuysen
Arboretum (see chapter 24) welcomes the season with a Gingerbread
Wonderland, a collection of structures made from gingerbread. Houses,
cabins, and even whole towns are entered in the annual contest. Look, but
don't taste!

Holiday concerts by the New Jersey Pops Orchestra, the Morris
Choral Society, and the Masterwork Chorus are among the season's seemingly nonstop musical presentations. The nearby Paper Mill Playhouse
offers *The Nutcracker* and Dickens' *A Christmas Carol.*

And, just when you're feeling seasonally warm and comfy, you can
remind yourself just how difficult it was to be a "common Joe" back in
1780 by joining a reenactment of the Mutiny Hike at Jockey Hollow

National Park. Jockey Hollow is where the enlisted boys shivered hungrily through that freezing, endless winter long ago. The mutiny hike follows their rebellious route as they started for Philadelphia.

The seasonal celebration in Morristown culminates with its First Night celebration (see chapter 50).

❄ ❄ ❄ ❄ ❄ ❄ ❄ ❄

DETAILS

The Historic Morris Visitors Center *(973-631-5151, www.morris tourism.org) at 6 Court Street prints a full seasonal calendar of cultural events for the area.*

Morristown National Historical Park *(973-539-2016, visitors center; 973-543-4030, Jockey Hollow Visitor Center; www.nps.gov/morr) consists of four noncontiguous units: Washington's Headquarters with the Ford Mansion and Headquarters Museum, the Fort Nonsense Unit, the Jockey Hollow Unit (including Wick Farm), and the New Jersey Brigade Area.*

Macculloch Hall Gardens *(973-538-2404, www.macculloch hall.org) is located at 45 Macculloch Avenue.*

The Morris Museum *(973-971-3700, www.morrismuseum.org) offers ongoing permanent and rotating exhibits, classes and special events. The museum is located at 6 Normandy Heights Road.*

Directions: *From the north, take I-287 south to exit 35. Turn left at the top of the ramp onto NJ 124 east (Madison Avenue). Turn left at the third traffic light (by Friendly's Restaurant) onto Normandy Heights Road. Proceed through the next light at Columbia Turnpike. The entrance to the Morris Museum is the first driveway on your left. From the south, take I-287 north to exit 36A. Turn right at the top of the ramp onto Morris Avenue. Stay right at the fork in the road and follow signs for CR 510 (Morris Avenue turns into Columbia Turnpike). Make a left at the first traffic light onto Normandy Heights Road; the Morris Museum will be on your immediate left.*

❄ ❄ ❄ ❄ ❄ ❄ ❄ ❄

CROSS-COUNTRY SKIING
High Point State Park and Fairview Lake

I F YOU'D LIKE TO DEVOTE A DAY or two to cross-country skiing in New Jersey and you need to rent equipment, you have but two choices: High Point Cross Country Ski Center in High Point State Park and the Fairview Lake Ski Touring Center in Stillwater Township. Many sites offer cross-country skiing, a few retailers offer rentals, but High Point and Fairview are the only places where you'll find both.

HIGH POINT CROSS-COUNTRY SKI CENTER

The sun flares in the cloudless sky. The snow glistens on the frozen lake. The pervading silence is broken only by the occasional birdcall or by branches rustling in the breeze. Beside the ice-covered water, a lone figure strides confidently on skis. Behind him the obelisk stands tall, marking the state's highest point. It's Monday morning at High Point Cross-Country Ski Center, and it doesn't get much more idyllic than this.

High Point State Park is known for its monument and panoramic views, for camping, picnicking, swimming, and hiking. It's less celebrated as a Nordic skiing center, which may explain why on this pristine Monday morning just three of us are on the trails—a gentleman from Ramsey, New Jersey, myself, and Kim Karlsen, who operates the ski center with her husband, Hans.

It's not always this empty, however. "On a good Saturday, we get up to

Kicking and gliding at High Point State Park

a thousand people," Hans told me on the phone a few days earlier. Kim confirms this as we ski together. "On weekends, the parking lot [350-car capacity] will be full."

I try to imagine the center's 16 kilometers of ski trails and 8 killometers for snowshoeing handling that many people. "Are there skier traffic problems on the weekends?" I ask.

"No," Kim says. "It gets a little crowded in the lodge, but not on the trails."

Hans, a native of Norway and former University of Vermont ski racer, nurtures a lifelong love of skiing. At High Point he and Kim have created a full-service Nordic center. Here you can rent skis, both skate and classic styles, and snowshoes. They groom for all three. They teach. They sell a selection of clothing, ski waxes, gloves, and other essentials. And, on weekends, they sell soups, stews, sandwiches, snacks, and drinks.

There's logic to setting a cross-country ski facility at High Point. The hiking trails readily convert to skiing. The kitchen-equipped lakeside concession building makes a fine ski lodge. And "We're in the best location," Hans said, "the snowiest and coldest spot in the state. And we have snowmaking. I don't think we would've tried without it."

While he'll readily admit that High Point can't boast the 50-kilometer scope of some centers in upstate New York or New England, he takes a backseat to nobody in quality. "We can make enough snow to cover about 3 kilometers," he continued, "and we use the same grooming machine that groomed for the Lillihammer Olympics. People who come up are returning, because everybody knows we go all out when it comes to maintaining top-shelf grooming conditions."

"I expected this to be more like the Catskills—rocky and rough," exclaimed the man from Ramsey, a first-time visitor, when he stopped to chat. "But these trails and conditions are great."

As with most ski operations, building weekday business requires some creativity. Kim recently organized a women's day in which she combined skiing, lessons, and yoga. Hans is considering promoting night skiing by headlamp. Weekend events highlight the season, among the most important is Winter Trails and Ski Fest, during which the center offers free lessons, door prizes, dog sledding and ski-joring demonstrations, winter hiking, ski waxing clinics, special food offerings, and giveaways and handouts.

Other state parks and forests have Nordic trails, but none contain a full-service center like High Point's or provide lessons and snowmaking. For occasional skiers, those who need to rent gear, or for skate skiers, the Karlsen's operation is perfect; for backcountry skiers, it's an excellent jumping off point to High Point's ungroomed trails. For nonskiers, snowshoeing affords an easy way to experience the winter woodlands. For everyone, the center provides a congenial, nearby winter escape.

FAIRVIEW LAKE SKI TOURING CENTER

Owned and operated by the YMCA, the center offers 12 miles of marked, groomed trails, open skiing on the lake, and a separate teaching area. Although the four trails are rated beginner, intermediate, and expert, Fairview will probably leave the hard-core Nordic practitioner out in the cold. For we occasional hackers, however, the Fairview experience proved just right.

The Y runs a sleepaway camp here in summer. Thus, the entire place has that rustic, temporal feeling that only summer-camp bunks and buildings can exude. After paying for our skis and trail pass at the main office, Penny and I were directed to obtain our equipment at the Program Lodge, a slightly musty and haphazardly furnished wood-and-stone building. The equipment keeper, a young man in his early 20s, helped us with pleasant enthusiasm. Before directing us to the trails, he welcomed us to "come back for hot chocolate or cider when you get cold or tired."

We embarked on an exploration of the Green trail, the area's easiest and longest. It led us first uphill into a grove of birch and maple, then rolled along easily, an abundance of mountain laurel lining its edges. We soon established a pleasant skiing rhythm, letting the woods' envelope us in a sense of freedom and quietude. There are few more pleasant feelings.

The trail ran south for, oh, perhaps a half mile, then dropped back down the hill and emptied out onto the lake. In front of us, to the west, the Kittitany Ridge, home to the Appalachian Trail, ran high above the frozen, snow-covered water, lending a wild and free sensibility. We followed the green blazes across the lake and onto the far shore. Suddenly we found ourselves gliding through a gathering of summer camp bunkhouses. An eerie, ghost-townish feeling. The trail paralleled then crossed a work road and finished with an exhilarating, if not all that difficult, single-track descent perched along the road's shoulder. We glided past the dining hall and back onto the lake. Altogether a pleasant run.

After a quick cider break at the lodge, I decided to take on one of the more difficult runs, the Blue trail. Alongside the trail I noticed several numbered markers, which corresponded to the summer camp's Discovery Nature Trail, for which I had obtained a guide in the lodge. Since the ski trail and the nature trail weren't exactly in sync, it was sometimes difficult to follow the guide. But I still managed to identify some tree species along the way. The ski trail was relatively short, but presented me with three good downhill stretches that got my adrenalin flowing.

OTHER OPTIONS

In abundant snow years, Nordic enthusiasts who own equipment will find excellent cross-country skiing in many parts of the state, especially in the state parks and forests. Perhaps best among them is Waywayanda State Park in the north-central reaches of Passaic County. A friend has characterized the Waywayanda skiing as "good enough to fool you into thinking you're in Vermont."

But you needn't go to the far north to enjoy backwoods sliding. The hiking trails of any state park or forest offer good skiing. Trails in Belleplain State Park and the sand roads in Wharton State Forest provide very enjoyable skiing. Along the Delaware River, Washington's Crossing State Park is another fine skiing locale. You can even ski along the banks of the Hudson River in Palisades Interstate Park.

But if you need to rent equipment, or you'd like a lesson, then High Point and Fairview Lake are for you.

DETAILS

For High Point Cross-Country Ski Center information *call 973-702-1222 or click on www.xcskihighpoint.com.* **Directions:** *Take NJ 23 west to the High Point State Park entrance.*

The Fairview Lake Ski Touring Center *(201-383-9282, www.fairviewlake.org) is located at 1035 Fairview Lake Road, Newton, NJ 07860.* **Directions:** *From the east, take I-80 to exit 25 and US 206 north into Newton, then go left onto NJ 94 south and drive approximately 3.5 miles to the blinking light. Turn right onto CR 610, which will become CR 521 north; follow 521 into Stillwater, pass the Stillwater Inn, then just beyond the elementary school on your right, take an uphill left onto CR 617; the center is on your left in 4 miles. From the west, take I-80 to exit 4 and NJ 94 north; at milepost 19, you'll come to a blinking light. Turn left onto CR 610 and follow the directions above from there.*

A HOLIDAY HOUSE TOUR

Spring Lake

The first time we stayed at the Hollycroft Inn, we couldn't find the place. It's hidden, you see. Hidden, as one reviewer put it, behind "towering oak, pine, and holly trees." The house is set back from the street, and after a touch of confusion, we turned into a twisting driveway. Following it around the bend, a log-and-stucco fairy-tale cottage was soon revealed.

Hollycroft, proprietors Mark and Linda Fessler will gladly tell you, was built in 1908 in the Arts and Crafts style. The simple wood and log beam construction was a reaction to opulent Victorian-era tastes. Come holiday time, the Fesslers garland their intriguing lodge with an array of decorations, including an eye-catching collection of grapevine figurines. Each room has its own miniature lighted tree, and Christmas music pervaded the open, rustic, but richly decorated dining room, living room, and brick-floored breakfast room on the main floor. The Fesslers offered seasonal crafts for sale.

The holly trees seem particularly appropriate in Christmas season, particularly if you're following the Spring Lake Bed & Breakfast Christmas Inn Tours.

The beauty of Spring Lake is its quiet simplicity. It's a pastoral, *Our Town* kind of a place, with wide, tree-lined streets, large, well-kept period homes set in manicured yards, an inviting mini-downtown four blocks long, a meticulously kept oceanfront, and of course, the two gemlike, spring-fed lakes (well, okay, some would call them ponds) that give the

Window dressing on the Spring Lake Bed & Breakfast Tour

village its name. When film director Milos Forman went looking for a place to set his movie version of *Ragtime*, an early-20th-century period piece, he chose Spring Lake.

Spring Lake entices visitors with one of the finest bed & breakfast collections in the state. The Christmas Inn Tours, on the first two weekends of December, are self-guided and offer an opportunity to see a handful of these hostelries dressed in their holiday finest. Two tours are offered: the Christmas Inn Tour, on December's first weekend, allows visitors to drop in at a half-dozen inns to admire ornate, whimsically arranged, and often antique holiday decorations; the Bed & Breakfast Candlelight Tour presents the same opportunity at a different group of establishments, along with hors d'oeuvres and deserts at each of the inns, donated by area restaurants. The combination of seasonal ornamentation and the buildings themselves—all beautifully restored with fine interior decorations—presents one eye-filling enjoyment after another.

Each bed & breakfast reflects the personality and tastes of its own-ers. At Victoria House, you enter a Victorian period piece that was been painstakingly and artfully restored by former owners Louise and Robert Goodall. The house dates from 1882 and was built in the Queen Anne style, highlighted by the original stained-glass windows. The current owners, Lynne and Alan Kaplan (no relation to the author, I'm sorry to say), have continued the Victorian interior theme and fill the place with tastefully elaborate seasonal decorations that enhance each room's indi-viduality. A favorite architectural detail of mine: the new tin ceiling in the foyer. The Kaplans offer two-night holiday tours packages that include gourmet breakfasts, tour tickets, a wine and cheese party (on the first Saturday) or a champagne and hors d'oeuvres party (on the second Saturday), evening cordials and chocolates, and health-club passes to work it all off.

During my last visit, a delightful French country theme was in evi-dence at La Maison, complete with a Père Noël (Santa) figure wearing wooden clogs and carrying a miniature basket filled with tiny traditional

❄ ❄ ❄ ❄ ❄ ❄ ❄ ❄

DETAILS

The Spring Lake Bed & Breakfast Christmas Inn Tour *takes place during the first Saturday in December from 1 to 4 PM. Tickets cost $25 each. The Candlelight Tour is staged during the second Saturday in December from 4 to 7 PM. There is limited ticket availability at $40 each. For tour and general information and for links to participating inns: www.springlake.org, 732-449-0577.*

Directions: *Take the Garden State Parkway to exit 34 and follow NJ 34 south to the first traffic circle. Follow the circle three-quarters of the way around and get on CR 524 east. From I-195 east, exit at NJ 34 south and do the same. Spring Lake can also be reached by train on New Jersey Transit's North Jersey Coast Line, or by bus from New York City's Port Authority Bus Terminal (1-800-626-RIDE, www.njtransit.com).*

❄ ❄ ❄ ❄ ❄ ❄ ❄ ❄

champagne bottles, standing atop the coffee table in the sitting room and a traditional *buche de Noel*—a rich chocolate Yule log cake—and two real bottles of champagne adorning the main dining table.

Tickets for the Christmas Inn Tour cost $25; Candlelight Tour tickets cost $40; all proceeds are donated to charity. The roster of participating inns can change from year to year , but no matter which properties partici-pate, the tour is fun and visually rewarding. To round out the tour per-fectly, book a room for one of the weekends and attend a performance of *Scrooge* at the Community House Theatre. This polished, annual commu-nity theater offering features, as one innkeeper put it, "just about every kid in town and adult residents who have been playing their parts for years."

As long as you're staying for the show, you may as well go downtown to shop. You'll enjoy sampling the handmade candies at Jean Louise's, browsing among the Irish goods at the Irish Centre, as well as visiting the unique toy and antiques shops. And indulging in homemade ice cream at Susan Murphy's is a must—even in winter.

THROUGH A GLASS BRIGHTLY

Wheaton Village at Christmas, Millville

WHILE BING CROSBY'S RENDITION of "White Christmas" may touch something deep within all of us, in south-central Jersey it's not snow but sand that holds sway. South Jerseyans have long fired that sand into glass, for both practical uses or just fanciful shapes. And nowhere is there a better celebration of glass in all its manifestations than in Millville's Wheaton Village.

My mom and I ventured to the American Museum of Glass during the holiday season to view the annual Christmas exhibit. The theme, which changes each year, was Christmas in New Jersey. A series of life-sized scenes depicted Christmas celebrations and decorations from different New Jersey times and places, including "Caroling in Hackensack, 1898" (complete with recorded musical accompaniment), and "Millville Christmas Parade, 1949." The museum's lobby, a re-creation of a turn-of-the-20th-century Cape May Mainstay Hotel, was dominated by an enormous Christmas tree.

Wheaton's Christmas exhibit is carefully researched and inventively created; it adds an appealing sense of historical depth to our celebration of the season. In truth, however, the museum commands a visit at any time of year. The permanent collection includes more than 6,500 pieces. They're displayed beautifully in four wings constituting nearly 20,000 square feet of exhibition space.

Progressing through the museum means traveling through time, beginning with early New Jersey glass pieces. The bottle room includes bottles designed to hold everything from soda and perfume to patent medicines to ink and babies' milk. Bottles for bitters alone, we learned, was at one time an $80 million industry.

Other exhibitions include art glass, a re-created Victorian kitchen, a New Jersey Room that features the work of local companies and artists, a research library, and a Paperweight Room.

Paperweights hold a place of special importance at Wheaton Village and, for that matter, among glass enthusiasts. Behind the museum, at the re-created T. C. Wheaton Glass Factory, paperweight-making demonstrations are almost always underway. The Creative Glass Center of America offers a select number of artists' fellowships to glassmakers, and these resident artists are among those who demonstrate their techniques for the public. The factory was constructed in 1972 as a replica of Wheaton's 1888 building. The main furnace is surrounded by a spectators' gallery from which visitors can watch narrated demonstrations. Usually these presentations include the creation of a paperweight and a piece of blown glass. If you'd like to purchase a paperweight, take a short walk back to the village's main street and stop in at the Arthur Gorham Paperweight Shop.

Or, better still, if you'd like to make one yourself, there is a program that will let you do just that. It operates by appointment and for a fee Tuesday and Friday afternoons, and all day on weekends.

Four shops and an art gallery line the main walkway. Here a variety of items—books, jewelry, crafts, collectibles, and of course, glass of all sorts—are available for purchase. The 19th-century village certainly is pretty, and a quaint antique effect is reached, albeit with a bit of a touristy overlay. More effective is the earthy Crafts and Trades Row, a rough, long building pieced together in three sections that houses working craftspeople, who demonstrate and explain their work in ceramics, flame-worked glass, woodcarving, and tinsmithing.

Other Wheaton Village installations include a railroad station, a half-scale steam train ride that circles the village, an 1876 schoolhouse, and a print shop.

Modern Millville, home to the Wheaton Glass Company world head-quarters, remains an international glassmaking capital, a role it has filled for a long time. Wheaton Village wonderfully expresses that history and spirit. And during the holiday season, it does so in a particularly festive way.

DETAILS

Wheaton Village *(609-825-6800 or 1-800-998-4552, www.wheatonvillage.org) is open from 10 to 5, Tuesday through Sunday from April through December; and from 10 to 5, Friday through Sunday in January, February, and March; closed Easter Sunday, Thanksgiving Day, Christmas Day, and New Year's Day. The Christmas exhibit is displayed from just after Thanksgiving until just after New Year's. Lodging is available next door at Country Inn by Carlson; for information or reservations, call 609-825-3100.*

Directions: *Take NJ 55 to NJ 49 and follow the signs.*

✤49✤

WASHINGTON'S CROSSING AND THE BATTLES OF TRENTON

Trenton

"How long does it take Washington to cross the Delaware?" I asked, which came out sounding like the set-up line for a joke.

"About five or ten minutes," replied the lady from the Washington's Crossing State Park. "Fifteen at the most."

Amazing. Back in 1776, Washington required all night to get across the river.

"You really want to get down here at least an hour or more before the crossing," she warned me generously. "That's when he inspects and addresses the troops. And besides, if you get here any later than that, you'll have to park at least a mile away."

Ah, George. Aren't you glad all you had to worry about was sub-zero cold, ice choking the river, operating with stealth in the dark of night, and boosting the rapidly sinking morale of your underfed, ill-clothed troops? You never had to suffer the consequences of limited parking.

Washington's Crossing and the Battles of Trenton represent a major turning point in the our nation's birth. Prior to Trenton, Washington and his beleaguered troops were vilified ; it was said they were capable only of retreat. These reenactments are made even more special by faithfully taking place on their actual anniversaries—Christmas Day and December 26—no matter how inconvenient that may be.

Crossing festivities begin with several screenings of a half-hour documentary in the Memorial Building on the Pennsylvania side of the river and a display featuring the famous painting entitled (appropriately enough) *Washington Crossing the Delaware*, by Emanuel Leutze. Promptly at 2 PM, more than 100 soldiers march one block from the McConkey Ferry Inn to the river, where Washington addresses them, and then they climb into authentic reproduction Durham boats for the cross-river row. After landing in New Jersey, the soldiers march to the John Honeyman Monument to pay their respects to the man who spied on the Hessians that night and gave Washington the information he needed to attack and win.

On December 26, 1776, Washington, after encountering many unexpected delays, managed to surprise the Hessians in Trenton. On our trip to the Battles of Trenton, Penny and I, too, encountered delays—a mysterious backup on the New Jersey Turnpike. Times change, delays change. We managed to arrive at Trenton's Old Barracks Museum just as the troops were hopping into their pickup trucks and minivans to head out for the fight.

We quickly followed. The distant sound of drums could be heard. The occasional costumed soldier could be seen running on the next block. We heard shots.

No sooner had we joined the other spectators at Mill Hill Park than the troops arrived. Standing in the bitter wind that whistled through the streets of Trenton that day and looking at this close approximation of the Continental Army's actual dress—woolen uniforms and knickers, leather boots and three-cornered hats (gloves optional)—evoked a sense of awe at the actual soldiers' hardiness; it's a wonder they didn't all die of exposure within that winter's first week.

Awe soon gave way to confusion. Some men were dressed in the expected British red coats. Others were in green. Hessians? Still others were in blue. It was impossible to tell the soldiers apart without a scorecard. The Americans seemed to be in retreat instead of taking the Brits by surprise.

Just as the cold-ache in our toes began to turn to numbness, the firing suddenly ceased. After light applause, one of the soldiers faced the crowd and began to explain what we had just seen: the second Battle of Trenton.

Hold it! You mean there were two of them? Yes. Buoyed by reinforce-
ments, the British made an attempt to get even with Washington's boys
several days after the surprise attack. They fought that day to a standoff.

It turns out that the turnpike traffic jam had caused us to miss the
first Battle of Trenton. I guess we should have come by Durham boat.

That explained, everyone quickly retreated back to the Old Barracks
Museum, the soldiers to act out a Retreat Ceremony that would officially
end their day's work, most of the spectators to get inside where it was warm.

MORE HISTORY

Trenton offers a treasure trove of historic sites. The Old Barracks
Museum was originally constructed in 1758 as one of five buildings to house
British soldiers who, in the colonies to fight the French and Indian War, had
been lodging in the colonist's homes—whether the homeowners welcomed
them or not. The building is the last existing colonial-period barracks, and it
houses permanent and changing exhibits illustrating colonial life, as well as a
guided tour that offers a first-person account of living in America circa 1777.

The William Trent House was built in 1719 on a 1,600-acre estate by
the man who laid out what he called Trent's Town. Mr. Trent's house was
later home to three New Jersey governors. It has been restored to its 18th-
century resplendence and boasts a noteworthy collection of William and
Mary–style furniture. Guided tours are offered daily.

The Trenton City Museum is located in an 1848, 34-room, Tuscan villa
called Ellarslie. The building houses a large collection of art and historical
objects. On the second floor, you can learn about Trenton's past role as a
pottery and manufacturing center. A particularly fascinating series of paintings depicting life in the John A. Roebling's Sons wire rope factory are kept
here. They were commissioned for the 1939 World's Fair, held in New York.

The New Jersey State Museum must be counted among the state's
finest resources, offering displays and programs relating to archaeology,
cultural history, natural history, and contemporary and classical art. The
museum holds a 150-seat planetarium and offers hands-on science programs for families and school groups (see chapter 43). It also hosts

student workshops in writing and the performing arts, as well as special events like the Super Science Weekend.

Downtown Trenton houses art galleries, more historical buildings, and a number of good restaurants. And of course, since Trenton is New Jersey's capital city, visitors can watch the state legislature in action— when it is in session, not stuck in traffic or rowing across the Delaware!

❋ ❋ ❋ ❋ ❋ ❋ ❋ ❋

DETAILS

Washington's Crossing *is reenacted every Christmas Day, beginning at noon. Call 215-493-4076 for directions and information.*

Events and ceremonies for the Battles of Trenton *run from 11 AM to 3 PM on December 26. A narrated walking tour of the battle is offered at 2 PM. Call 609-396-1776.*

The Old Barracks Museum *(609-396-1776 or 609-777-3599, www.barracks.org), located on Barrack Street, is open daily 10–5; closed Easter Sunday, Thanksgiving Day, Christmas Eve, Christmas Day, and New Year's Day.*

The William Trent House *(609-989-3027; www.williamtrent house.org) is at 15 Market Street; it's open from 12:30 to 4 PM daily, but closed on major holidays.*

Ellarslie, the Trenton City Museum *(609-989-3632, www.ellarslie.org) is located in Cadwalader Park and is open Tuesday through Saturday 11–3, Sunday 1–4, closed Monday and major holidays.*

The New Jersey State Museum *(609-292-6308 or 609-292-6464, www.state.nj.us/state/museum) is at 205 W. State Street; it operates from Tuesday through Saturday, 9–4:45, and Sunday noon–5; closed holidays.*

Useful general information *is available from the Trenton Downtown Association, (609-393-8998, www.trenton-downtown.com) and from the City of Trenton's official Web site: www.ci.trenton.nj.us.*

❋ ❋ ❋ ❋ ❋ ❋ ❋ ❋

❄50❄

CHRISTMAS WITH THE DICKENS AT THE HERMITAGE

Ho-Ho-Kus

I T'S A COLD DECEMBER EVENING, just perfect for visiting friends in their warm and cheerfully decorated home. So you drive over to visit the Dickens at their large stone house with the steep, wood-shingled roof, pinnacled dormers, and the gingerbread trim. As you step across the threshold, you not only receive a cordial welcome, you pass through time, as well. You've entered the world of master novelist, Mr. Charles Dickens, circa 1843.

Mr. Dickens and family greet you graciously, but urgency is in the air. For tonight Charles will be sharing his newest work, specially written for the holidays. He calls it *A Christmas Carol*. Dickens can't wait to read it to you. As he does, other family members and friends will act out the parts. First presented in 1986, the Hermitage's adaption of *A Christmas Carol* draws inspiration from Dickens' own custom of reading his latest chapters to friends and family before sending it off to the publisher. Dickens sometimes read all the parts, and sometimes the group acted out the roles. At the Hermitage's annual reading, a cast comprised of Ramapo College Theatre students portray the familiar characters.

Christmas Dickens has become a holiday custom at the Hermitage, the only 19th-century Bergen County house to earn designation as a national historic landmark. Dickens' *A Christmas Carol*, relating as it does the miraculous personal salvation undergone by Scrooge, is somehow particularly appropriate here. The Hermitage, too, represents something of a miraculous deliverance. All done up for the holiday season, with authentic Victorian ornaments—pine ropes, garlands across the ceiling, gilding everywhere, and a kissing ball of entwined mistletoe, berries, ivy, and holly hanging from above—it's hard to imagine that for years this magnificent home was the scariest place in suburbia. But, it was . . . .

The Hermitage's first incarnation was built about 1750 as a two-story Georgian house along the New York–to–Albany post road. The owners, Colonel James Marcus and Mrs. Theodosia Prevost, hosted George Washington here for a celebration weekend shortly after the American victory at the Battle of Monmouth. Theodosia was widowed in 1780, but she remarried in the house in 1782—to one Aaron Burr, future vice president of the United States and victor over Alexander Hamilton in the country's most infamous duel.

In 1807, the Hermitage was purchased by Dr. Elijah Rosencranz, one of the first physicians to reside in the area. Dr. Rosencranz then built a highly successful cotton mill on nearby Ho-Ho-Kus Brook. The Rosencranzes remodeled the house significantly during the mid-19th century. Most of the original home was leveled, and the Victorian Gothic design we see today was created. For its time, the home was state-of-the-art, employing such advanced technology as indoor plumbing and central heating, and closets, too, at a time when most stored their clothes in wardrobes.

The house stayed in the Rosencranz family for more than a century and a half. But, by the 1960s, the building had deteriorated badly. Lone surviving family member Mary Elizabeth Rosencranz and her companion, Kathryn Zahner, lived there in near-poverty, occupying only one of the house's 19 rooms. Elizabeth refused many lucrative offers for the 4.9-acre property and, upon her death in 1970, the house and grounds were willed to the state. By then the Hermitage was known among the neighborhood kids as "the Ghost House." If this place wasn't something right out of *The Addams Family*, then nothing was. I remember well the derelict, haunted house on Franklin Turnpike from my own high school days. "What is that place?" we'd ask as we cruised by on a Saturday night. None of us knew.

Luckily, there were people who did know—not only what that place was, but how valuable it could be. They formed an organization, called themselves Friends of The Hermitage, and set about restoring it to its former grandeur. The Friends have brought back the luster and made the Hermitage into a living museum. They have developed an impressive archive that includes more than 10,000 items—textiles and period clothing, photographs (most taken by the shutter-happy Rosencranz family), letters, maps, toys, and historical documents that were found on the premises. The collection has made the Hermitage into a vital historical resource for the region.

The Friends draw on those resources to create events and raise funds. Which is how you might find yourself enjoying an evening of Christmas parlor theater with Charles Dickens, or participating in a Victorian dinner party whodunit murder mystery in the spring, or attending a symposium on the Victorian era and a Victorian fashion show, or shopping at the twice-yearly crafts shows, or just dropping by on a Sunday afternoon for a docent-led tour and a coffee at the Hermitage's small café in the smaller, adjacent, 1892 John Rosencranz House.

History buffs can combine a Hermitage visit with stops at two important nearby sites: Steuben House in Hackensack, a sandstone home sited on the banks of the Hackensack River that dates from the early 1700s and that now serves as a museum of early Dutch-American culture, as well as for the headquarters for the Bergen County Historical Society; and Lambert Castle, the elegant, Belle Vista residence of silk manufacturer Catholina Lambert built in 1892 atop Garrett Mountain overlooking downtown Paterson.

The Hermitage is yet another New Jersey treasure amid the seemingly endless suburban sprawl that is too easily overlooked. It took me more than 20 years to stop in. It won't be long before I return.

❄ ❄ ❄ ❄ ❄ ❄ ❄ ❄

DETAILS

The Hermitage *(201-445-8311, www.thehermitage.org), located at 335 N. Franklin Turnpike in Ho-Ho-Kus, is open for guided tours Wednesday through Sunday from 1 to 4, with the last tour starting at 3:15.* **Directions:** *From exit 165 on the Garden State Parkway, take Ridgewood Avenue westbound (toward Ridgewood) for 0.3 mile to NJ 17 north to the Hollywood Avenue exit. Bear left after exiting and follow Hollywood Avenue westbound to the Franklin Turnpike. Turn right onto Franklin Turnpike (north) and go 0.5 mile to the Hermitage, which will be on the left.*

The Steuben House *(201-487-1739; www.bergencountyhistory.org) is open Wednesday through Saturday, 10–noon and 1–5, and Sunday 2–5; call ahead to confirm the museum is open.*

Directions: *From the Garden State Parkway northbound, take exit 161 and follow NJ 4 east for about 2 miles. Exit at Hackensack Avenue north and proceed through two traffic lights, then take the exit for Main Street, River Edge. Turn right onto Main Street. Steuben House and New Bridge Landing is on the left. From the Garden State Parkway southbound, take exit 163 onto NJ 17 south to NJ 4 east, and follow the directions above.*

Lambert Castle *(973-247-0085, www.lambertcastle.com or www.lambertcastle.org) is open Wednesday through Sunday, 1–4; the castle grounds, the Garret Mountain Reservation and Rifle Camp Park, are open daily from dawn to dusk.*

Directions: *From I-80 take exit 57A onto NJ 19 south for a 0.5 mile and exit at Valley Road. Turn right and go about 100 feet to entrance for Lambert Castle. From the Garden State Parkway southbound, take exit 159 onto I-80 west and follow the directions above. From the Garden State Parkway northbound, take exit 155P onto NJ 19 north to the first exit onto Broad Street. Turn right onto Broad Street and travel to the first traffic light. Turn left onto Fenner Avenue. At the first light turn right onto Valley Road and travel five blocks to the museum entrance.*

❄ ❄ ❄ ❄ ❄ ❄ ❄ ❄

FIRST NIGHT

Montclair

AS A FRESHMAN IN COLLEGE, I spent New Year's Eve at Times Square, sideways drunk. When I awoke on New Year's Day, the ringing pain in my head said, "There's got to be a better way." There is.

On that same New Year's Eve, December 31, 1967, a group of folks in Boston were creating it. They called their celebration First Night. The idea was to forget the alcohol and spend the evening in a more meaningful celebration, with art exhibits, musical performances, theater, and dance. There are currently well over 100 First Night celebrations in North America, and in terms of the number of official First Night events, New Jersey, with about a dozen sites, ranks among the leading states.

First Night came to New Jersey in 1987 in Montclair. Suburban in nature, the town nevertheless harbors an active cultural, arts, and performance community, including the excellent Montclair Museum, an international array of restaurants, several music clubs, and professional theaters. Numerous musicians and performers live here. Indeed, for a relatively small suburb, Montclair is downright cosmopolitan.

We went to see what it was all about.

Darkness fell, and so did the rain. Well, more like a heavy mist. We momentarily reconsidered our New Year's Eve plans.

"What happens to a festival in which you walk around town when it rains?" we wondered.

The answer was—nothing. The show goes on.

Celebrants circulated through the town, never missing a beat; they just put their umbrellas up and down as the weather demanded. We joined right in.

That night First Night Montclair took place at some 33 venues, ranging from school auditoriums to churches to the Montclair Museum. In recent years, the event has been staged entirely on the multi-building high-school campus. For us, choosing among the dozens of events was the hardest part. We started with a visit to the George Innis Theater at the high school—mostly because we were standing right there when it was time for jazz singer Jeannie Bryson to take the stage. Between numbers, people wandered in and out as they pleased. They were coming from and leaving for other venues. The informal quality was much like being at a party and breaking off a conversation in one room to converse with someone else in the next.

We left Ms. Bryson after a handful of songs and wandered down Park Street, a street bordered by huge houses and lined with large trees. We were heading downtown, but we were attracted to musical sounds emanating from the Central Presbyterian Church. We ducked inside. The New Jersey Children's Choir was performing. A baby cried incessantly. A girl in the choir's second row dealt with a perpetual nose itch. But, the kids sounded just fine as they finished with a moving chorus of "Should auld acquaintance be forgot . . ."

The room emptied. We consulted our schedules. If we moved quickly, we'd be just in time to see the stand-up comics. I love stand-up comics. We walked. By the time we made it up the Bloomfield Avenue hill (which took a while, and maybe that's one reason everything is now staged in one place), we were walking in a crowd.

The lobby was choked with folks waiting. We poked our heads into the academy's auditorium. On stage, two or three dozen kids and a few young adults were dancing with pure youthful exuberance. We took seats.

To an upbeat and moving lyric that said "We are one," the troupe filled the auditorium with life. *Ceremony in Dance* was an event created especially for First Night through a program that places professional performers in the local middle school to work with the kids. The energy alone made the show wonderful to watch.

Ceremony in Dance was followed by the stand-up comics. They drew an standing-room-only crowd. It wasn't raucous, like a nightclub, and the humor was pretty clean. But, it was funny. These guys were doing two

DETAILS

The First Night name *is a trademark registered to First Night International, the umbrella organization that fosters the First Night concept in 131 cities in the United States, Canada, Great Britain, and New Zealand. The most current list of New Jersey First Night celebrations can be found at their Web site: www.firstnight.com.*

In 2003, New Jersey hosted *about a dozen First Night Celebrations in the following: Mount Holly (609-914-0811, www.mainstreet mountholly.com), Teaneck (201-287-9730, www.tcacarts.org), Ridgewood (201-689-1473, www.firstnightridgewood.org), Summit (908-522-1722 ext. 22, www.firstnightsummit.org), Maplewood/South Orange (973-763-4778, www.firstnightmapso.org), Montclair (973-509-4910, www.firstnightmontclair.org), Morris County (primarily in Morristown, 973-455-0708, www.firstnightmorris.com), Haddonfield (856-429-4700 ext. 3000, www.firstnighthaddonfield.org), Ocean County (Seaside Heights and Toms River, 732-286-1889, www.first nightoceancounty.org), Ocean City (609-525-9292 or 609-525-9300, www.firstnightoceancitynj.com).*

In addition, *many communities create local, unofficial versions of this event. For more information on First Night and local events, click on www.jerseyarts.com or www.firstnightnewjersey.com (1-800-THE-ARTS).*

shows, and the crowd outside when we left looked bigger than our crowd. Good luck finding seats.

We hurried next to see the Silk City Quartet, an eclectic string band that combines country sounds with klezmer, swing, bluegrass, and Brazilian music. Alas, we reached the door just in time to be told there was no more room.

Moving along, we came across a church that literally rocked with revivalist singing. A combo—electric piano, a priest on sax, and a full complement of trumpets, drums, trombones, and singers—had folks dancing in the aisles. We'd thought to go watch a magician perform. Distracted by the music, we never made it. Indeed, we never made it to half the things we'd have found interesting—the sky show at the school planetarium, the ice show at the skating rink, the square dancing at the high school, the paper cutting demo on the promenade, the New Jersey Chamber Music Society at the First Congregational Church . . . .

You get the idea.

We got the idea, too. A community at one, all ages, bidding adieu to the old year, welcoming the new, enjoying each other's joys and talents. And, even if the newest First Night version is done on a smaller scale, it sure beats being drunk in Times Square.

CABIN FEVER CURE
The Flower, Garden & Outdoor Living Show of New Jersey—Edison

THE SKIES HUNG A HEAVY GRAY. The mercury in the thermometer was dropping, and the weatherman warned of yet another snowstorm. The ice on the ground had congealed there long enough to grow dirty and mean. Warm weather couldn't have seemed further away. What better time to thumb your nose at the cold? What better way to do that than by tip-toeing through thousands of tulips?

I gathered up my wife and headed for the Flower, Garden & Outdoor Living Show of New Jersey, staged each year at the New Jersey Convention Center in Edison. The hall is located in a commercial complex that seemed an unlikely site to celebrate nature. Parking is a bit quirky, and the main lot is a five- to seven-minute walk away. A bus will run you between the lot and the hall, but sometimes it takes longer to wait for the bus than to walk. We regarded seriously the admonition to get there early and encountered no delay or problems.

To enter the Flower & Garden Show was to travel instantly from a gray winter's day to a bright, warm springtime afternoon bathed in a riot of color. Each year, the show centers on a theme. The first time I'd attended, it was 400 Years of Garden Magic, featuring "gardens from the Netherlands" that celebrated the 400th anniversary of the cultivation of the tulip. This last time, it was A Garden State of Mind and featured an

Memories of summer

entrancing range of gardens, from a traditional English garden to the whimsical "Peek-A-Boo" and "Walking In a Water Wonderland" entries. I had to admit to my summer-loving wife that even a winter-loving boy like me got a lift from moving so quickly from the drab cold to this warm, bright array of color.

I best liked a design entitled "It's May, It's May, The Lovely Month of May," created by The Garden Club of New Jersey. The program notes said it was "an educational display garden that demonstrates the age-old customs of May Day baskets and Maypoles which are enjoying a resurgence in the United States." I don't know about that. But it sure was pretty. A lot of folks were gravitating to that "Walking in a Water Wonderland" creation, no doubt drawn to the trickling sound of running water coming

Taking time to smell the roses at the Garden Show

from its natural stone waterfall and an actual meandering stream. The "Garden of Enchantment" proved another favorite of mine. I mean, how could you not like a place populated not only with real, live monarch butterflies, but also was inhabited by a pretty young lady dressed up as a butterfly? Frankly, it's amazing what summery environments can be created indoors in midwinter.

The Garden Show isn't only about ogling gorgeous floral spectacles. Education is part of it as well. Tucked into the far corner of the hall, hidden behind some dreary dark green cloth room dividers was a space in which experts from the Rutgers Cooperative Extension (RCE) provided information and tips about a surprising range of horticultural topics. We took a seat just at the end of a seminar on grape growing (did you know that New Jersey receives an average of 27 inches of rain between Memorial Day and Labor Day alone, and that's why attention to mold prevention on grape vines is vital?), which was followed immediately by a session on pruning. Pruning, we learned from Ross Karr, horticulturalist for RCE of Middlesex County, should be regarded as "controlled wounding" of the plant, and there are definite right and wrong ways to go about it.

Over the 10-day course of the show, well more than two dozen such seminars were staged, their topics ranging from Growing the Best Tomatoes to Edible and Ornamental Landscape Plants. A highlight was the appearance of Joan Hamburg and Arthur Schwartz, who did a live taping of *Weekend*, their WOR radio program. The sessions were offered at half-hour increments in two separate spaces throughout the show and, during the ones we sat in on, attendees showed rapt attention and fascination.

Fascinating in another way was the array of exhibitors in the Marketplace area. Here, we could buy everything from a cup of Starbuck's coffee to double-glazed windows. Okay, I admit it, I was astounded by the Incredible Rubber Broom, intrigued by the eye-opening array of gadgets of all kinds, attracted to the fascinating architectural artifacts sold by Olde Good Things, and pleased to purchase a pair of decorative insects on copper staffs to bob in the breeze in our garden, while the missus purchased from the Home Department display a few small potted plants. Plenty of jewelry, gee-gaws, sun catchers, and gardening tools caught our eyes, but we managed to exercise some restraint with our credit card. The presence of some vendors was logical, while others' participation seemed rather obtuse and arcane. I can understand how flower-show goers might comprise a likely market for plant shops, garden and home centers, deck makers, and solarium manufacturers. Or that they might buy pussy willows from Rosemary's Pussy Ranch. I don't know why anyone would come here to purchase timeshares from the Marriott Vacation Club or subscription cell-phone services. It was, however, great fun to stroll the aisles and watch the vendors at work.

The show also offered a handful of ongoing children's activities. I surreptitiously observed a brother-and-sister team hunt down the "bird singing in the tree," the "bunny laying on the ground," and other secrets in the Peek-A-Boo Garden, and how they stopped to have their "Children's

Garden Hunt" guide stamped at each discovery site. I was tempted to enter the Garden of Enchantment coloring contest, but feared I'd be ruled too old to qualify for one of the first-place prizes—a $100 U.S. Savings Bond.

We were qualified to vote for that garden as our selection for the People's Choice Award, however. It was definitely my favorite—probably because I thought the lady in the butterfly suit was cute as could be. (I was pleased to learn later that I'd voted for the winner.)

Exiting, one more survey of the flowers and display gardens provided a last dazzling burst of sunlight and color and a refreshing glimpse of spring's bounty as we'd soon enjoy it outdoors. It was all a tease, of course. To quote one woman from our first visit who, while waiting by the exit to be picked up by her senior citizens' group bus, looked gloomily into the wind-swirling snow that had begun falling during our stay. "Oh well," she said. "Back to reality."

DETAILS

The Flower, Garden & Outdoor Living Show of New Jersey
(1-800-332-3976, www.macevents.com) takes place for four days in mid-February at the New Jersey Convention Center in Edison. Show hours are 11 AM–9 PM on Thursday, 10 AM–9 PM on Friday and Saturday, and 10 AM–6 PM on Sunday. Admission is charged, but children under 12 are admitted free with a paying adult.

Directions: *From the New Jersey Turnpike, take exit 10 and follow CR 514 west to Raritan Center. Take the first exit marked Raritan Center and follow signs to the Expo Hall. From the Garden State Parkway northbound, take exit 127 to I-287 north and onto CR 514 west, then follow the directions given above. From the Garden State Parkway southbound, take exit 129 to I-287 north. From I-287 southbound, take the exit signed "Bonhamtown Only—Route 514 West" (just after the New Jersey Turnpike exit) to the first Raritan Center exit and follow signs to the Expo Hall.*

INDEX